THE PROCESS OF INVESTMENT
IN THE SOVIET UNION

SOVIET AND EAST EUROPEAN STUDIES

Books in the series

THE PROCESS OF
INVESTMENT IN THE
SOVIET UNION

DAVID A. DYKER

CAMBRIDGE UNIVERSITY PRESS

CAMBRIDGE

LONDON NEW YORK NEW ROCHELLE

MELBOURNE SYDNEY

Published by the Press Syndicate of the University of Cambridge
The Pitt Building, Trumpington Street, Cambridge CB2 1RP
32 East 57th Street, New York, NY 10022, USA
296 Beaconsfield Parade, Middle Park, Melbourne 3206, Australia

First published 1983

Printed in Great Britain at
the University Press, Cambridge

Library of Congress catalogue card number: 82–14600

British Library cataloguing in publication data
Dyker, David A.
The process of investment in the Soviet Union.
—(Soviet and East European studies)
1. Investments—Soviet Union
I. Title   II. Series
332.6′0947   HG5572

ISBN 0 521 24831 0

Contents

Preface

The present work is the final stage of a research project which has already seen the light of day in a number of preliminary forms. It started off as a *referat* to the Department of Industrial Economics, Institute of National Economy, Tashkent, USSR, presented in 1968. An outline of the analytical approach was mapped out in an article entitled 'Industrial location in the Tadzhik republic', published in *Soviet Studies*, vol. xxi, no. 4, April 1970. My thanks are due to the editors of that journal for permission to reproduce material from the article. In 1978 a D.Phil. thesis entitled 'The planning of investment in the Soviet Union' was presented at the University of Sussex.

Many people have helped me through a gestation period long even by Soviet standards, and I have space to mention only the most notable. Professor Tibor Barna and Dr Peter Holmes of the School of European Studies, University of Sussex, Professor Peter Wiles of the LSE, Michael Kaser of St Antony's College, Oxford, and Roger Clarke of the Institute of Soviet and East European Studies, University of Glasgow, all read the manuscript and provided invaluable comments. Professor Michael Ellman of the Department of Micro-economics, University of Amsterdam, gave advice on Chapter 5. Though responsibility for the end product is mine alone, these colleagues have made contributions without which I should surely never have brought the work to a conclusion. The maps were drawn by Chris Heaps of the University of Sussex and by Naomi-Jane Dyker. Lastly my thanks are due to Elsa Gibbins of London, and Helen Howard and Yvette Stone of the University of Sussex, who typed the manuscript.

DAVID A. DYKER

1

A conceptual framework for the study of investment activity in the Soviet Union

INTRODUCTION

It is the primary aim of this study to examine and evaluate, using empirical material, the whole process of investment in the Soviet Union – from policy formation and planning *stricto sensu* through to the actual construction site. The availability of empirical material is, however, extremely uneven, particularly in relation to policy and plan formation. It is simply not possible (at least for a westerner, but probably even for a Soviet scholar) to study the Soviet investment process directly. Decision-taking procedures are shrouded in obscurity, the detailed content of decisions is rarely published, and even at the 'non-strategic' level of, say, the management procedures current in building enterprises, the material available is bitty and impressionistic, albeit relatively rich. The most important source is the 'problem-orientated' article from p. 2 of *Pravda* or p. 9 of *Ekonomicheskaya Gazeta*, and scholarly or technico-specialist journals like *Voprosy Ekonomiki*, *Planovoe Khozyaistvo* and *Ekonomika Stroitel'stva*. In many cases, then, one has to try to work back from the problem to the underlying state of affairs in terms of organisation etc. In order to do this, some kind of clearly-defined *a priori* frame of reference is more than useful. In relation to questions concerning, for example, the basis on which the central organs of the Soviet state formulate investment plans, a subject on which there is an almost complete lack of even this problem-orientated literature, *a priori* reasoning becomes absolutely essential. The term *a priori* is, however, being used here in a fairly broad sense. It implies 'on the basis of general considerations, given what we know about universal economic tendencies, human nature, the Soviet economic system *and* the Soviet socio-political system'. Thus this first chapter, in which the *a priori* basis of the study is laid down, presumes a great deal of general empirical knowledge on

1

the part of the reader. Even the overall complexion of the Soviet
economic system is only discussed explicitly when it relates directly to
some aspect of the investment process as such, and this principle is
maintained in later chapters.

The culmination, if not the conclusion, of the work is the collection
of case studies presented in Chapter 6, and these case studies
represent the final stage in the transition from *a priori* reasoning to
systematic presentation of interrelated complexes of facts – the
manifest imbalance of the case studies, with two hydro-electric
stations, one oil/gas and one coal complex, and one local jumble of
small-scale engineering plants, reflects, of course, the fact that this
transition can only be made in the few cases where, for special reasons,
much more than the usual amount of information is available. In
between Chapter 6 and these present opening remarks there is,
however, a gradual escalation in terms of selective empirical content.
In subsequent sections of this chapter occasional empirical elements
are explicitly introduced. More frequently, 'insightful' quotations
from western writers are used to back up the *a priori* reasoning.
Chapters 2–5 discuss in greater detail the implementational end of the
investment process, and in Chapter 2, which deals with the implications of the economic system as a whole for the investment sector, the
selective empirical element is already considerable. In Chapters 3 and
4, in which we look at design and construction, this element becomes
predominant.

In proceeding, then, to 'set up the enquiry', we are faced initially
with two main problems. Firstly, what are the goals of the authorities
controlling investment? Secondly, what principle can we use for the
assessment, from a resource allocation point of view, of the implementation of aims, once ascertained, in the context of an imperfectly
known and dynamic world? The next two sections of this chapter treat
these questions in turn, though in the case of the first still in a very
general way.

THE AIMS OF SOVIET INVESTMENT POLICY – A GENERAL TREATMENT

There is no good reason to believe that investment policy in the Soviet
Union is not, to a considerable extent, oriented to the satisfaction of
individual consumer preferences – though in the context of a command economy there can be no automaticity about this. As far as

collective consumption goods and communal services are concerned, there is no evidence that the Soviet authorities systematically consult the Soviet population before taking decisions, whether on public parks or on nuclear missiles. Again, however, this creates no problems as far as the *nature and purpose* of the given good or service is concerned, though it might incline us to believe that *paternalism* could play a major rôle in this particular sphere of decision-taking.

But what of categories of aims coming under the conventional title of 'social objectives'? The fact that distributions of income etc. are not tangibles, while certainly disqualifying them from being called 'goods', does not alter the fact that the basic phenomenon being dealt with is similar to that of collective goods and services. Just as only groups of people can have defence systems, so only groups of people can have distributions of income. Pearce has remarked, in connection with cost-benefit analysis:

in applying a hypothetical compensation principle, cost-benefit implicitly assumes away any effects that will result from the change in income distribution consequent upon a project. The problem is that, whereas 'efficiency' benefits are defined in terms of some aggregate of individual preferences, there is no comparable criterion for judging distributional changes. This seems odd to the extent that the value judgement of consumers' sovereignty underlies the concept of an efficiency benefit: there would appear to be no logical reason for refusing to extend the principle to permitting social preferences to determine whether a distributional change is good or bad. Precisely the same argument applies to *any* objective preferred by society and which is not reflected in efficiency benefits and costs.[1]

A state such as the Soviet, with its high degree of general economic, political and social control, is virtually obliged to have more or less clearly-defined social objectives. After all, it *cannot help* determining the distribution of income. One might be reluctant to use the term 'social preferences' (of this more later), but once again there are no problems as far as the nature and purpose of the given objective is concerned.

There are, however, difficulties involved in the distinction between individual and collective aims which impinge strongly on any consideration of the investment sphere, and which play a good deal of havoc with the clarity of the preceding presentation. Firstly, individuals may have what in the past, in a singular misuse of terminology, has been referred to as 'irrational' aims. Stalin's obsession with canals, for instance, seems to have had very little to do with the solution of transport problems. One might be tempted to make a similar comment about the Concorde project in Britain and France. Again, the building of skyscrapers in African capitals seems to be motivated only secondarily by a desire to solve accommodation problems. Cases such as these, however, are no more instances of irrationality than is my former habit of smoking large numbers of cigarettes. The concept of rationality is, of course, relevant only when the mutual consistency of a number of stated aims, or the means of implementing given aims, is under discussion. Aims themselves by definition cannot be rational or irrational. They may or may not be considered 'sensible' by third parties, but this is merely to say that the preference maps of individuals may differ widely. The difficulty is that, in cases of what I have referred to in the past as '*investment good fetishism*',[2] where direct psychological satisfaction is derived from objects whose *raison d'être* would appear to be in terms of derived demands, the traditional distinction between consumption and investment goods breaks down. Since, for obvious reasons, no one ever admits to being an investment good fetishist (he may in any case be only dimly aware of the fact) and in the absence of the opportunity to psychoanalyse the people involved, certainly a reasonable assumption when one is dealing with the Soviet Union, it can become very difficult to ascertain just what the desired bundle of goods and services etc. is. The only way to cope with this difficulty, though it is not a very satisfactory one, is simply to go ahead on the assumption that investment good fetishism does not exist, and to bring it in in cases which cannot be adequately explained in any other terms.

Methodological messiness should not, however, be permitted to induce us to pigeon-hole this kind of thing as merely an 'interesting aberration'. George Orwell, for example, was deeply aware of its great political significance:

the Socialist who finds his children playing with tin soldiers is usually upset, but is never able to think of a substitute for the tin soldiers; tin pacifists somehow won't do. Hitler, because in his joyless mind he feels it with exceptional strength, knows that human beings don't only want comfort, safety, short working hours, hygiene, birth-control and, in general, common sense; they also, at least intermittently, want struggle and self-sacrifice, not to mention drums, flags and loyalty-parades. However they may be as economic theories, Fascism and Nazism are psychologically far sounder than any hedonistic conception of life. The same is probably true of Stalin's militarised version of Socialism.[3]

There is no intention here to suggest that the Soviet, or any other régime, is similar, in a general political sense, to the Nazi. The point is simply to emphasise that certain very fundamental psychological tendencies exist, and that skyscrapers and supersonic airliners may fulfil in one age a rôle that in another age was fulfilled by flags and loyalty-parades. Following

Orwell, I would suggest that the *a priori* importance of investment good fetishism is universal, and in no way contingent on special aspects of Soviet reality.

The second difficulty that arises with our basic analysis of individual and collective aims is that *monistic* elements may be present in the political superstructure, i.e. that the state or community may be deemed to have interests and concerns over and above those of its individual members, however summed. There is an obvious temptation to tie this in with investment good fetishism, but it is important to see that the two concepts are, in principle, quite distinct. Monism does not so much blur the distinction between private and collective consumption goods and services as introduce a third category. For this reason it is methodologically much easier to cope with. Some readers would no doubt prefer that all defence expenditures were treated as monistic. I have chosen not to do this, but to count defence as an 'orthodox' collective service. Even if this exclusion is allowed, however, the peculiarities of the Soviet state, and in particular the essentially mystical view of itself that it purveys, must incline us to attach considerable importance to monism as an *a priori* element in the formation of Soviet investment policies.

Up to now discussion has proceeded on the basis of the assumption that all conceivable aims can be traded off against each other. This obviously may not always be the case. Aims may take the form of constraints rather than maximands, and this might tend particularly to be the case with non-goods-and-services desiderata. Distributional preferences, for example, would surely normally be expressed through a constraint taking the form of a maximum acceptable degree of inequality. In the context of contemporary theory, however, none of this presents any conceptual difficulties though, as we shall see later, some practical problems do arise.

One major issue remains to be discussed before we leave the question of final aims in its most general form, namely that of time periods. The three-fold classification which I have used in the past, though in a narrower context, runs, rather clumsily, in terms of the *short-term, medium-term* and *long-term planning horizons.*[4] The short-term planning horizon is taken to be shorter than the gestation period of new plants, so that investment is restricted to *minor* extensions or replacements in existing plants. (*Major* extensions or replacements may, of course, take much longer than the construction of new plants. See below, pp. 43–4.) The medium-term planning horizon allows for the construction of new plants, but only the long-term planning horizon permits consideration of the possibility of significant *external economies of scale*. These are of two main types: (a) significant permanent changes in levels of productivity of sectoral, regional or national labour forces, not *directly* attributable to specific new investments and/or instances of technical progress; (b) locational economies, reaped as the building-up of activity complexes reduces transport costs. The general analytical issues raised by this concept will be discussed in a moment. For the present it is important only to note that the planning horizon must be open-ended in an 'outwards' direction. Normally, one might expect it to be of the order of 10–20 years, but this period could plausibly be extended to around 30 years in given cases, especially in relation to (a) above. An awkward case in relation to (b) is that of a single investment *in transport itself*, for example, a motorway project, which would reduce transport costs, shrink distances and thus possibly create a complex where none existed before, without any new enterprises having to be constructed, and therefore in a fairly short period.

The long-term planning horizon must, then, be defined in terms of what are *typically* the temporal conditions for the emergence of external economies of scale. In general the planning horizon 'mix' is a fairly clear-cut concept, and will obviously be a major element influencing the desired bundle of goods and services etc. at a given point in time, whether formal time-discounting procedures are used or not. In terms of standard Soviet planning practice the medium-term planning horizon can be taken to correspond to the five-year, medium-term plan. As we shall see in Chapter 2, however, the total investment cycle (in Soviet planning terminology *prodolzhitel' nost' stroitel' stva* – duration of construction)[5] averages at least 5–7 years. Even the stage of construction proper (*vremya stroitel' nogo proizvodstva* – building time) may average more than 5 years. The equation of five-year plan with medium-term planning horizon is, then, certainly in contemporary Soviet conditions, only an approximate one. So-called long-term programmes work in terms of a horizon of about 15 years, and this is clearly not very different from my long-term planning horizon.

THE YARDSTICK

There seems, then, to be no reason why aims other than the traditionally respectable one of satisfying individual wants to the fullest possible extent should not in principle be treated by the normal tools of economic analysis. Whether one would be justified in using some such orthodox concept as 'Pareto optimum', or 'welfare optimum' in an analysis of investment under Soviet conditions is another matter. Monism in any form is surely incompatible with any such concept, and Heal argues that the Pareto condition 'rules out any overtly paternalistic approach'.[6] Elsewhere it has been explicitly argued that conventional welfare criteria involve assumptions about the primacy of individual desires and their satisfaction that are incompatible with the facts of Soviet reality.[7] For this reason, it seems wise to remain content with some rather lower-level concept when dealing with such subject matter.[8] As a starting point, let us take the formal definition of *allocative efficiency*. 'An attainable bundle of basic activities is called an *efficient* bundle if there exists no attainable bundle which produces more of some desired commodity and no less of any other desired commodity.'[9] Because the concept 'takes as given the immediate purpose of production – to produce desired commodities – without getting involved in the details of further postulates of a theory of consumers' choice to explain for what purposes, up to what limit, and in what relative degrees the commodities in question are desired by consumers',[10] it avoids the difficulties involved in welfare concepts. Formal allocative efficiency is not, however, directly usable as a criterion in the present context, and this for a number of reasons.

Firstly, there is the problem of defining a good, a problem which can become virtually insuperable in the context of a high degree of product differentiation. This is less of a problem in a Soviet-type economy, with its fairly utilitarian approach to the production of consumer goods, but it does mean that empirical material has to be carefully chosen. In fact, most of the empirical material in this work relates to more or less homogenous intermediate goods, with their relationship to final production largely taken for granted.

Secondly, allocative efficiency is an essentially static concept, while our subject material is by definition dynamic, however much we may try, initially, to assume away the complications that this involves. One important aspect of this difficulty concerns locational patterns. Formal activity analysis strictly treats technologically identical goods produced or consumed in different locations as different goods.[11] In a context where we are particularly concerned to call into question the advisability of existing locational patterns, this is clearly an inappropriate restriction, though it can be removed only at the cost of 'fuzzing up' the definition of efficiency considerably. Equally important is the question of discounting the future. In principle, since the bundle of goods and services etc. is given, the savings/investment rate should also be given. Thus there must always be an implicit rate of interest which, when used in conjunction with the Present Value criterion for project assessment, would provide a basis for choosing between different projects and different variants for given projects, in such a way as just to exhaust the planned level of aggregate investment while fulfilling the requirements of the formal efficiency definition. There are, however, special problems here, relating to certain empirical characteristics of the Soviet economic system, and these will be discussed later on in this section.

The third main problem with formal efficiency is that it is difficult to free it completely from welfare implications, for example with regard to the length of the working week. Clearly it should always be possible to produce more of some desired commodities and no less of any others simply by compelling, or inducing, people to work at weekends. It does not in fact seem possible to arrive at any conception of equilibrium work/leisure mix without becoming involved in welfare considerations.

The fourth principal difficulty with the formal allocative efficiency criterion is that, as Leibenstein notes, 'the empirical evidence, while far from exhaustive, certainly suggests that the welfare gains that can be achieved by increasing *only* allocative efficiency are usually exceedingly small, at least in capitalist countries'.[12] The potential gains, in welfare or any other terms, may be more considerable in a Soviet-type economy, but the key point in the present context is the importance of what Leibenstein calls 'X-efficiency', i.e. essentially organisational and motivational efficiency.

Firms and economies do not operate on an outer-bound production possibility surface consistent with their resources. Rather they actually work on a production surface that is well within that outer bound. This means that for a variety of reasons people and organizations normally work neither as hard nor as effectively as they could. In situations where competitive pressure is light, many people will trade the disutility of greater effort, of search, and the control of other people's activities for the utility of feeling less pressure and of better interpersonal relations. But in situations where competitive pressures are high, and hence the costs of such trades are also high, they will exchange less of the disutility of effort for the utility of freedom from pressure etc. [Note how the welfare complication comes in again – D.A.D.] Two general types of movements are possible. One is along a production surface towards greater allocative efficiency and the other is from a lower to a higher one that involves greater degrees of X-efficiency.[13]

X-efficiency is clearly a concept whose content can easily escalate, and in the present context it is very important to exclude completely any major form of technical progress, which is one of the most common bases for moving onto a higher production surface. But organisational efficiency is a key issue in Soviet-type economies, and some level of organisational efficiency, including being more or less at the existing 'normal' level of technology, must be included within any useful definition of efficiency for the analysis of such economies. In so doing we once again, however, lose a degree of precision in the formulation.

Fifthly, we have the problem of externalities. Let us begin discussion of this difficult issue with some definitions. An *external production diseconomy* arises when a specific process at one point directly and deleteriously affects a specific process at another. It may result immediately (i.e. within the short-term planning horizon) from the installation of a new piece of equipment in factory A, if that creates an effluent discharged into a river the waters of which constitute a raw material for factory B. Normally, however, serious effects could be expected only with the construction of new plants (i.e. on the medium-term planning horizon). The peculiarity of *external economies of scale*, the concept introduced on p. 6, is that they are a function, not of the scale of an individual plant or organisation, but of an entire spatial complex of activities. If we treat the complex as the 'basic unit' they reduce to a straightforward category of internal economy of scale. Scitovsky, in his famous article,[14] subsumed production externalities and some categories of external economies of scale under the general title of *technological externalities*. We find it useful to use a narrower categorisation, but it must be admitted that the distinction does in some cases become blurred. What, for example, of the pollution problem which only reaches significant proportions beyond a critical level of spatial concentration? Our procedure is to use the terms external economy/diseconomy of scale only for phenomena which are *purely* a function of the scale variable. This, in effect, limits them to the labour force and transport dimensions. Transport economies relating to reduction in distances may, of course, ultimately be cancelled out by diseconomies of congestion and delay. This appears to be the only significant form of 'pure' external *diseconomy* of scale. We have, it will be remembered, already relegated external economies of scale to the long-term planning horizon by definition.

Scitovsky's other category of 'pecuniary' externalities is again a broad one, but Holland's more precise definition of the concept in terms of 'reductions in unit costs for an individual producer in securing inputs from technologically related firms whose internal economies of scale permit them to produce the inputs at lower cost than the producer who purchases them' gives us a useful point of departure.[15] The word 'pecuniary' is clearly inappropriate to discussion of an essentially non-market economy, but some such concept is as necessary to an analysis of the investment process in the Soviet Union as it would be in any other context. Construction of project A may affect the cost conditions of plants in the same region by permitting them to exploit internal economies of scale, and the time-lag need only be as long as the time needed to install new equipment (again, within the short-term planning horizon), though presumably significant effects would only come with the construction of new plants. The impossibly long-winded title I would prefer for this category of externality is 'externally conditioned internal economies of scale'. They are not *in principle* locationally conditioned in the way that external economies of scale are – the scale of oil extraction in the Middle East, for example, must surely affect potential economies of scale in European oil refineries. When Holland points to 'the over-estimation of the role of external economies in the location process, and a failure to admit the extent to which medium- to large-sized firms of the kind which have the highest growth promotion potential for less-developed regions either internalise production economies, or are assured of major external production economies through regularised long-term contracts with other producers',[16] he is surely thinking primarily of externally conditioned internal economies of scale. But these economies will normally be geographically limited, and will normally interact closely with external economies of scale to form the totality of the 'agglomeration effect'.[17] For this reason I will refer to externally conditioned internal economies of scale more conveniently and shortly as *secondary agglomeration effects*.[18]

These effects could clearly be 'forwards' or 'backwards'. The backwards effect, where a big project creates new demands on a large scale, is the more obvious, but the forwards effect, where a new, large-scale source of, say, cheap electricity, makes it possible to build plants for energy-intensive processes on a scale not otherwise possible, might be equally important. It is, however, clear that the forwards effect could not be expected to have any significance except on the medium-term or long-term planning horizons. We must, of course, bear in mind that in a centrally planned system someone above the level of the enterprise must make a decision to construct a new plant. The same may be the case even with the installation of a new piece of equipment in an existing enterprise. There is, therefore, no question of this kind of externality 'spontaneously' occurring in the way that production externalities may.

Consideration of the fact that planning in the Soviet Union has been persistently 'taut' introduces for consideration another kind of 'externality' or, more properly, 'spill-over' effect, since intrinsic production possibilities are not affected as such. Any system which tries to plan 15,500 commodity groups centrally, as does the Soviet,[19] is going to have a lot of trouble in achieving even approximate internal consistency in plans. To make things worse, a system which bases targets on depositions coming from executive bodies will clearly encourage these bodies to tailor information to the private desideratum of an easy plan – this in addition to the informational problems of a purely organisational nature which a high degree of centralisation must involve. As we shall see presently these problems have been significant factors in elements of inefficiency in the system. But the very inflexibility of attitudes on this matter has introduced a positive to be counted against the negative. What taut planning basically involves is a simple rule that, in case of inconsistencies appearing, downward adjustments should be made only as a very last resort, and that the basic tactic should be simply *to instruct producers of deficit goods to produce more, irrespective of the implications of information to hand.*[20]

To take an example from the investment sphere, the construction of enterprise A might demand, for supply reasons, the construction of enterprise B. Funds for the construction of the latter enterprise may, however, be 'impossibly' deficient. The response, however, is simply to leave this gap in the plan, in the hope, pious or otherwise, that either enterprise B will indeed be constructed on the basis of 'sought-out' reserves or decentralised funds, or that the supplies will be forthcoming, by hook or by crook, from elsewhere. Creation of this sort of tension, which keeps planners on their toes as much as producers, since it compels them continually to seek out reserves of one kind or another, has been succinctly described as 'goading the goaders'.[21] The point is, of course, that, given the high degree of informational uncertainty, the 'impossible' may well be achievable, as the history of the Soviet economy in the 1930s amply showed.

Thus, through the implementation of something bearing a considerable resemblance to Hirschmanian 'unbalanced growth' tactics,[22] through the creation of bottlenecks and tension, overall output indices for given sectors or regions may have been raised through the implementation of a general policy which has had the inevitable result of making projects look inefficient on a partial basis, in cases where the 'impossible' has, in fact, proven quite unattainable. Following Hirschman, we shall use the term *linkage* to decribe this phenomenon. The nub of the matter is that, particularly in a developmental context, information is by definition very vague, whatever the economic system, if only for sociological reasons, and concepts of full capacity rather artificial. There is, therefore, plenty of scope for upward pressure from the planners, in order to ensure maximisaton of total output. Whether this effect will more than cancel out accompanying negative effects must depend largely on the structure and complexity of the economy. It seems clear that as the economy matures, so the virtues of balance will tend increasingly to outweigh the enticements of imbalance. Inter-sectoral relationships become more complex and delicate, and supply constraints are increasingly felt, in materials and labour markets, not to mention the market for imported technology.[23]

Of these four types of externality or quasi-externality, one does not cause problems as far as the formulation of an efficiency-based yardstick is concerned. Linkage effects are very important, and will be discussed again in the last chapter. But they are clearly *macro-economic* effects, and so are not relevant to what remains, however much we move away from the formal allocational definition, a purely microeconomic approach. Backwards secondary agglomeration effects do not present serious problems in market economies because they can be expected, under normal conditions, to be largely internalised by the 'moving' enterprise, as prices of the goods and services of the 'secondary' enterprise fall. In a Soviet-type economy, where prices are administratively fixed, however, such an internalisation is unlikely to occur. It is not clear to what extent forwards secondary agglomeration effects can be expected to be internalised to the mover in a market economy, but it is clear that they will not be in a command economy, less because of inflexible prices than because of the primacy of obligatory output targets, which tends to push clients and potential clients into the background as far as the attitudes and actions of a given enterprise are concerned. (See discussion below on pp. 15–17 and 32–5.) Production externalities are, of course, crucially relevant to any kind of efficiency concept, whatever the economic system. Between them, then, secondary agglomeration effects and production externalities may make it very difficult to pin-point any optima, so that once more we have to lower our sights as far as precision is concerned. External economies of scale, on the other hand, could haze up the picture to an impossible extent, and it is fortunate that we can assume their importance on the medium-term planning horizon to be minimal.

The problem of prices is, of course, a completely general one, with implications that go beyond the narrow sphere of secondary agglomeration effects. It is simply not possible at the present level of computer technology to plan systematically the number of prices that are fixed by one planning body or another in the Soviet Union. (For detailed discussion see pp. 101–2.) From a resource allocation point of view the Soviet price system is, consequently, fairly unreliable, and this unavoidably creates further practical obstacles to the precise application of any kind of efficiency concept.

One would imagine that the kind of 'externality' involving forced saving of one kind or another is not one that should have any relevance to a command system where the savings/investment rate is centrally determined. It is, nevertheless, clear that the famous 'priority principle', which has played such an important rôle in the practice of Soviet planning, has tended to produce deviations in the proportion of actual investment expenditure in total National Income from the corresponding planned levels. Hunter has shown the tremendous importance of the priority principle in the pre-war Soviet period.[24] The basic rationale of the principle rests in terms of minimising the potential dislocation which may result from taut planning. If in the course of plan implementation it becomes clear that the plan as a whole cannot be fulfilled, resources are simply physically shifted out of non-priority into priority sectors. Hence the priority principle is primarily simply an aspect of the linkage effect discussed above on pp. 11–12. But it does also have implications for basic macro-economic proportions. The priority sectors have been the investment, intermediate and defence goods sectors, while consumer goods sectors have been the non-priority sectors. Thus the priority principle has tended, *inter alia*, to push up *de facto* investment rates.

How this can be interpreted in policy terms is a matter of some difficulty. Perhaps it is as simple as this: any priority system which works at the expense of, rather than to the advantage of, investment may be considered to be ultimately self-defeating, since investment goods are required for the production of almost everything; in any case, the origin of the whole business is taut planning, which is aimed at fostering growth, and any reduction in investment would, *ceteris paribus*, contradict that aim. But other considerations may have been important. Given the priority on defence, the priority on investment could be argued to be essentially a 'derived' priority, on the ground that most investment is, in one way or another, connected with defence. This latter argument gets stronger the larger the investment component in National Income, for the larger that component, the larger the proportion of total investment that has to go into the investment goods industries, i.e. primarily engineering.

Depending on how we lay emphasis on these or other interpretations, we will come to differing conclusions on the extent to which the macro-economic effects of the priority principle have been a matter of conscious policy, and to what extent merely a by-product of other policies. But irrespective of these conclusions the operation of the priority principle does call into question the validity of any conception of a fixed rate of time-preference in the Soviet context. As we shall see in Chapter 5, there are plenty of more specific reasons, connected with official state doctrine, why concepts and procedures relating to the rate of interest have been somewhat vaguely and ambivalently spelled out in the Soviet Union. It is important that we recognise at this point that there is some 'objective', system-based, vagueness in this regard as well. *A propos* of the earlier discussion of time discounting, this means that there is an element which fuzzes up the *reality* of the rate of interest, as distinct from the *perception* of that reality.

In the light of all these problems with the formal concept of efficiency it seems best to take an essentially commonsense approach as the basis for the yardstick which we need to analyse the case studies. The term 'efficiency' will be retained, but will from now on be taken to imply simply executing a given task in, as far as the 'naked eye' can see, the cheapest possible way, subject to reasonable constraints about quality. The more abstruse semantic problems about how precisely the given 'task' should be defined will simply be ignored, and in practice it will be complexes of related tasks (e.g. production + transport) that will most frequently be considered. The length of the standard working week and a 'normal' incidence of overtime will simply be taken as given. Since the aim of the study is a critical evaluation of investment activity we will obviously not treat investment goods as final goods. We are, then, using the term in a sense which subsumes both allocative and 'X-' efficiency elements, and which would surely not differ much from what a western businessman conceives of as efficiency.

In order to avoid complications with external economies of scale we will narrow down the yardstick to 'medium-term-planning-horizon (hereafter m-t-p-h) efficiency'. Even so, however, the naked eye may be seriously deceived by the complexities relating to organisational efficiency, some types of externalities, price distortions, etc. discussed above. Accordingly only case material showing very clear deviations from the yardstick has been used. This has not excluded the use of any outstandingly interesting body of material, except perhaps that relating to the Urals-Kuznetsk combine. One final simplification that is adopted for the sake of ease of analysis is that the yardstick is defined net of 'unorthodox' goods and services etc. In practice aims on, for example, distribution are often not clearly enunciated, while their costs may be virtually impossible to quantify. In addition, the fact that they may often take the form of constraints is more easily handled with the yardstick approach if they are viewed as represent-ing a special category. To underline that there is no implication that distributional aims are by definition inefficient, the definition of the yardstick is further narrowed down by the introduction of the epithet 'simple'. To sum up, then, simple m-t-p-h efficiency relates to the purveyance, at least cost, of the given bundle of orthodox goods and services, including defence goods and other communal consumption goods and services, ignoring all long-term complications. This, then, is the *yardstick* and it would be nice to be able to say that it is a yardstick completely devoid of normative significance. Given the welfare complications in the definition of efficiency, however, this would be an unjustified statement. What we can say is that the yardstick is sufficiently non-normative to serve as a starting point for enquiry. Finally the term 'deviation' must clearly, in terms of our definition, be understood as being completely free from the pejorative connotations it has in normal usage, and having no intrinsic normative implica-tions. The analytical approach taken will, however, facilitate a clear differentiation between deviations reflecting policy aims and devia-tions that occur *despite* policy aims.

SOME KEY ASPECTS OF THE SOVIET ECONOMIC SYSTEM

We have already spent a considerable amount of time trying to analyse the bases of different possible aims in investment policy, and we concluded the last section with a reference to the question of deviations from the yardstick, the origin of which has nothing to do with policy aims, and which policy might indeed dearly love to eliminate. These are the 'real' deviations, with their origin lying in the operational inefficiency of the Soviet economic system, and a large part of this work will be devoted to their detailed analysis. At this point, I want merely to outline two crucial features of Soviet-type economies which in fact between them provide a very large element in the conditioning of the various operational inefficiency factors.

The technical problems involved in achieving internal plan consistency with a high degree of centralisation have already been mentioned, as have the practices of 'taut' planning. The negative aspect of taut planning is obviously potential dislocation through non-arrival of 'planned' consignments etc. The problem has been intensified in a number of ways through the operation of the plan implementation system. Primary emphasis on output targets of one kind or another has inevitably meant that enterprises etc., having achieved their set target, have had no market incentive to produce more, if the degree of tautness has indeed left them any 'spare'. They have, furthermore, felt some positive disincentive, given the tendency of the planners, understandable in the light of informational problems, to respond to high levels of plan overfulfilment by jacking up targets for the subsequent plan period ('ratchet planning'). This disincentive has generally outweighed the incentive of special bonuses for overfulfilment. Thus there have been built-in obstacles to any 'filling in of gaps' through decentralised action.

These obstacles have always been unofficially modified through the activity of 'pushers', operating semi-legally, or even outrightly illegally, on the supplies market. The introduction of profit-based success-indicators in the post-1965 period should in principle have done something to modify the situation formally, to the extent that high levels of sales would also produce high levels of profit, thus having a 'double' effect on bonuses. In practice the application of the ratchet principle to plans for profits themselves, and the continued tendency to instability in norms for deductions into incentive funds, has tended to neutralise any such effect. More recently profit-based success-indicators have in any case been progressively de-emphasised.[25] Some ingenious experimental incentive schemes tried out in the late 1960s and early 1970s obviated, at least in principle, the problem of asymmetry in the plan implementation system, whereby even marginal underfulfilment would mean complete loss of bonuses. But they offered little inducement to managers to 'trust' planners more in relation to the ratchet. It is, in fact, clear that the 'ratchet' effect continues to operate powerfully throughout the planning system, not surprisingly given that the system remains so highly centralised that the planners cannot eschew the help of some such 'rule of thumb'.[26]

But methods of plan implementation have had much wider effects than this. The primacy of output targets has meant that producers have had little incentive to study the needs of customers in terms of specification and/or quality.[27] Thus added to the danger of non-delivery has been the danger of delivery of unsuitable or substandard goods. All in all, then, generalised supply uncertainty has been a chronic tendency of the system.

The other principal feature of the system which we must note here is the tendency for cost constraints to be only partially effective. Once again, the matter is basically one of success-indicators. Output indicators are as insensitive to cost considerations as they are to quality and specification considerations. Modifications to the success-indicator system in the post-1965 period have not fundamentally altered the fact that there is some tendency for *all* costs to be externalised in the Soviet system – a paradoxical enough result in a centrally planned system. Detailed discussion of the operation of this tendency requires a certain degree of institutional detail, so it is best left to Chapter 2.

SPECIFIC FACTORS LIKELY, A PRIORI, TO INDUCE DEVIATIONS FROM SIMPLE M-T-P-H EFFICIENCY

Bringing together, then, the conclusions of the second and fourth sections of this chapter and bearing in mind the difficulties discussed in the third section, we can proceed to a taxonomy of factors whose operation could result in deviations from the yardstick. This list is, of course, exhaustive only in terms of the elements, speculative and empirical, subsumed under the term of *a priori*, as defined earlier. As far as policy aims are concerned, long- and short-term planning horizons are classified together into a separate A group, while a miscellany of factors whose ultimate rationale must lie in paternalistic or monistic attitudes on the part of the authorities are likewise listed together as B group factors. Factors relating to elements of generalised operational inefficiency in the economic system as a whole are classified as C group factors, while elements of operational inefficiency in the design and construction sectors themselves are classified as, respectively, Factors D and E. This leaves some 'awkward customers' which will be discussed in due course.

A factors: different planning horizons. The potential importance of the *long-term planning horizon* (Factor A1) is obvious. Any policy of moving industrial activity into hitherto undeveloped areas can be expected to be based to a major extent on expectations of eventual external economies of scale. Clearly the long-term planning horizon could normally only have operational force in cases where 'normal' time discount procedures were bypassed. Of less obvious importance is the *short-term planning horizon* (Factor A2). The only likely conditions under which the authorities' horizons might be shortened to such an extent as to rule out the construction of new plants are those of wartime, but there is no reason of principle why this should be so, so that it seems best to keep it quite separate from the strategic factor proper.

B factors: possible additional elements in, and constraints affecting, the desired bundle of goods and services etc. The *strategic factor* (Factor B1) is complex in that there is no obvious unique direction in which it must operate. By definition it is essentially a matter of location, and by our own definitions it takes the form of a constraint, since military goods themselves are included in the 'simple' bundle of goods. In its most elementary form it is easily enough handled – the authorities may go for a greater degree of national self-sufficiency than that conforming to the yardstick. When we come to a consideration of internal locational patterns, we see that the factor might operate in diametrically opposing directions. Investment might be directed towards the Soviet heartland, the Volga–Urals–West Siberia area, as the region most immune from attack from any quarter, or alternatively to thinly populated and partially developed border regions, such as Eastern Siberia and the Far East, in order to strengthen the frontier. It could also operate in quite specific and peculiar ways, such as in the evacuation of equipment from the western to the eastern regions of the USSR in the path of the invading German forces in 1941. There were, of course, elements of short-term planning horizon as well as of pure strategic factor in that policy.

In principle a centrally planned economy should be able to determine matters of distribution of income independently of investment policy. In practice this may be difficult, and in any case might not represent the least-cost solution to distributional problems. Investment policy as an instrument of *distributional policy* (Factor B2) would again normally come in a locational form. Investment might be directed to poor and under-developed areas, quite apart from any consideration of long-term planning horizon, or to areas of unemployment not amenable to a 'workers to the work' solution, for example in cases of female unemployment in a metallurgy centre or male unemployment in a textile centre. In the former case investment might be in more labour-intensive directions than would conform to the yardstick, quite apart from the question of the total amount of funds going to a given area. In the latter case the same would apply, and investment would clearly have to be in certain specific sectors. Factor B2 could come in the form of a constraint, or of a constrained maximand.

A similar but separate cause for deviation from the yardstick might be the pursuit of *cultural policy* (Factor B3). It is possible in principle to solve the purely distributional problems of poor and under-developed areas through a 'workers to the work' policy. If, however, the authorities are concerned to maintain the cultural identity of a region, a factor of great potential importance in a country like the USSR, with its vast number of geographically concentrated national minorities, this solution would be automatically excluded. In practice the effects of such a policy would be similar to those of distributional policy, except that one would expect the tendency towards labour intensity to be stronger.

Exactly the same kind of results might flow from a concern on the part of the central authorities to *maintain political stability* in national minority, or other peripheral regions (Factor B4). To some extent this ties in with the strategic factor, since internal political stability is obviously an important element in defence preparedness, but it could operate as an independent desideratum. Factors B2–B4 clearly form a sub-group which, in American political terminology, would be called 'pork-barrel'.[28]

Foreign policy, a desire to impress the outside world, especially the developing part of it, might induce the authorities to place more investment funds in formerly backward areas than would conform to the simple m-t-p-h efficiency yardstick (Factor B5). A preference for labour-intensity in techniques might be induced by the operation of this factor also, though we must bear in mind that 'grand' projects are usually fairly capital-intensive ones.

The Soviet Union is not a wholly non-pluralistic state, though it may aspire to be, and may have got nearer to that aspiration than most states. I am not speaking here of the lack of total control over the way in which centrally determined aims are implemented, of which more in a moment, nor about the concessions that the central authorities may make to groups outside the decision-making process for one reason or another (see B2–B5 above), but about the extent to which an individual participating in the decision-making process may go for particular variants because they correspond to desiderata felt by himself, or some group which he feels he represents. For example, a provincial or republican party secretary with good *blat*, i.e. influence, connections, who-you-know, etc.,[29] might be able to get more investment funds, or a more labour-intensive investment profile if he were worried about depopulation, than would correspond to the yardstick, not because the central authorities are concerned with anything under B2–B5, or through any distortion of the implementation process, but simply because he is a part of the process of deciding what the bundle of goods and services etc. will be. It would be incorrect to include this as a separate 'factor',[30] since the motivation of the individual must be classifiable under B1–B5, or possibly A1–A2, or one of the 'ideological' factors to be discussed presently. The point is simply that one cannot assume that decisions which finally emerge are wholly-integrated, nationally-based decisions.

It will in practice be very difficult, at least on the basis of looking only at decisions, rather than at decision-making, to distinguish the operation of one factor from that of another, as far as the B2–B5 sub-group is concerned. This need not worry us too much, however, and the analytical distinctions remain valuable, if only as an indication of how desirable it would be to be able to get comprehensive material on the decision-making processes themselves.

We come now to a preliminary discussion of the most complex of the factors likely to result in deviations from the yardstick – those related to elements of operational inefficiency in the Soviet economic system itself. The essential background to the treatment of these factors is the discussion of supply uncertainty and lack of effective cost constraints in the previous section (pp. 15–17). At this point we extend the analysis as far as classifying specific factors, while still leaving the detailed analysis of how these factors work themselves out in practice to later chapters.

C factors: generalised elements of operational inefficiency in the economic system as a whole. These elements relate to all non-specialised (from the point of view of investment) subordinate executive bodies, i.e. intermediate planning bodies and actual enterprises of all types. Firstly, we have the *tendency to overbid for investment resources* (Factor C1). The overall weakness of cost constraints has given general scope for the operation of this factor, but before 1965 a specific anomaly in the price structure, namely the absence of any kind of capital charge on fixed investment, made the system particularly vulnerable in this way. Connoisseurs of the way in which university departments bid for new posts and other resources will not be surprised by the complexity and importance of this factor. Then there is the *tendency to organisational autarky* (Factor C2). As a way of trying to minimise supply uncertainty, with no pressing need to concern themselves overly with considerations of economies of scale or minimisation of transport costs, non-specialised executive bodies have often proceeded on the basis of 'if you can't trust someone else to do the job, do it yourself'.

This brings us to *cost/benefit externalisation* proper (Factor C3), which covers 'orthodox' production externality cases, where the tendency to cost externalisation is completely untrammelled. Production externalities have already been discussed as an element which could blur perception of efficiency points. Here we introduce the possibility that in a given case the intensity of the externality effect may be so great as to create a plainly visible deviation. The peculiar aspect of this factor in the Soviet context turns on the virtual absence, throughout the post-industrialisation period, of systematic land-rental elements in the price system.

Detailed discussion of the precise ways in which these different C group factors work themselves out will come in Chapter 2. In the meantime we must turn to preliminary discussion of elements of operational inefficiency in the economic system which originate from, or manifest themselves in, the activity of the specialised bodies operating in the investment field.

Factor D: elements of operational inefficiency at the design stage. Detailed plans for particular investment projects are worked out by specialised, non-executive bodies called *proektnye organizatsii* (design organisations). In Chapter 3 we will study the salient points in their organisation and mode of working, with a view to establishing in precisely what ways they may be responsible for the appearance of deviations from the yardstick.

Factor E: elements of operational inefficiency at the construction stage. Our approach to this, the specialised, executive sector, is more or less as with the design organisations, and the details will be sorted out in Chapter 4. Strictly speaking, the specialist executive sector includes machine building and the building materials industry as well as construction proper. The reader will not, however, find systematic coverage of these industrial branches in Chapter 4. Partly to avoid excessive length of treatment, partly because, once you start looking at supply, input-output realities may demand that you study very nearly *every* sector of the economy, I decided to discuss machine building and building materials only selectively, as they impinge on the various activities directly related to investment. The specially important theme of imported equipment will be discussed in the Appendix.

We come now to what are, from the purely conceptual point of view, the most difficult factors to deal with, namely *official state doctrine* and *investment good fetishism*. There are in the Soviet Union officially approved guidelines on matters such as investment criteria, location policy, etc. which, as we shall see in Chapter 5, could be expected to induce deviations from the yardstick. Though the need, *ipso facto*, to study chapter and verse means that a special chapter has to be devoted to the purely technical aspects of this, the latter are, in fact, easily enough worked out. Indeed, to anticipate, the conclusion emerges that state-doctrinal factors have probably been of fairly marginal importance. The difficulty arises in trying to classify this factor, and in trying to pin-point its relationship to investment good fetishism. State doctrine is very obviously implemented, to the extent that it is implemented, through state policy. Are we then to look on state doctrine as an end in itself, and thus as an item in the final bundle of aims? The operation of most of the A and B group factors could, in fact, be defended on state-doctrinal grounds, but could equally well be defended without any reference to them at all. Here we are concerned with the *net* state-doctrinal factor. By definition, therefore, we are dealing with something which can hardly be pinned down in terms of *form*, even if it can in terms of *effect*. If we believe that the factor operates because the authorities believe that it gives 'correct' solutions, then clearly it should be classed as an *a priori* error factor. If we believe that it operates because the authorities see an independent value in the observance of a set of doctrinal principles it should equally clearly be classified as a B group factor. The point is, of course, that we have absolutely no basis for believing one thing or the other, or even that the issue is and has been clear in the minds of Soviet leaderships. The best solution, then, though it is a pragmatic one, is to *classify the state-doctrinal factor as a separate Factor F*. This solution does, however, have the effect of postponing detailed discussion of the state-doctrinal factor to a rather late stage, and some readers may feel it appropriate to acquaint themselves at least with the material on investment appraisal techniques right from the start.

What of the problem of the relationship of investment good fetishism to the state-doctrinal factor? It is clear that both have a fair amount to do with what is usually vaguely referred to as 'ideology'. Is the distinction, then, an artificial one? In a purely psychological sense it probably is, though a psychologist would presumably be interested in distinguishing between explicit guides to action, on the one hand, and not fully self-conscious tendencies whose origin may lie in the general ideational milieu of a society on the other. For present purposes, in any case, the distinction is surely valid and important. If grand industrial objects are fetishised, the temptation to tie this in with Marxist ideology, given the great weight which it attaches to industrialisation, is strong. Quite apart from the issue of question-begging, however, there is plenty of evidence to suggest that investment good fetishism is not a monopoly of officially Marxist societies (see above, pp. 3–5), whereas explicit Marxist doctrine is, at least as far as central authorities are concerned. Even more important for immediate purposes, there is no great difficulty in pin-pointing the operation of the state-doctrinal factor, simply because it is explicit. With investment good fetishism we must, for the reasons adduced in the second section of this chapter, proceed on a residual basis. It seems best, then, to give *investment good fetishism the status of a separate Factor G*.

The full list of factors likely, *a priori*, to induce deviations from the yardstick, is, then, as follows:

Factor A1: *long-term planning horizon*
Factor A2: *short-term planning horizon*
Factor B1: *strategic factor*
Factor B2: *distributional policy*
Factor B3: *cultural policy*
Factor B4: *maintenance of political stability*
Factor B5: *foreign policy*

Factor C1: *tendency to overbid for investment resources*
Factor C2: *tendency to organisational autarky*
Factor C3: *tendency to cost/benefit externalisation*
Factor D: *elements of operational inefficiency at the design stage*
Factor E: *elements of operational inefficiency at the construction stage*
Factor F: *state-doctrinal factor*
Factor G: *investment good fetishism*

That, then, provides the basic framework within which we will analyse the case material. The next four chapters are, however, devoted to expanding and elucidating the operation of factor groups C to F. Before concluding this chapter a few further words of explanation of what will *not* be found in these four chapters are perhaps in order. Here we return to a theme which occurred on the first page, namely the mystery which surrounds the modes of operation of the central Soviet authorities with respect to investment. As far as Party/Government policy is concerned, we have provided ourselves with an *a priori* framework of reasonably solid construction. But what of the central organs which concern themselves with investment planning as such, i.e. Gosplan, the State Planning Commission, and Gosstroi, the State Committee for Construction? These organisations are not subject to the kind of day-to-day problems and pressures that ministries and enterprises suffer, but there must be some expectation that organisational inefficiency may sometimes be an important element in their 'contribution' to the investment scene. *A priori* analysis does not, however, take us very far here, and it is simply not possible to fill the gap systematically on the basis of empirical material. There should have been a separate chapter on Gosplan and Gosstroi. Instead, the reader will discover occasional references to them in chapters devoted to other institutions, in cases where some concrete information is available. But only in the last chapter will we try to make any generalisations on the central planning bodies.

It is perhaps hardly necessary to emphasise the partial and essentially taxonomic nature of the approach which has been laid out. One of the purposes of the case studies is indeed to bring a higher degree of generality and dynamism into the analysis, by presenting more or less complete 'pictures', but it is only in the concluding chapter that the really knotty problems of the relationship of charac-teristics of the investment scene to the great issues of economic development will be discussed, inevitably in an essentially qualitative way.

2

The economic system as a whole: non-specialised, subordinate executive bodies

THE FORMAL STRUCTURE OF APPROVAL AND CONFIRMATION OF INVESTMENT PROJECTS

Intermediate executive bodies, whether ministry or *sovnarkhoz*, and to a lesser extent *ob"edineniya*, enterprises and regional planning authorities (Fig. 2.1), play an important direct rôle in the determination of investment patterns.

The categorisation of investment in the Soviet Union, from the point of view of incidence of formal decision-taking responsibility, is, however, complex to the point of obscurity, and has gone through a number of changes. The most important broad category has been that

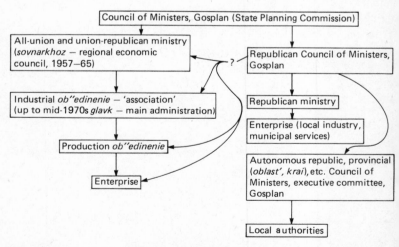

Figure 2.1 General organisational structure of the Soviet economic system.

of *centralised* investment, historically simply investment which is included in the plan. All other investment is *decentralised*. The centralised category is subdivided into *above-limit* and *below-limit* investment. Individual approval by Gosplan is required for the *titul'nye spiski* (singular *titul'nyi spisok* – 'title list') of projects large enough to be placed in the above-limit category, though the 1979 planning decree introduced the principle of joint approval by Gosplan and ministries etc.[1] The *titul'nyi spisok* is a fairly brief document, normally of about six pages, covering the basic technical, locational and cost characteristics of a given project. The planning decree of 1979 has aimed to increase the specificity and status of title lists. They are now to include breakdowns of volumes of construction work by year,[2] and are to acquire some kind of binding force, for suppliers as well as construction organisations.[3] These measures serve to underline how limited an instrument of central control the *titul'nyi spisok* has been until very recently. With below-limit investment, central approval is required only for the aggregate volumes of funds going to each sector, and in the past there has been no tie-up between planned aggregate investment and planned increment to output by sector.[4] To make matters more complex the actual designs of very big projects have to be approved centrally – but of this more in the next chapter.

Immediately after the 1965 planning reform the *titul'nyi spisok* 'limit' seems to have been set at between 5 and 25 million rubles, depending on the sector,[5] but it was quickly reduced to 2.5 million rubles.[6] Since the early 1970s it has been fixed at 3.0 million rubles.[7] In former times it has been as low as 1 million rubles,[8] and during the *sovnarkhoz* period it stood at 1.5 million rubles.[9] In 1966 65 per cent of total industrial investment was above-limit, though sectoral variations were sharp, with the figures for chemicals and non-ferrous metallurgy standing at, respectively, 98.6 per cent and 95.9 per cent, and that for the food industry at only 40 per cent.[10]

As of 1966, centralised, material-sphere capital investments in enterprises under all-union ministries and industrial and construction union-republican ministries went through the ministries, with *titul'nye spiski* for below-limit projects subject to their approval or general supervision. For enterprises under other union-republican ministries investment was included in the republican plan, unless the enterprise involved was 'directly subordinate to the ministry'. The rest of centralised investment went through the republics,[11] with *titul'nye spiski* of below-limit projects subject to the approval of republican or lower-level territorial authorities. Ziyadullaev, the chairman of the Uzbek SSR Gosplan, clarified the relative standing of republican planning authorities in the late 1960s, when he stated in 1968 that 'republican planning organs do not calculate, nor does Gosplan USSR consider in respect of republics, . . . any indicators for labour, profits, costs, research. . . . All these indicators, as well as the breakdown of plans for industrial production and investment in respect of republics, are confirmed by the appropriate all-union ministries and departments, without consultation with Gosplan USSR or the Councils of Ministries of union republics.'[12]

Since then, there has been some movement towards an increase in the effective rôle of territorial authorities in this connection. By the early 1970s the republics appear to have acquired new specific powers in relation to small material-sphere projects.[13] The contemporary policy emphasis on the importance of *complex spatial development*, underlined in the 1979 planning decree,[14] has served to raise the general status of territorial authorities, and the long-term regional plan has been emphatically endorsed by the central authorities as a key element in the improvement of the general level of planning.[15] It would be dangerous, however, to over-identify territorial *plan* with territorial *authority*. One scholarly source states that 'the basis for working out a complex plan comes from the territorial breakdown of sectoral plans, worked out by ministries and departments, which fix production tasks and material and financial resources, in the first instance by enterprise, and then on a territorial basis'.[16] More bluntly, 'it stands to reason that a territorial capital investment plan for a *raion* cannot be anything else than a summing of the capital investment plans of the various departments'.[17] Certainly some recent reports have accused territorial authorities of a degree of 'localism' in relation to investment matters reminiscent of the *sovnarkhoz* period (see below, pp. 39–43), and implying a considerable degree of effective 'muscle', whatever the formal position.[18] But it is only at the rather humble level of housing and municipal services that real organisational teeth have been given to local bodies through investiture of the capital investment department (*otdel* or *upravlenie kapital'nogo stroitel'stva*, OKS or UKS) of the local government with the status of 'single client' (*edinyi zakazchik*) for all related investment projects built on the 'in-house' basis (see below, p. 75), whatever the organisation that is actually doing the financing.[19] Even at this level, however, the ministries can pull their weight. When the Tyumen' *gorispolkom* (city government) recently refused to pass some blocks of flats built by the Gas Ministry because they did not have proper plumbing, water supply or central heating, the Ministry simply sent its workers in to squat.[20] In general, then, there seems no reason to doubt the continued prevalence of the departmental principle in the organisation of capital investment planning.

Cutting across these rules on who approves what is the breakdown of centralised investment by *source of finance*. Table 2.1 presents a nearly contemporary picture of the centralised investment finance situation by ministry.

Before the 1965 planning reform budgetary grants were the predominant form of finance for centralised investment. The reform stressed both retained profits and bank credit as alternative modes. As Table 2.1 indicates, the former has tended to emerge much more strongly than the latter as a key source of finance. There is, of course, no reason why above-limit investments should not be financed from retentions or bank credit, and the figures in Table 2.1 should not be taken to imply that, for example, the Ministry for Instrument-making is completely free of central tutelage with respect to its investment plans, or that its subdivisions can ignore ministerial preferences on below-limit projects. Reliance on own finance must, surely, *de facto* give initiating organisations some greater degree of effective influence over allocation, whatever the formal planning procedure, but on the whole trends in investment finance have probably been most important in relation to the general question of the effectiveness of cost constraints (see below).

The decentralised investment category was brought into prominence by the Kosygin reform, and increased in value from 5 to 10 milliard rubles between 1965 and 1968.[21] By 1972 it accounted for almost 20 per cent of total state investment.[22] The primary source of finance for decentralised investment is the *production-development fund*, an autonomously managed fund financed from profits. Every executive organisation on *khozraschet* (for a detailed explanation of this term see below, pp. 32–4) normally has a production-development fund. Decentralised investment projects can also be financed from bank credit. As of the immediately post-reform period, the only constraint on complete freedom on the part of executive organisations with respect to this kind of investment was their own financial position and a planned level for total decentralised investment. The history of decentralised investment over the past decade has been chequered.

Table 2.1. *Centralised investment in Soviet industry by financial source (percentage distribution)*

Ministry	1972 Budgetary grants	1972 Own funds	1972 Credit	1974 Budgetary grants	1974 Own funds	1974 Credit
Oil	47.3	52.7	—	46.04	53.96	—
Oil-refining and Petrochemicals USSR	9.0	72.3	18.7	6.98	61.46	31.56
Gas	42.7	42.9	14.4	55.51	27.38	17.11
Chemicals	29.3	63.1	7.6	23.64	69.27	7.09
Coal USSR	53.0	47.0	—	44.18	55.82	—
Heavy Machine Building	25.6	70.4	4.0	31.93	63.36	4.71
Electricity	22.9	66.3	10.8	21.20	66.57	12.23
Chemical and Oil Machine Building	24.6	54.2	21.2	26.42	43.30	30.28
Machine Tools and Tools	36.1	61.4	2.5	33.62	59.14	7.24
Instrument-making	—	100.0	—	—	100.00	—
Vehicles	50.4	40.0	9.6	47.09	44.31	8.60
Agricultural Machine Building	28.5	50.9	20.6	29.02	52.68	18.30
Construction Machine Building	24.3	67.3	8.3	24.33	67.63	8.04
Light Machine Building*	20.0	64.0	16.0	17.65	63.34	19.01
Forestry USSR	25.5	61.4	13.0	31.65	67.19	1.16
Paper	32.4	57.9	9.7	35.03	55.95	9.02
Building Materials USSR	43.6	52.5	3.9	40.29	57.62	2.09
Ferrous Metallurgy USSR	27.3	72.7	—	31.47	68.53	—
Non-ferrous Metallurgy USSR	24.5	72.4	3.1	25.01	73.69	1.30
Light Industry RSFSR	20.8	79.1	0.1	31.51	68.49	—
Food Processing RSFSR	8.3	87.8	3.9	17.37	68.99	13.64
Meat and Dairy RSFSR	1.1	98.1	0.8	1.52	98.48	—
Fisheries RSFSR	62.6	37.4	—	71.99	28.01	—
TOTAL	33.8	60.0	6.2	34.63	57.69	7.68

* The full title of this organisation is 'Ministry of machine building for light industry and the food and household appliances industries'

After initial supply problems the overall decentralised investment plan was overfulfilled in 1971 by 26 per cent, while the centralised investment plan was underfulfilled by 4 per cent.[23] This prompted a reaction from the central authorities that has resulted in a progressive emasculation of the decentralised category. From 1971 total amounts of decentralised investment by ministry, republic and sector were planned centrally,[24] while the 1971–75 plan included a 'unified supply plan' for centralised and decentralised investment,[25] though this appears to have been ineffectual.[26] In 1973 overfulfilment of decentralised investment plans was banned,[27] and provisions made for the siphoning-off of idle balances from decentralised sources into an 'all-state fund of financial resources'.[28] By 1975 production-development funds were being commonly used to finance centralised investment,[29] while the proportion of total state investment financed on a decentralised basis fell to just 15 per cent in that year.[30] As from 1977, ministerial, *ob"edinenie* and enterprise planned aggregates for investment are confirmed without sub-division into centralised and decentralised categories,[31] and it is now 'a pure formality that investments implemented on the basis of the production-development fund . . . are called decentralised'.[32]

For the late 1960s and early 1970s, then, we have to be careful to distinguish between decentralised and centralised investment, and in particular to avoid confusing centralised investment financed directly from retained profits, and decentralised investment financed from the production-development fund. In the past the category of decentralised investment has given *khozraschet* organisations a very significant area of manoeuvre in the investment field. This is no longer the case and for practical purposes decentralised investment can probably now be treated as a subdivision of below-limit centralised investment, though the 1979 planning decree may herald some movement back towards the position of the late 1960s.

What emerges from this rather complex picture, then, is that the intermediate executive body has enjoyed a direct rôle in the determination of investment patterns second only to that of the central planners. Some rôle has been played by *ob"edineniya*, enterprises and republican planning authorities, and its importance for each of these types of organisation has varied from one period to another. One should not, of course, ignore the indirect influence that lower-level bodies must have on all categories of investment, simply by virtue of the fact that the central and intermediate planners are heavily dependent upon them for information regarding investment possibilities etc.

WEAKNESS OF COST CONSTRAINTS – THE DETAILS

As was briefly indicated in Chapter 1, there are three main ways in which the milieu in which they operate induces non-specialised, subordinate executive bodies to take decisions likely to lead to deviations from the yardstick – overbidding for investment resources, autarkical tendencies and cost/benefit externalisation. The operation of the first two of these factors is encouraged by the emphasis on output performance, necessitated by the prevalence of supply uncertainty, and permitted by the tendency for all cost constraints to be weak. Before passing on to a detailed discussion of Factors C1 and C2 let us run quickly through the history of formal cost constraints in the planning system.

Up till 1959, though cost plans were handed out to enterprises, the gross output plan was of overriding importance as far as bonuses were concerned. Being on *khozraschet* (*khozyaistvennyi raschet* – 'business accounting'), as all industrial enterprises were, meant that orthodox business accounting procedures were followed, and enterprises were expected to avoid making losses. Many enterprises were, however, 'planned loss-makers', so that the cost-minimising element in *khozraschet* should not be overstressed. The other main element in *khozraschet* – having formal success-indicator/bonus systems – simply strengthened the orientation to the prevalent gross output success-indicator. Ministries and *sovnarkhozy* were not on *khozraschet*, and presumably did not operate under a formal success-indicator/bonus system. It is, however, fairly clear that gross output considerations outweighed cost considerations with intermediate bodies as much as with enterprises. Cost reduction was introduced explicitly into enterprise bonus systems in 1959, but it is unclear whether this change ever really 'took'. Certainly, the Soviet authorities quickly became conscious of the defects of the new success-indicator, in particular the intensified quality problems it tended to produce.[33] The position as it affected intermediate bodies (at that time *sovnarkhozy*) may have in any case remained unchanged, though there is some uncertainty about this.[34]

The 1965 reform returned to the problem of making cost constraints more effective, this time indirectly, through the introduction of profit and profit-rate success-indicators for enterprises. Output considerations remained, however, at least equally important, though in the modified form of a sales (*realizatsiya*) success-indicator, and the continued prevalence of *shturmovshchina* ('storming' – the mad rush at the end of the plan period to fulfil the production target at any cost) indicates how the priorities sorted themselves out under this régime in times of stress. In the early and mid-1970s explicit cost-reduction targets were progressively reintroduced in a number of sectors,[35] and they continue to have some status for particular sectors under the 1979 planning decree.[36] These trends partly reflect the growing confidence on the part of the Soviet planners, explicitly expressed in the 1979 planning decree, in their ability to measure quality directly. On the other hand, there seems to be no question of trying to re-establish cost reduction as a key success-indicator at the general level. Rather the current policy emphasis is on the development of a new planning indicator – normed net output (*normativnaya chistaya produktsiya*, hereafter NNO) – as a form of synthetic indicator embodying cost-reduction elements. A value-added indicator based on a definition of net output that includes wage costs and profit only, NNO obviously excludes the incentive to 'grossness' – 'ample' utilisation of bought-in materials from other organisations – implicit in the older output success-indicators. Because payments into funds are on the basis of the *normed* relationship of net output to sales, an enterprise which achieves a given level of *realizatsiya* on the basis of less-than-normed labour inputs will gain. Thus the 'excess labour intensity' deviation which is built into crude value-added indicators is obviated, and the enterprise does, in fact, have an incentive to minimise processing costs, subject to the fulfilment of the NNO target.[37] But application of this indicator is still only at the experimental stage. Other elements in a rather contradictory planning decree, particularly the emphasis on *proizvodstvo produktsii v natural'nom vyrazhenii* (production in physical terms) as a key indicator,[38] suggest a continued orientation to 'grossness' which may neutralise the cost-minimising properties of NNO, where it is introduced. As far as the enterprise is concerned, then, there has been a growing tendency to introduce explicit or implicit cost-reduction elements into the system of planning indicators. Up to now this tendency has not been sufficiently strong to transform the basic situation.

As far as intermediate bodies (now again ministries etc.) are concerned, the position is less clear. Initially at least, ministries seem to have continued to operate largely on a totally non-*khozraschet*, gross output basis.[39] The 1968 plan, however, was, according to one source,[40] to include sales and profits plans for ministries. Another report, from 1970, describing the situation in a 'reformed' ministry, namely the Ministry of Instrument-making, talks vaguely of 'elements of *khozraschet*', and indicates that profit would not be an explicit success-indicator, though enterprise profit was clearly to be a source of general finance to the ministry.[41] In 1976 the Ministry for Road Transport of the Kazakh republic was put onto a fairly full form of *khozraschet*,[42] though a similar system introduced in the Belorussian Ministry for Road Transport a couple of years earlier had not operated very satisfactorily.[43] It is in any case not clear what this kind of development means in terms of the big all-union industrial ministries. More definite steps were taken in the immediately post-reform period towards the introduction of *khozraschet* at the level of the *glavk* ('main administration', plural *glavki*).

With the *ob"edinenie* decree of 1973, however, the *khozraschetnyi glavk* seems to have been largely superseded. The new system is complex in the extreme. In the Ministry of Light Machine Building, for example, some production *ob"edineniya*, all scientific-production *ob"edineniya*, and even some large enterprises are directly subordinate to the ministry. More normally production *ob"edineniya* and large enterprises are directly subordinate to so-called *industrial ob"edineniya*, which are in turn directly subordinate to the ministry,[44] though in 1979 still only 46 per cent of total industrial sales were accounted for by *ob"edineniya*.[45] That all production *ob"edineniya* are on *khozraschet* is indubitable, and the situation would appear to be the same with the industrial *ob"edineniya*.[46] What is certainly the case is that the introduction of *khozraschet* into sub-intermediate bodies has in a number of cases run into trouble precisely because the ministries still operate largely on a traditional, *val*-based (gross-output-based), system.[47] Ministerial *khozraschet* is once again emphasised in the 1979 planning decree, but it has been made clear that this is not to mean much more than just having formal incentive and research funds.[48] How effectively, then, cost constraints have been introduced into the intermediate planning hierarchy remains something of a moot point.

Another change introduced in 1965 was the establishment of the principle of payment for use of capital – in other words of an interest charge. As we have seen, this was paralleled by the introduction of bank credit as a basis for financing centralised investment. With costs that are recorded in an accounting sense we can speak only of a tendency for them to be ignored. Even when costs did not affect bonus arrangements, excessive rises in costs might bring down the wrath of control agencies and central authorities upon the organisation responsible. But before 1965 there was really no reason whatsoever for an organisation to concern itself about capital scarcity, except to the extent that it affected output performance. This is of particular importance with respect to *raspylenie sredstv* (*raspylenie* – 'dispersion', or 'spreading' of investment resources). In the present context, then, the introduction of a capital charge, and interest payments on investment credits, is an interesting aspect of the 1965 reform. It is hardly of major importance, however, given the low level at which interest rates have been set, the very large number of exemptions, and the still marginal, though growing, quantitative importance of long-term credits. And, once again, it may, in any case, not have affected the ministries very much. The rapid emergence of retained profits as a major form of investment finance noted in Table 2.1 may represent a more important, though surely still minor, inducement to cost-consciousness.

As far as republican planning authorities are concerned, it is not clear what effect any of this has had. It is not clear to what extent they have been concerned with plan fulfilment as such at all, whatever the terms in which the plan might be expressed. Republican governments are concerned with plan fulfilment, though they presumably do not get actual bonuses for it, and they may put pressure on local planners.

Planning developments since 1965 have, then, done something to introduce effective cost constraints, but there is still a heavy emphasis on output performance, and this emphasis becomes heavier the more one moves up the planning hierarchy, i.e. the more one moves towards the major *loci* of investment decision-taking. There is no reason, then, to believe that the situation has changed fundamentally from that prevalent in the pre-reform period. On the basis of this we can proceed to examine in detail how the first two C group factors operate in practice.

FACTOR C1: TENDENCY TO OVERBID FOR INVESTMENT RESOURCES

Alone of the three factors, C1 has no direct locational implications. It simply has the effect of introducing *raspylenie sredstv*, prolonging gestation periods, and indirectly increasing the costs of capital projects. Krasovskii cited in 1967 a figure of 7–8 years as the average total lead-time, from design assignment/technical design (see pp. 52–3) through to capacity operation, for large enterprises, while Maevskii and Maevskii, writing about the same time, suggest a corresponding figure of 5–7 years for all enterprises.[49] Both these sources claim that this is 2–2.5 times longer than what, on the basis of foreign experience, could be called 'normal'. Evidence from the 1970s suggests that, if anything, the situation may have worsened. Gnatov and Uvarov give a figure, corresponding exactly in coverage to the Maevskii and Maevskii one, of 8–10 years, while Hanson and Hill, in their survey of chemicals turnkey projects exported from the UK to the USSR, came up with an average total lead-time, 'from first enquiry to completion (handing over)', of 6 years and 10 months, as compared to a corresponding figure, for projects done in Western Europe, of 2.25–3.5 years.[50] Gnatov and Uvarov break their figure down in terms of 2–3 years for designing, more than 5 for actual construction, and 2–3 for attainment of full capacity. Some of the 'excess' in the case of the chemicals turnkey projects relates to negotiating time, but even the contract–completion stage took 2.5–3 years longer than it would in Western Europe. For 'priority' projects (but of this more later), this seems a very big gap. The Soviet planners themselves recently estimated that lead-times could be reduced by 1.8 times in the period up to 1990.[51]

It is this problem which sometimes seems almost to mock Soviet attempts to plan investment. Fifty per cent of projects do not meet their planned completion dates,[52] even though planned lead-times are often anything but demanding. On average for the Ukrainian Ministry for Ferrous Metallurgy, for example, the planned gestation period is 8.1 years, as against a 'normative' period of 4.5 years.[53] The grey area of 'on-streaming operations' (*puskonaladochnye raboty*) is subject to few norms, and its inclusion in calculations of total lead-times introduces an additional element of vagueness (and also, of course, more scope for 'getting away with' *raspylenie*).[54] Unfinished construction as a proportion of annual investment reached 69 per cent in 1965, 75 per cent in 1975, and 85 per cent in 1977.[55]

What lies behind the phenomenon? Briefly, organisations, in the quest for output maximisation, try to get as many investment projects as possible started in period 1, because this will make it easier to get more investment funds in period 2. But *raspylenie* is not wholly a function of the operation of non-specialised, subordinate executive bodies. As we shall see in later chapters, specialised, subordinate executive bodies – *proektnye organisatsii* and building enterprises – have their share of responsibility. Again, as long as supply uncertainty persists there is bound to be some tendency to overshoot planned completion dates. But supply uncertainty also has an indirect effect, which operates *through* non-specialised, subordinate executive bodies, inasmuch as it makes it desirable for them to have a large number of projects on the go, in order to raise their chances of always being in a position to finish some projects, whatever the supply situation.

There is, in fact, fairly strong evidence that overbidding on the part of intermediate bodies has been of considerable quantitative importance within the general tendency to *raspylenie*. Year after year, plans for the introduction of new capacity are underfulfilled, while output plans continue to be fulfilled.[56] Major articles on the problem of *raspylenie* mention the need to improve efficiency in planning and building, but place emphasis on the rôle of the ministries and local planning organs, and one authoritative survey states simply that 'this dispersion of capital investments flows from a number of causes, but primarily from localistic and departmentalist tendencies on the part of ministries and departments and also union republics'.[57] These organisations proposed 1,000 major new investment projects for 1970, of which only 300 were eventually adopted.[58] Enterprise managements operate in exactly the same way, viz:

(industrial enterprise manager to building manager) 'We've just got to have a new unit. Could you help us?'

'What have you got apart from plans.'

'We've got a little money. A design is being done. The ministry is promising to help with equipment.'

'OK, when you've got everything ready, then we'll talk about it.'

The old hand in the management game is nothing dismayed by this kind of treatment. Waving written guarantees and requests from his ministry, he beats on the door of the construction *glavk*, and appeals to the city and *oblast'* [province, plural *oblasti*] authorities.

'You've got to help me! Otherwise they'll give the money to somebody else.'

Usually they do help, although they know in advance what the result will be . . .[59]

It has been shown that in 1970 there were 2.5–3 times as many investment projects under way as the economy could handle, even with 'normal' building times,[60] and more recent figures suggest no dramatic change in this respect.[61] In 1975 the total estimated value of projects in the plan was gauged at 1.7 times its optimal level,[62] and that does not include projects that have been started, even though they are not in the plan – there were 362 such projects in 1976.[63] This represents strong confirmation of the importance of overbidding on the part of non-specialised, subordinate executive bodies, i.e., if you like, of the 'pure' *raspylenie* factor.

One interesting point which it is worth pausing over is the way in which *raspylenie* seems to have got worse during the *sovnarkhoz* period. Krasovskii blames this largely on difficulties encountered in the 'localisation' of the building industry. 'The majority of construction organisations were handed over to the *sovnarkhozy*, but proved unprepared for the solution of the new, complex tasks set by the seven-year plan. Local construction organisations did not have the necessary production base, and lacked special cadres with experience in the construction of complex projects connected with new technology and large-scale lines of communication.'[64] Solomin points out that 1963 was a particularly bad year, and blames this on a 'lowering in the degree of responsibility displayed by the *sovnarkhozy* in the period of their amalgamation',[65] though one wonders whether, in fact, the *sovnarkhozy* still controlled much investment in 1963. Perhaps the most important factor here was simply the worsening, for reasons well known, of the supply problem in the *sovnarkhoz* period. Nove argues this strongly,[66] and quotes Dymshits in support: 'planning organs, *sovnarkhozy*, enterprises, construction trusts, do not satisfactorily link investment plans with plans for producing and delivering equipment. As a result of such defects in the planning and organisation of construction, more building projects are in hand at any given moment than can be supplied with metal, cement and equipment.'[67] It seems clear, at any rate, that there is no need to see the worsening of the situation in the *sovnarkhoz* period in terms of an increase in the intensity of the tendency to overbid for investment resources.

FACTOR C2: TENDENCY TO ORGANISATIONAL AUTARKY

This phenomenon has received wide coverage in the literature,[68] and all that is necessary here is to point out some of its more interesting locational aspects. At the level of the enterprise there is a tendency to sacrifice economies of scale through the institution of 'dwarf-work-shops'. 'The typical Leningrad (engineering) factory of today is an enterprise with a full range of subsidiary production lines. It has its own "mini-castings shop", smithy and plastics department. It makes its own chisels, bolts and screws, and does its own maintenance work on equipment. This is fantastically expensive. The production of chisels for turners at the Yegorov factory costs 12 times as much as at a specialised factory, and at the Reduktor factory 22 times as much. The question arises, why spend money in this way, why not go out and buy the articles? But there is nowhere to buy them. There are still very few specialised factories turning out articles of general application in the engineering industry.'[69] Managers are forced to act in a way which to the uninitiated or tendentious might seem like cynicism. 'Just look at what a good guy I am, and how passionately I support the idea of specialisation. But for old times' sake – let me build just a wee castings shop at the factory . . .'[70] According to one source, enterprises make more than three-quarters of the instruments and equipment they need themselves.[71] The cost relatives from the Leningrad example are extreme examples, but on the basis of a recent survey of all dwarf-workshops producing castings etc. in the Belorussian republic it was estimated that costs in such units were 1.5–2.0 times the republican average.[72] Supply organs, unable to do anything very much about supply uncertainty, advise enterprises to organise production of 'bits and pieces' locally.[73]

Intermediate bodies are not, of course, especially in favour of 'dwarf-workshops', and would rather organise this kind of production on a sectoral or regional basis. In 1969, for example, the Ministry for the Oil Industry launched a campaign for the rationalisation of auxiliary services.[74] But intermediate bodies have the same problem of control over enterprises as the centre has over intermediate bodies, and in cases where the sums involved in investment are small, enterprises can clearly get away with a great deal.

The way in which the autarkical tendency works out with ministries and *sovnarkhozy* is more complex and more interesting. The basic elements in the situation are as follows: ministries try to acquire production capacity in lines on which they depend for supplies, and this tends to lead to sacrifices in economies of scale, in the same way as it does with enterprises. Because ministries are Union-wide organisations, it also tends to lead to an excessively 'transport-inten-sive' locational pattern. 'The ministries see the Irtysh steppe as just a site for enterprises. Having built the factories, they usually start to supply them from afar with "their own" raw materials, though these are produced in adequate quantities in Pavlodar – but by other ministries.'[75] Transport organisations, still heavily oriented to gross-output-type success-indicators, have no incentive to minimise hauls, and in any case transport capacity is one of the things that ministries tend to 'collect'. An inspection in 1976 of nine *oblasti* in the RSFSR, for example, revealed that over the previous two years departmental lorry parks had grown by a total of 470,000, while those of specialised transport organisations had grown by only 62,000, this despite the fact that costs in the former are 1.2–2.3 times what they are in the latter.[76] In some cases, one particular ministry may be practically 'annihilated' by the autarkical tendencies of others. More than 70 ministries and departments produce timber products, for example, and the Forestry Ministry accounts for only 37 per cent of total timber output.[77] *Sovnarkhozy* had the same tendencies, except that the problem of excessive transport hauls did not arise, for obvious reasons. On the other hand, the problem of comparative advantage, or its absence, could clearly have become important. Had the *sovnarkhoz* system survived, it is possible that Central Asia would eventually have succeeded in expanding its ferrous metallurgy sector which, given the absence of significant deposits of iron ore in the region, would have been inefficient from a national economic point of view, whatever the scale of the venture.

Sometimes these tendencies work themselves out through the construction of new enterprises. For example, separate cable factories and general metal goods (*metiz*) factories were built in each of the Central Asian republics in the early *sovnarkhoz* period, when *sovnarkhoz* boundaries corresponded to republican boundaries in that region.[78] Clearly, the fact that new construction must normally come under the head of above-limit investment may make it fairly difficult for intermediate bodies to get away with this. There is, however, a way in which it can be made easier. 'There have been cases where estimates have been deliberately scaled down by design workers to sums of under 1.5 million rubles, in order that the *proekty* [designs, singular *proekt*] could be confirmed on the spot – by the *sovnarkhoz*.'[79] When Promstroiproekt (general industrial design organisation), for example, estimated the cost of the production block of Sibgipromez (specialist ferrous-metallurgy design organisation) in Kemerevo at 5.2 million rubles, the Ministry for Ferrous Metallurgy simply cut this to 2.5 million rubles – the then limit – on confirmation. In the end the project cost 5.8 million rubles.[80] This, of course, throws considerable light on the problem of rising estimates, of which more in a later chapter.

Sometimes the transferral of an enterprise from one ministry to another is involved, as, for example, with the Ordzhonikidze engineering factory in Tadzhikistan, which was taken over by the Ministry for the Oil Industry in 1942.[81] In cases like this, however, a factory will usually have to be reconstructed to suit the needs of the ministry – in the case just mentioned the factory was switched from general repair and maintenance work (locally orientated) to the production of heavy fittings for the oil industry (there is virtually no oil in Tadzhikistan) – and it is quite clear that, whether the allegiance of an enterprise changes or no, 'reconstruction and expansion' is the normal way in which ministries and *sovnarkhozy* pursue their autarkical ends. Whatever the precise location of the limit, it is clear that more often than not this will come under the head of below-limit investment, so that it is not surprising that 'analysis shows that part of the funds going to so-called "below-limit" construction is used irrationally. Growth of production capacity, replacement of morally and physically worn-out equipment and removal of bottlenecks in existing enterprises, does not always take place, and work is carried out on the expansion and reconstruction of existing enterprises with less efficient results than with new construction.'[82] There is, furthermore, evidence to suggest that it certainly used to be easier to get a reconstruction through than a new enterprise, even with an above-limit investment.[83] It is, of course, very difficult for the central authorities to enunciate a clear definition of 'reconstruction and expansion'.

Let us look at the *proekt* for the reconstruction of the Karlovka mechanical factory of the former Khar'kov *sovnarkhoz*. A small factory, with productive fixed capital before reconstruction of 861,000 rubles, it turned out machinery for the food industry at the rate of 1.8 million rubles per annum . . . The *proekt* foresees the construction on the territory of this factory of the following new buildings: a metal-construction department of area 9,000 m^2; an assembly department of area 2,500 m^2; an engineering building of area 4,200 m^2; a restaurant and food shop of area 1,000 m^2: funds have also been set aside for the construction of a kindergarten, nurseries, a school, a Pioneer camp, a laundry, an *univermag* [department store], and a tailors' shop. Production in existing departments is to cease . . . As a result of reconstruction, the productive floor space of the factory will increase from 2,800 to 16,100 m^2, i.e. by almost six times.

We are not concerned here with the question of whether it was basically necessary to build this factory or no, whether the expenditures on its construction are being used effectively. The *proekt* for the reconstruction of the Karlovka factory proves only one thing; this is not reconstruction of an existing factory, but construction of a new, contemporary enterprise on the vacated territory of a small existing enterprise. Expenditures on the construction of new projects within the factory make up more than 4/5 of the estimated outlays. Nevertheless, work on this factory goes into the plan and the accounts under the heading 'reconstruction and expansion of existing enterprises'.[84]

Gosplan and Gosstroi (see below, pp. 48–50) have issued special instructions in which the categories 'reconstruction' (*rekonstruktsiya*), 'technical re-equipment' (*tekhnicheskoe perevooruzhenie*), expansion (*rasshirenie*) and new construction (*novoe stroitel' stvo*) are defined.[85] Nevertheless 'even now, they try to get things involving expansion or new construction into the plan under the rubric of reconstruction in the Ministry for Machine-tool Production',[86] and 'analysis of capital investment in ferrous metallurgy enterprises in the Central Urals shows that in practice analogous work is counted as reconstruction in some factories and extension in others'.[87] A standard methodology on calculating the effectiveness of reconstruction and expansion, worked out by the Urals Scientific Centre of the USSR Academy of Sciences, has been severely criticised for its 'extreme vagueness on the definition of the concept of "reconstruction"'.[88]

The ways in which this freedom enjoyed with respect to reconstruction has been used is well documented. A source from 1965, just about the time the ministerial system was being reintroduced, describes how:

recently the *proekt* for the development of the Chelyabinsk metallurgical factory, which envisages a three-fold increase in production, was examined. Implementation of the *proekt* would require expenditures of more than a milliard rubles. The *proekt* appears properly completed in accordance with the needs of the customer. But if its content is analysed, it is not difficult to see that the decision taken is anything but satisfactory. The factory does not have a reliable ore base. Fuel is transported from the Kuzbass. There is a deficit of electrical energy. Users of the metal are situated thousands of miles from the Urals.

The Chelyabinsk factory specialises in the production of high-quality metal, but expansion of capacity is in fact aimed at increasing production of ordinary rolled steel.

Thus, the strongly-held wish of the client to expand the Chelyabinsk factory apart, there are no weighty arguments in favour of the decision which has been taken – which, by the way, is being most energetically implemented.[89]

The transport-intensity of this particular decision is typical of departmental (in this case presumably one of the 'State Production Committees' which filled in between the effective demise of the *sovnarkhoz* system and the formal reintroduction of the ministerial system in September, 1965) autarky, and the switch in emphasis in production profile from a more to a less 'finished' product, from a more specialised to a more general product, surely represented a switch towards *greater emphasis on supplying other enterprises in the same or closely allied industrial sectors*.

Moving back in time to the *sovnarkhoz* period, the same source comes up with another example from Leningrad.

In 1962 it was decided to go ahead with the reconstruction of the Leningrad carburettor factory im. Kuibysheva, as an exceptional case, in order to increase the output of carburettors and apparatus for the oil industry. Three-shift work was envisaged for the factory, so that the number of workers should not be increased, and capital expenditures reduced to a minimum. This would also mean completion of reconstruction in the shortest possible time.

However, the design-constructor bureau of the Leningrad *sovnarkhoz*, Lenstankoproekt, produced a *proektnoe zadanie* [design assignment] envisaging the development of production of a whole range of articles currently being produced by the factory, but having no connection whatsoever with the production of carburettors and apparatus for the oil industry. The design workers foresaw a quite unnecessary expansion of iron castings production, with 90 per cent of production being marketed, which will lead to the pollution of the atmosphere in Leningrad. Demolition of capital buildings area 4,900 m^2 and construction of new buildings area 32,000 m^2 was envisaged . . . Two-shift instead of three-shift work is planned in the *proekt*, and the programme has been enlarged by 39 per cent, with estimated costs more than doubling. Naturally, the *proekt* was not confirmed.[90]

This last sentence reminds us, of course, that we are talking about tendencies which the centre can do something to control and restrict. But the case stands as an outstanding instance of a *sovnarkhoz* trying to 'despecialise' a factory, and reorient its production profiles towards notoriously scarce products like castings, in order to improve supplies of these products within the *sovnarkhoz*.

The whole business of reconstructions is made the more interesting inasmuch as the Soviet authorities have been trying over recent years, for reasons that have nothing to do with autarkical practices, to encourage reconstruction at the expense of new construction, and the share of reconstructions in total investment grew from 58 to 65 per cent 1970–73,[91] and is planned to exceed 70 per cent for the period 1976–80.[92] The reasoning behind this policy has been that reconstructions, at least when accompanied by full-scale modernisation and technological updating, yield lower capital-output ratios than the corresponding 'new' constructions. This is certainly not borne out by data on reconstructions from the early and middle 1960s. At the Zhdanov factory *Tyazhmash* the output-capital ratio fell from 2 to 1.36 after reconstruction, a result unlikely to be explicable purely in terms of a change in the capital-labour ratio.[93] The capital cost of expanding the Chelyabinsk auto-mechanical factory was 60 per cent above the norm for analogous new enterprises.[94] A survey of 50 reconstructions done by Stroibank USSR in 1962 showed that in the majority of cases production increases were achieved purely through expansion of the production area, with the capital-output ratio worsening, but a second survey conducted in 1964 came up with the interesting result that the return on investment is higher where expansion of production area is minimal, i.e. presumably in genuinely 'technological' reconstructions.[95] Part of the reason for this is that 'in enterprises where new construction goes on under the rubric of reconstruction, it tends to drag out over long periods'.[96]

It is the technology-oriented reconstructions that the authorities have been trying to encourage in recent years. It may not be an exaggeration to say that what they have been attempting to do is to change the whole nature of reconstruction, to transform it into a vehicle for cheap high technology. They have encountered a number of problems in doing this, not least the fact that design organisations and regular (*podryadni* – contract) building organisations, which would naturally be favoured for a genuinely 'centralised' project over ministerial or enterprise 'own' building organisations, find reconstruction 'fiddly' and bad for success-indicators.[97] The 1979 planning decree envisages the introduction of special norms for fund-forming etc. in construction enterprises to try to counteract this tendency.[98] Enterprises too tend, *ceteris paribus*, to be unsympathetic towards reconstruction, because it interferes with current production and may jeopardise plan fulfilment.[99] A 1975 source notes that in the leather-processing sector the average gestation period for reconstructions is 77 months, as against 39 months for new plants,[100] while criticism of the low level of construction technology used in many reconstructions continues to be heard.[101] There must, therefore, be some doubts as to how successfully the reconstruction campaign is changing the whole nature of reconstruction. For our present purposes, however, the important point is that current policy must, at least in principle, open up even greater scope for ministerial etc. 'own' policies, the more so to the extent that the degree of effective control in the investment field remains well below its 'planned' level. In this connection, an authoritative article from 1976 merely states that 'the share of funds going to genuine reconstruction and technical re-equipment is significantly lower than (the official figure for reconstructions as a whole)'.[102]

The reconstruction syndrome has some interesting implications, perhaps not at first sight obvious, particularly for ministries. A ministry which was totally independent as far as investment decisions are concerned would be able to arrange itself supply-wise without necessarily causing excessive transport activity, and without necessarily building up production capacity in unsuitable environments. Economies of scale would still, of course, be sacrificed, and there would still be little positive incentive to keep down lengths of hauls. But it is the peculiar half-way house which characterises Soviet central planning which conditions the outstanding features of *vedomstvennost'* (departmentalism). Ministries are constrained to work with a more or less all-union network of establishments, big and small. For historical reasons the big establishments tend to be in the big cities, so that considerations of internal economies of scale and of some aspects of external economies of scale (e.g. availability of labour) conspire to induce a strong preference to concentrate main activities in the big centres, while the small, peripheral plants are left to produce the 'nuts and bolts'.

Before leaving this topic, it is worth pausing to speculate over an interesting question. It is fairly clear that autarkical tendencies were stronger under the *sovnarkhozy* than they are, or have been, under the ministries. Why? Three possible explanations spring to mind. Firstly, as noted earlier, the mixture of territorial and sectoral principles which characterised the period 1957–65 intensified the problem of supply. Secondly, the lack of any real economic rationale in the way in which *sovnarkhoz* boundaries were drawn made the phenomenon potentially much more pernicious. Thirdly, the fact that many *sovnarkhozy* corresponded to national areas probably meant that, to some extent, autarkical phenomena in this period reflected investment good fetishism rather than a concern with supply problems. For, of course, if authorities in contiguous areas fetishise the same things, the result is autarky, even if this is not an aim in itself, as the experience of Yugoslavia has shown. It is interesting in this connection to note that in the *sovnarkhozy* in Central Asia, where, of course, *sovnarkhoz* boundaries corresponded to republican and national boundaries, autarkical tendencies were very pronounced indeed. Finally, it is clear that autarkical tendencies feed on themselves, because they create supply problems for others, so that any marginal tendency for the *sovnarkhoz* system to be worse in this respect would have been magnified, more or less automatically.

FACTOR C3: COST/BENEFIT EXTERNALISATION

To repeat, there is some tendency to externalise all costs in the Soviet system and this fact is of great importance in the operation of Factors C1 and C2, just discussed. Under the present heading we are concerned with a narrower category, basically similar to the concept of production externalities used with reference to market economies, where specific costs and benefits are imposed upon fairly specific third parties. As noted earlier, the major peculiarity of the concept as it will be used here is that it includes opportunity costs of land and natural resources in a way in which it would not if we were dealing with a market system with a reasonably rational rent structure. Zoned agricultural procurement prices have in the past provided some rental element in the Soviet system, but, of course, have not implied any transfer price for land if, say, it moves from agricultural to industrial usage. The 1965 reform brought with it some attempts to charge for the use of unique natural advantages,[103] but nothing systematic resulted, and the 1979 planning decree does little more than introduce a generalised water charge for enterprises.[104] It could be argued that the state-doctrinal factor is present here, inasmuch as the absence of requirement of rental payments is tied up with Marxist theory. Clearly, however, the central authorities would, if they could, counteract the kind of tendencies to be discussed in greater detail in a moment. If, of course, the central authorities themselves take decisions which ignore external costs or benefits, the case is quite different.

Because of their lack of a territorial identity the ministries have inevitably exhibited stronger tendencies to cost-externalisation, and lack of consideration of external benefits, than did the *sovnarkhozy*. Normally the latter could have been expected to do so only where the cost was externalised outside the territory of the *sovnarkhoz*, and this was certainly a bigger problem than it need have been in the *sovnarkhoz* period because of the economically meaningless way in which boundaries were drawn. But the ministry has no reason at all to concern itself with any effects outside its own sector, whether they be costs or benefits, hence a strong ministerial preference for construction in old-established industrial areas, whatever the cost in terms of land and clean air. Enterprises can be expected to have similar tendencies to those of ministries.

The most long-suffering third party to cost-externalisation is agriculture. One of the outcomes of the highly complex and interesting Nurek hydro-electric scheme (Tadzhikistan), of which more later, was the eventual decision to build an electro-chemical factory at Yavan. The Yavan valley is one of the few places in the Soviet Union where high-grade cotton can be grown, and the factory would inevitably have deleterious effects on crops.[105] More often, of course, it is directly through the transfer of land out of agricultural use that agriculture is affected, and it is important to emphasise that this does not affect exclusively the state and collective sectors.

In the choosing of the site for the Tashkent GRES [local power station] no thought whatsoever was given to the question of the routes for the high-tension transmission lines of 110 and 220 kilovolts. Furthermore, this question received no clarification even in the *proekt* of the GRES, worked out by TashTEP [specialist energy project design organisation]. Let us remember that there are 14 of these lines, and that they have to be laid through the densely populated territory of the Ordzhonikidze *raion* [district], with its big gardens, so that it will be necessary to dig up as much as 300 hectares of orchards. This can hardly be considered sensible.[106]

Nor is this the only case affecting Tashkent orchard lands. In the early 1960s a factory of refractory and heat-resistant metals was built on the same type of site. All together, in the period 1953–63, 10,000 hectares of cultivated land in the suburban zone of Tashkent was taken over for construction purposes.[107] It is worth noting that both these specific cases come from the *sovnarkhoz* period. *Sovnarkhozy* were not responsible for agriculture, so that in cases where that sector was affected they had no more reason to concern themselves than ministries would have.

Within the production field, costs may be externalised from one specific project or sub-sector to another. The proposed construction of the mid-Yenisei hydro-electric station (HES) at Abalakovo, controversial but heavily promoted by the energy ministry, would submerge large volumes of high-quality timber, and a considerable amount of valuable agricultural land, including market garden areas.[108] Delays in completing purifying installations of the Caspian, crucially important for the fishing and other industries, are blamed on oil producing and prospecting organisations, which are unwilling to place top priority on 'unproductive' projects.[109] More usually, however, it is localities rather than sectors which suffer, and here we come to a problem which is all too common in the West. The ministries have always been particularly culpable in this respect. The authorities have consistently attempted to control the ministerial penchant for concentrating investment in heavily populated, old-established industrial areas. At present there is a list of 34 towns in the Russian republic, plus all the towns of Moscow *oblast'*, where construction of new or expansion of existing enterprises is forbidden.[110] The trouble is, of course, the old problem of controlling reconstructions.

The swifter development of industry in Tashkent and Tashkent *oblast'* was to a significant extent connected with the practice of attaching new enterprises to an already existing industrial base, and also with the growth of what were, in essence, new enterprises, built on the pretext of reconstruction of existing enterprises, or as a result of quite voluntaristic decisions, not based on facts. This locational tendency among enterprises was usually defended on the grounds of lower costs. The development of industry in Tashkent was also helped by the departmental structure of industrial administration, industrial enterprises being, in the main, subordinate to all-union ministries. For them Uzbekistan was often reducible to a single point – Tashkent.[111]

One is left speculating on the extent to which the ministries may have presented powerful vested opposition to schemes for the general introduction of rental payments!

MONITORING OF THE INVESTMENT DECISION-TAKING OF NON-SPECIALISED EXECUTIVE BODIES

It would, of course, be quite erroneous to believe that these various tendencies enjoy untrammelled scope for expression. Just because, for example, a project is below-limit does not mean that an intermediate executive body is totally immune from outside interference on micro-economic matters. The bulk of the critical material on which our type of analysis is based is, after all, made up of reports of cases where some body has intervened, and at least tried to modify the operation of, in this case, Factors C1–C3.

What, then, are the forces of *kontrol'* (monitoring)? The Communist Party and its subsidiary organisations, notably the Trade Unions and Komsomol, are often sharply effective in criticising and changing patterns which emerge from the middle level of the planning bureaucracy. Indeed the sins of the ministries is a favourite theme in critical articles published on p. 2 of *Pravda*. At the same time lower-level Party cadres are systematically ambivalent about 'distortions' because of their personal involvement in plan fulfilment. I have seen no evidence of Communist Party organs *within* a ministry providing a major vehicle for the modification of the systematic tendencies under discussion. Intervention from the higher echelons of the political dimension is obviously by definition occasional, so that in practice it can do little more than give a lead to the more specialised planning/control organisations operating in the investment field. The most important of these are Gosstroi and Stroibank.

Gosstroi USSR (*Gosudarstvennyi komitet Soveta Ministrov SSSR po delam stroitel'stva* – state committee of the USSR Council of Ministers for construction affairs) was created on 9 May 1950. Republican Gosstroi also exist. Much of the work of Gosstroi relates specifically to design and building organisations, and will be discussed in the succeeding two chapters. In the present context it is the work of organs of *ekspertiza* (design-monitoring organisation), in most cases subordinate to USSR or republican Gosstroi, that is of primary importance. These organs normally have to pass all designs for centralised investments. Apart from the question of quality of design work as such, which will be discussed in the next chapter, *ekspertiza* organs do have the power to reject projects outright, on grounds of general efficiency considerations. All the evidence suggests that this does not happen very often, and when it does happen, the determined ministerial administrator may be more than a match for his colleagues in *ekspertiza*. When, for example, Glavgosekspertiza (Main State *ekspertiza*) recently threw out the design for a building materials factory on the grounds that two existing factories of the same type had shown disappointing results, the ministry simply changed tack, and submitted designs for *two* similar factories in different areas.[112] The lowest level of *ekspertiza* organ is, in fact, actually subordinate to the ministry, rather than to any body in the Gosstroi system,[113] so that very little indeed could be expected of it at the strategic decision-taking level. This surely reflects the basic weakness in the *ekspertiza* system, namely that it is sorely overstretched, disposing of neither the human or material resources that the ministries command. However valuable as a source of *information*, the system has not proven to be a highly effective instrument of *inspection* in relation to intermediate executive bodies.

Stroibank (Construction Bank) was created on 7 April 1959, taking over the competences of a number of specialised banks, including the Agricultural and Industrial Banks. All investment finance for state organisations goes through Stroibank (investment finance for collective farms goes through Gosbank (the State Bank)), which gives the bank broad scope for monitoring the investment process. Stroibank systematically exercises its right to veto dubious projects. In 1971, 342 new projects were excluded from the plan on the suggestion of Stroibank.[114] Sometimes the bank makes positive proposals for specific investment undertakings.[115] To the extent that bank credit continues to increase its share in total investment finance, we can expect that the arm of Stroibank would be strengthened, as its rôle developed beyond that of simply bursar and accountant. It is interesting that Stroibank data show that with 278 enterprises using long-term credits to finance centralised investment in 1974, 58.3 per cent of the investments were put on-stream on or before time.[116] While the work of Stroibank is far from neutralising the powerful tendencies discussed in this chapter, it does clearly introduce a significant corrective.

To recapitulate the main points in this chapter, then:
(1) Intermediate bodies and enterprises have a significant degree of control over the process of investment.
(2) The basic characteristics of the Soviet economic system – the predominance of output success-indicators, prevalent supply uncertainty and ineffectiveness of cost constraints – lead to the emergence of definite distortive tendencies in the investment process. Notable characteristics are:

Factor C1: tendency to overbid for investment resources.

Factor C2: tendency to organisational autarky.

Factor C3: cost/benefit externalisation. Under this rubric, we include the normal tendency for organisations to ignore considerations of production externalities. Because of the general absence of rent payments in the Soviet Union this factor operates more widely than in market economies.

All these tendencies result in the emergence of quite distinctive patterns in terms of location, production profile and cost characteristics of investment undertakings, depending on the type of organisation involved. The work of organisations like Gosstroi and Stroibank limits, but does not neutralise, the operation of these tendencies.

3

Specialised, subordinate non-executive bodies – design organisations

Design organisations (*proektnye organizatsii* – POs, singular *proektnaya organizatsiya*) are the bodies which handle the 'blue-print' stage of the investment process. They have no powers of approval or rejection of projects. There are three basic types of design organisation – territorial, sectoral or technological, and specialised. The first are concerned with the planning of industrial nodes. The second concentrate on work for particular sectors, while the last work on particular kinds of construction, for example, industrial construction or transport construction.[1] In principle design organisations concerned with actual construction are normally subordinate to Gosstroi, while others are subordinate to ministries etc. In practice the bulk of industrial design seems to be done by organisations within the ministerial structure.[2] Organisations are grouped together in associations (*ob"edineniya*), led by a head (*golovnoi*) institute. We are thus presented with a highly complicated and often overlapping system.[3] Gosstroi is, indeed, currently reviewing the whole structure of the sector.[4] In 1966 there were 450,000 people working in design and survey organisations,[5] and by 1981 this had risen to more than 800,000.[6] In 1970 there were 1,420 *proektnye organizatsii*.[7] By 1981 the number had reached 1,800.[8] We cannot be absolutely sure of the coverage of these figures. There are organisations called constructor bureaux (*konstruktorskie byuro*), which design non-standardised machines and also operate as general purpose design organisations at enterprise level. These are intermediate between the design and R and D sectors, and could be counted under either head.

BASIC MODE OF OPERATION

Since 1971 design organisations have played a rôle in the elaboration of sectoral and territorial 'development and location schemes'.[9] They could, in the case of large and important projects, until recently be involved in the preliminary stage of 'examination of the technico-economic advisability of the envisaged project' (*tekhniko-ekonomicheskie obosnovaniya*, TEOs – feasibility studies), this work being otherwise done by the ministries. By a decree of 1981 TEOs will now cease to exist as such, their content being effectively integrated back into the development and location schemes.[10] Once a client has a clear idea of what he wants, he presents the design organisation with an 'assignment for design work' (*zadanie na proektirovanie*), and this forms the basis for initial requests by clients for funds.[11] The new decree places considerable stress on the assignment for design work as an instrument for raising the technological content of design work, and for ensuring implementation of sectoral development and location schemes. Fairly detailed 'technical assignments' (*tekhnicheskie zadaniya* – singular *tekhnicheskoe zadanie*) are required when clients request the design of non-standard pieces of equipment.

The first stage proper in the compilation of the 'design and financial documentation' of a project was, up to 1969, the 'design assignment' (*proektnoe zadanie*), which included 'basic technical decisions aimed at securing the most efficient utilisation of labour, material and financial resources, in the operation of the envisaged project and in its actual construction'.[12] In normal, two-stage design work, the completion of the design assignment was followed immediately by the stage of working drawings and 'estimates for each separate building and installation'. It was on the basis of these working drawings that the building organisation entrusted with the project compiled its 'design for the implementation of construction and installation work' (*proekt proizvodstva stroitel'no-montazhnykh rabot*).[13] With projects involving major innovations and/or special difficulties in terms of site, however, three-stage design work was the rule. The additional stage, intermediate between the standard two, was the *tekhnicheskii proekt* (technical design). Standardised (*tipovye*) designs were used as much as possible in cases where no special complications were foreseen in a project. By a decree of 1969 the design assignment was abolished, and the technical design elevated to the key position in the planning system. In addition, a new emphasis was placed on standard designs, with provision that, in cases where no special difficulties were envisaged, the technical design and working drawings stages could be conflated into a single 'technico-working design' (*tekhno-rabochii proekt*).[14] The 1981 decree once again changes the terminology, with 'design with aggregated estimate cost of construction' (*proekt so svodnym smetnym raschetom stoimosti stroitel'stva*) replacing the technical design, and one-stage designing, now scheduled to become the predominant form, dubbed 'working design with aggregated estimate cost of construction' (*rabochii proekt so svodnym smetnym raschetom stoimosti stroitel'stva*).

PLANNING AND FINANCE

Previously financed from union, republican or local budgets,[15] design organisations went onto *khozraschet* on 1 October 1959.[16] What this meant essentially was that finance for the work of the organisations would now come largely from the capital investment funds, i.e. that the cost of design work would now be included as part of the cost of the given project.[17] Traditionally the principal success-indicator used in this sector of investment planning has been 'volume of design work' – a variant of the standard gross-output success-indicator, measured in value terms.[18] In the 1959–65 period cost reduction figured as a major indicator in design work, as it did in industry.[19] The situation in the post-reform period remains unresolved. In 1966 an experiment covering 65 design organisations introduced the principle of payment for completed stages of design work – previously tranches of 'volume of work' had been calculated as a simple percentage of the total work to be done, and organisations could and did receive payment for work that was in a quite unusable state.[20] Sources from the late 1960s indicate no rapid extension of the experiment, however,[21] and in 1971 just 18 organisations were put onto 'the new system', which appears to have been essentially a regularisation of the 1966 experiment,[22] with the number due to expand to 35–40 in 1972.[23] Only 200 *proektnye organizatsii* were reformed at the end of 1975.[24] Apart from the change in the manner of definition of 'volume of work', profit was introduced at an early stage as a major success-indicator for POs, so that organisations working on the old 'volume of work' definition may be 'reformed' as far as profit is concerned.[25] A change envisaged for the 1976–80 five-year plan is transferral of the financing of design work to a credit basis.[26] This seems to have been going on gradually, and the 1979 planning decree predicates completion of the process, with credit being extended for completed designs, rather than stages, at least in the majority of cases.[27] That decree once again announces the general transition of design organisations onto *khozraschet*, to be completed by 1980,[28] and this no doubt reflects the evolving scope of that term in Soviet planning usage. (Note, however, that, for example, POs will still not pay the capital charge.)[29] Under the new regulations providing incentives for on- or before-time completion, which also involve quality coefficients (for detailed discussion see Chapter 4), design organisations are to receive 5 per cent of total bonuses paid on that count.[30] This may sound rather mean, but the proposed introduction of competitive tendering for design work would represent a very significant change.[31] Surprisingly, *proektnye organizatsii* are only now to have their own five-year plans.[32]

As is normal in other sectors of the Soviet economy, the upper echelons of design organisations are paid on a time-rate basis, but with supplementary premia being paid in the event of fulfilment or overfulfilment of plans. The principal success-indicators used in design work have been already discussed, but it should be noted that special premia are also paid for raising the quality of designs, reducing the time spent on particular projects, cost reduction (post-1965), etc.[33] Such premia do not, however, appear to have played a crucial rôle in behavioural patterns. Lower-status workers in design organisations may receive some share of special bonuses, but are largely paid on a piece-rate basis. This does, of course, mean that, whatever the nature of the success-indicators for the organisations as a whole, they work on the basis of crude volume of work.[34] The overall level of remuneration of design workers has been comparatively low in the past, and this is one of the problems that the 1981 decree tries to tackle.

DISTORTIONS INDUCED BY THE PLANNING AND MANAGEMENT RÉGIME

The types of distortion which success-indicators of one kind or another tend to encourage have already been discussed in their general context, and the work of design organisations has not proven atypical in this connection. The most fundamental problem has been that the emphasis on volume of work has tended to result in neglect of quality and cost considerations, and of the specific needs of customers. Manifestations of this can take on veritably Crocodilian crudeness. Some design organisations have had plans for drawings fixed in physical terms, giving them a direct incentive to maximise the number of drawings made out.[35] In the *postanovlenie* (decree) of the CC CPSU (Central Committee of the Communist Party of the Soviet

Union) and Council of Ministers dated 4 November 1955 'On the elimination of extravagance in design work and construction', 'the hugely extravagant obsession with the superficial side of architecture was subjected to sharp criticism. Many designs included excessively large buildings and uneconomical layouts, unjustified increases in the numbers and dimensions of auxiliary buildings, quite indefensible decorations, numerous columns and porticoes, complicated cornices and other expensive details.'[36] Stalin's personal tastes in architecture may have been reflected here to some extent, but a strong prevalence among design workers of the 'cult of the gross' is surely also indicated. A more recent source complains that:

architects, design workers and builders frequently underestimate the importance of economic questions. Good examples of this sort of thing are the obsession with the construction of very high buildings, the excessive use of glass on outside walls, the construction of massive, 'material-intensive' porches and entrances to buildings, and the totally unjustified use on façades of various kinds of mock constructions, panels and bas-reliefs. All this leads to more expensive construction, and in addition frequently makes buildings less convenient to use.[37]

The problem of quality under such a planning and management régime was neatly summed up in another recent article, which noted that the category of defective work (*brak*) is not recognised in design organisations — only that of 'creative misfortune' (*tvorcheskaya neudacha*).[38]

Neglect of cost considerations affects both the cost of the actual design work and the costs, capital and operating, of the project being designed. It may seem extraordinary that, for example, 'statistical comparison of projected and actual production costs is not carried out',[39] but consideration of elements of interaction with other stages of the investment process help to place this sort of thing in perspective. 'Design workers know that in the majority of cases the completion of a new factory will take three, five, or even ten years, and that consequently control over estimated production costs is really not possible. As far as estimated capital cost is concerned, it will in any case be reconsidered in the course of construction!'[40] To the extent, of course, that *raspylenie* is itself caused by low quality in design work, the process of mutual interaction becomes even more complex!

But the inherent deficiencies of the 'volume of work' success-indicator have been compounded, certainly in the past, by inadequacies in the *Handbook of Aggregated Indicators* (*Spravochnik ukrupnennykh pokazatelei*), which serves as a basis for calculating volume of work.

In many sectors of industry technology is developing at rapid tempi, and techniques of production improving, which in turn gives rise to the need to design more complex buildings and structures. But this is not reflected in the Handbook. As a result, sectors 'advantageous' and 'disadvantageous' from the point of view of fulfilment of the planned indicators of design organisations have appeared. For example, the value of the design work on the Bratsk aluminium factory, worked out on the basis of Part V of the Handbook, came to only 0.65 per cent [of the value of the project itself – D.A.D.]. The design work on this project has, consequently, turned out to be loss-making for our institute.

The value of design work on the construction side of the anode mass of the factory, consisting of six separate installations, is, according to the Handbook, roughly equal to that of one building of a higher educational establishment. It is consequently not surprising that actual labour expenditure on the design work on this project exceeds the estimates, in money terms, by three times.[41]

A new Handbook, which appeared in. 1965,[42] may have cleared up some of these points, but contemporary sources indicate the survival of a number of serious problems in relation to procedures for valuing the projects themselves. Gosstroi USSR started work in 1970 on a system of 'aggregated estimating norms' (*ukrupnennye smetnye normy* – USN), but by 1976 these were being used for only 20–25 per cent of total estimating work.[43] Ministries are now charged with working out their own 'sectoral aggregated construction cost indicators' (*ukrupnennye pokazateli stoimosti stroitel' stva* – UPSS), and we may speculate that this represents a degree of decentralisation to the intermediate level aimed at lessening the burden on Gosstroi and introducing more technological reality into the basis of costing.[44] But design organisations are berated for their extreme tardiness in implementing UPSS, while the need to 'further perfect' UPSS is admitted.[45] Surely progress is being made here, but it is slow, and of little importance in analysis of the past and present.

In addition to these problems of cost, quality and specification, there has been the characteristic disincentive to innovation. As Khikmatov points out,[46] design organisations, faced with the need to fulfil quantitatively defined tasks in a set time period, cannot afford to spend a lot of time in trying to discover original and better ways of solving given technical problems. It was hoped that the switch to *khozraschet* financing in 1959 would 'compel clients, i.e. enterprises and economic organisations involved in construction, to keep a close watch on the course of design work, and to check the quality of the documentation produced, which in the last analysis guarantees the introduction into designs of the latest techniques and technology'.[47] That this did not happen to any significant extent is hardly surprising, seeing that the success-indicator system of both design organisations and client enterprises, ministries, etc. remained basically unchanged. Contemporary reports indicate that the problem remains a serious one. A *Pravda* editorial from 1974 noted that seven blast furnaces, plus the convertor departments at the Karaganda, West Siberian and Chelyabinsk steel works, all commissioned in 1973, did not have automatic control systems, and blamed designers for this.[48] A 1978 report blames conservatism on the part of POs in relation to new materials for excess capacity in new, advanced construction material factories.[49] It should be noted, however, that existing regulations in some cases forbid design organisations to use light construction materials.[50]

Until such time as the post-reform situation with respect to success-indicators solidifies, it will remain impossible to say what improvements may be possible through modification of the traditional system. Payment by completed stages should increase sensitivity on the part of design organisations to customer needs somewhat, and, in addition to reinforcing the above, the profit success-indicator should introduce an effective cost constraint. But implementation of reformed principles has run into all sorts of difficulties, and this is no doubt a major reason why they have still not been generalised. The half- or rather quarter-way house that has prevailed since 1965 seems often simply to add confusion to traditional problems. It is clear that there is a great deal of vagueness about rules for premia, and that volume of work and profit plans are often badly coordinated. In the early post-reform days top management (*rukovoditeli*) was being awarded bonuses for fulfilment of profits plans, while others continued to be paid by quantitative results. As a consequence management sometimes got no bonuses while everyone else was getting them.[51] Arrangements for the payment of special bonuses for quality seem even at the present time to be in complete confusion.[52] Podshivalenko noted in 1968 that:

in many cases transition to accounting by stages is being made difficult because design organisations continue to deliver estimate documentation without any breakdown of work by stages, while clients and contracting organisations do not demand from the design workers the inclusion in the estimates of these important indicators. Moreover, design organisations often demand additional payment, i.e. more than the value of design-survey work according to the price list, for breaking down estimates into stages of work.[53]

Four years later the same author noted a tendency to arbitrariness in the breaking-down of designs, with stages sometimes being defined simply as a given percentage of the total work involved.[54] More recent sources confirm this picture. Breakdown into stages is often excessive, bearing no relationship to technological realities.[55] An experiment involving exclusive use of 'fully complete design-estimate documentation' as a basis for the credit finance of design was started in 1974, and apparently showed good results.[56] It initially involved only four organisations, but was subsequently extended, again with reported success.[57] As noted earlier, the 1979 planning decree envisages a general transition to this system. Quite apart from questions of implementation, however, measures of this nature have to be interpreted with caution. The 1979 decree is quite explicit that *design work itself* will continue to be broken down into stages, measured on the basis of *tovarnaya produktsiya* (marketable output).[58] That concept represents a weak form of *realizatsiya*, implying saleability, but not necessarily sale. All this means, of course, that basic plan fulfilment will continue to be assessed in terms of conventionally defined stages. The new credit arrangements could mean that design organisations might find themselves without the means to pay in cases where a given 'advantageous' stage was yielding inflated putative bonuses, and would certainly counter any tendencies to simply drop 'disadvantageous' stages. But as long as the command principle continues to reign supreme they cannot directly affect success-indicators as such. The creation of integrated design-construction *ob"edineniya*, currently fashionable,[59] seems to miss the point that it is the relationship with the *client* which is crucial, for design and construction organisations alike. As the next chapter will show, there is little enough prospect that POs will unlearn their faults under the tutelage of builders.

To the extent that operationalisation may really become a key success-indicator for design organisations, under the new regulations described earlier, the command principle is, indeed, weakened in that the command is generalised to 'give the client what he wants'. Competitive tendering for design work would introduce a positive element of marketisation which, if backed up by similar arrangements at other points in the investment cycle, would certainly revolutionise the situation and give real teeth to radical financial and accounting procedures. But the sheer complexity of the 'good' involved in design work would surely require a much more radical move towards the market than is likely in the present climate of Soviet economic policy, if classic success-indicator problems are to be completely excised. It is interesting in this connection that one Soviet director has expressed the view that the development of *khozraschet* relationships in the design sector is likely to intensify rather than to alleviate the tendency to maximize paper output, suggesting that, paradoxically, over-timid marketisation may exacerbate the classic problems of the command principle.[60] In any case, our present purpose is primarily to analyse the present and past, and all available materials from the 1970s suggest that here we can feel quite safe in continuing to expect, *a priori*, strong manifestations of *val*-induced distortions among design organisations.

In addition to specific success-indicator issues, *proektnye organizatsii* have tended to suffer from more general problems. These may be induced partially by the success-indicator régime but also tie up with broader organisational issues.

DELAYS IN THE DELIVERY OF TECHNICAL DOCUMENTATION

These present perennial difficulties. Hold-ups in the delivery of documentation affected 1,293 projects, with a total estimated value of 58 milliard rubles, in 1979.[61] It is quite common for projects scheduled for operationalisation during the given plan year (*puskovye ob"ekty*) to be without working drawings. The priority blocks for 1969 of the Lipetsk metallurgical factory expansion were only 25 per cent furnished with technical documentation at the end of 1968.[62] Examples could be multiplied a hundredfold,[63] and this is quantitatively one of the most important problems facing design organisations, and indeed the implementation of investment plans in general. It is clearly an important element in *raspylenie* problems, all the more so since organisations are obliged to stop work on a given design once the official time limit has run out, and go on to the next one planned for them, though they may return to unfinished designs later.[64] What is equally clear, however, is that the problem is also to some extent a reflection of *raspylenie* factors originating elsewhere. The tendency, discussed in Chapter 2, for ministries etc. to overbid for investment resources means that design organisations are continually faced with a volume of work corresponding to a level of physical investment activity which the economy is not able to support. Indeed Khikmatov sees this as the major factor in the problem.[65] But other factors, inherent in the design organisation system itself, have surely been of equal importance, and one source blames design organisations for 20 per cent of cases of failure to meet planned completion dates.[66]

Firstly, as was mentioned at the beginning of the chapter, the structure of the system of design organisations has been excessively complex. It is the rule, rather than the exception, for the design work on big projects to be shared among a number, sometimes a large number, of organisations. No less than 59 *proektnye organizatsii* were, for example, involved in the design for the Krivoi Rog blast furnace No. 9,[67] and it seems to be not uncommon for the figure to go as high as 50–70.[68] Despite the multitude of different organisations, rational specialisation has often been lacking. For instance, there are no large-scale specialised organisations serving construction in internal trade and catering.[69] But apparent lack of organisation is, at least in some cases, more properly interpreted as organisation distorted by autarkical tendencies on the part of non-specialist intermediate bodies.

. . . dwarf design organisations, duplicating the work of existing units, continue to sprout in our town. Three years ago, for example, a section of Soyuzkurortproekt [specialist tourist industry design organisation] and a design 'workshop' [*masterskaya*] of the Leningrad *oblast'* council for tourism and excursions were opened. Each has an annual turnover of work of no more than half a million rubles, and a staff of less than 200. In practical terms they do exactly the same kind of designs as LenZNIIEP, a large-scale, specialised organisation designing cultural and amenity projects. It would appear that this happens because of some deep-seated tendency to departmentalism. So the organisation's small, well at least it's mine.[70]

A recent trend towards the setting-up of 'technical groups' and 'bureaux for checking and improving design decisions' (*byuro ekspertizy i sovershenstovovaniya proektnykh reshenii*) within construction organisations or *glavki*, to re-work and improve design documentation, is an understandable enough reaction to general problems of quality of design work.[71] But this sort of thing could very easily be the thin end of the wedge of further departmentalisation and atomisation in design.

As of the late 1960s only 20–35 per cent of the working time of design workers was taken up by actual work on the designs.[72] By the mid–late 1970s, this proportion seems to have improved to 40–60 per cent,[73] though this is still considered too low. The rest of the time goes on the process of getting approval for designs from various organs. Now clearly the existence of the success-indicator problem makes it important that close scrutiny over design organisations should be maintained (see discussion of Gosstroi and Stroibank below). But 'multi-level' checking by other subordinate organisations, each with their own axe to grind, cannot be expected to yield high returns to the extra time 'invested'.

Shiryaev makes the point that excessive 'petty tutelage' over design organisations may be a hangover from a time when the average level of qualifications of a design worker was much lower.[74] Interestingly enough, Krasovskii makes exactly the same point in connection with the relationship between design organisations and the building industry. 'Nowadays, when we have a large number of technically qualified engineers and technicians in construction, petty tutelage by design organisations over construction personnel has outlived its usefulness.'[75] The organisations may, then, be trying to elaborate projects to a degree of detail which is no longer necessary, even within the context of a centrally planned economy. The design for the Lipetsk metallurgical factory filled 91 volumes and 70,000 pages,[76] and that of the Baranovichi automatic production line factory 220 volumes.[77] In addition, there is an element of sheer clumsiness in the way forms have to be filled in that may increase the apparent incidence of both kinds of petty tutelage, meanwhile wasting a good deal of time. Constructor bureaux have to fill in two sets of forms, called respectively the constructor's documentation and the technological documentation. There is a 30–40 per cent overlap in the content of these two sets, and the latter involves no less than 120 different types of form![78] But of course one must bear in mind that the success-indicator/bonus system does encourage maximisation of the 'weight' of the design documentation. The 1981 decree predicates an easing-up of multi-level checking, and a two- to three-fold reduction in the volume of design materials. How powerfully these exhortations will affect the situation remains to be seen.

Then there is the fact that design organisations do a great deal of work on projects that have not been finally approved. In 1967 the working drawings for the Voronezh gypsum factory were 87 per cent completed, though a final decision on whether to build the factory had still not been reached. In 1974 the institute Giprotraktorosel'khoz-mash (specialist design organisation for agricultural machine build-ing) produced documentation for construction work worth 307 million rubles, only 159 million of which was covered by *titul'nye spiski*.[79] Over the period 1971–75 the Coal Ministry failed to use design documentation prepared for a total of 43 new enterprises.[80] The inevitable result of this sort of thing is that a large proportion of design documentation is never in fact used. Between 1962 and 1966, 240 million rubles' worth of design work on above-limit projects valued at 12 milliard rubles was left unused.[81] In the Uzbek republic, 6–7 million rubles' worth of design work is thrown away each year.[82] Ministerial overbidding for investment resources could, of course, be a contributing factor here, since the prior existence of detailed documentation may be a good card to play in this particular game. In 1979 the Chemicals Ministry had on its files four times the 'normal' quantity of design documentation.[83] It is interesting that in the Giprotraktorosel'khozmash case there was 116 million rubles' worth of work in ministerial plans not covered by *titul'nye spiski*. A side-effect of all this is that, with the best will in the world, the technology embodied in many designs is obsolescent by the time the design documentation is used.[84]

Lastly, the way in which design work is actually carried out remains fairly primitive. Modern techniques based on model-building and photography are still not widely used in Soviet design work,[85] and Krasovskii argues that this is a major reason why the design stage takes so much longer in the USSR than in the USA, where such techniques are widely used.[86] Success-indicators no doubt operate as a disincentive to innovation in design techniques, as they operate as a disincentive to innovations in designs themselves. But inadequate production of photocopying machinery etc. has also been an impor-tant factor here.[87] There seems also to be room for purely organisa-tional innovation within design organisations. It has been estimated that 'rationalisation of work', a phrase which presumably excludes major changes in actual technology, would permit an increase in 'output' by design organisations of 10–15 million rubles' worth of design work per annum, covering 150–200 million rubles' worth of investment.[88] One observer of the design scene noted, a few years ago, a case where automation had indeed been introduced – in the form of closed-circuit television to the end of permitting the chief designer to keep a closer eye on his subordinates![89] Clearly the technology and 'petty tutelage' themes may provide some counterpoint to each other.

Under the experimental system discussed earlier whereby design organisations are paid only once projects have been completed and passed, delivery dates for documentation have been reduced by 20–30 per cent.[90] This is impressive, but it relates to an experiment with very limited coverage. The analysis of this section has emphasised the extent to which problems of delivery of documentation go beyond the narrow sphere of success-indicator distortions, and even sometimes beyond the sphere of Factor D proper. The 1979 planning decree stipulates that from 1981 only projects with full documentation confirmed six months in advance may be included in annual plans. This seems a quite unrealistic aim.

INACCURACY IN ESTIMATES

The capital cost estimates in designs are frequently greatly exceeded in the implementation stage. Some escalation of estimates is characteristic of all economies, but a 1966 survey of 1,741 Soviet projects showed an average increase on estimated capital costs of 32.5 per cent, while one conducted in 1968, covering 2,100 projects, gave a corresponding figure of 41 per cent.[91] A sample of 850 projects reported an average cost escalation of about 30 per cent 1971–75.[92] Table 3.1 gives

Table 3.1. *Cost escalations on selected projects*

	Estimated costs	
	Envisaged in the 5-year plan for 1973	Confirmed by the annual plan for 1973
	(in millions of rubles)	
Ust'-Ilim HES	690.3	1,025.0
Oil pipeline Ust'-Balyk–Kurgan–Ufa–Al'met'evsk	520.0	649.9
Oil pipeline Kuibyshev–Tikhoretskaya	143.5	267.0
Abakan rolling-stock factory	293.0	500.9
Tuvaasbest combine	43.2	91.9
Rybina printing equipment factory	25.5	44.2
Kostroma cylinder and piston factory	52.9	236.4

Source: V. Isaev, 'Puti povysheniya effektivnosti kapital'nykh vlozhenii', in *Voprosy Ekonomiki*, No. 8, 1973, p. 33

an impression of the scope of the problem in a number of outstanding cases. Design organisations are adept at 'covering up' particularly serious cost hikes, so that these figures may, indeed, not fully reflect the extent of the phenomenon.

As we shall see later, there is a strong *a priori* argument in terms of the responsibility of the building industry for these overruns. In addition, the tendency for 'temporary' prices of special pieces of equipment not covered in the standard price lists to be inflated beyond the level of 'comparable items' often knocks out calculations.[93] But Soviet sources frequently attach at least partial blame to design organisations,[94] though a 1974 survey, covering admittedly only 150 projects, blamed them for only 12 per cent of the total escalation of costs.[95] It is, however, perhaps misleading to attempt too rigid a separation of individual elements here. One article on the problem of escalating machinery prices noted that 'because the majority of estimates for the acquisition of equipment are put out by design workers without adequate detail, it is in practice impossible to verify them'.[96] The importance of this point is thrown into relief in the light of the general tendency for detail in designs to be excessive, and it seems likely that the 'increases in machinery prices' item is sometimes used as a cover-up for other forms of cost escalation. The 1971–75 survey quoted above simply lumped design errors and increases in machinery prices together, and blamed them for almost a quarter of capital cost escalations.[97]

We have already seen that POs are not encouraged by the success-indicator/bonus system to minimise costs, and that estimating procedures are very imperfect, but this is no reason why estimates should habitually understate real costs, unless general carelessness about costs does, for some reason, tend to operate in a skewed way. As Krasovskii succinctly enquires 'one wonders why "making estimates more specific" always involves increases, and why this occurs every year'.[98] It must, of course, be borne in mind that design organisations have to work closely with ministries etc., which are in many cases the approving bodies appropriate for projects that particular organisations may be working on, and it has already been noted that these bodies may put pressure on a design organisation deliberately to under-estimate capital costs in order that the given projects should fall into the below-limit category. 'To get construction started at any cost, and that means having to prove that the given project is economically highly attractive – that is in many cases the unspoken behest to the design worker.'[99] In cases like these no inefficiency would necessarily be present, since the real costs of the project may still represent an optimal variant. But such 'cheating' usually reflects a ministry or *sovnarkhoz* looking after its own interests, in the way discussed in Chapter 2, so that there must be a fair presumption of some inefficiency, though it may be more in terms of whether the project as such is preferable to other projects, rather than in terms of implementation of the given project. In any case, this really represents the operation of C group factors, with design organisations playing an essentially subsidiary rôle.

Do we then simply come back to the basic problem of quality of design documentation? Bad design work must obviously tend to lead to rises in capital cost estimates. The fact that the estimated cost of the fenol-acetone and nitric acid departments of the Saratov chemical combine rose by 10.5 million rubles is clearly not unconnected with the 1,700 changes and corrections that had to be made to the design.[100] But it should be borne in mind also that delays in the delivery of technical documentation, apart from their obvious effect on gestation periods, must also lead to rises in cost estimates, through the disruption of production and supply plans. In other words, general organisational factors as well as success-indicator problems may be at the back of these 'inflationary' tendencies in capital cost estimates.

Not only capital, but also running cost estimates are frequently greatly exceeded in practice,[101] and we noted earlier the weakness of planning procedures in this connection. As in the case of capital costs, pressure applied on design organisations by clients to make projects appear more attractive to the central authorities may be a factor here,[102] and to this extent the phenomenon can be subsumed under Factors C1 and C2. Likewise, the building industry may be to some extent to blame, though one would imagine, on *a priori* grounds, to a lesser degree than with capital costs. Again, the general lack of incentive to keep costs down which has been prevalent throughout the economy during much of the period under consideration means that inflated running costs may be to a considerable extent a function of the way the completed factory is run, thus falling outside the field of investment as such. To the extent that design organisations are responsible to a serious degree for this tendency, and there is not a great deal of direct evidence on this point,[103] one would presume that it is primarily connected with poor quality in design documentation and/or technological 'conservatism', cf. the blast furnaces and convertors discussed earlier (p. 57).

THE SPECIAL PROBLEM OF 'SCHEMES' AND FEASIBILITY STUDIES

This is an aspect of the quality of documentation problem which merits particular attention. Design organisations tend to treat the initial stages of design work as being of secondary importance. Development and location schemes have only come into prominence in the 1970s, and a good deal of progress has been made in the computerised 'optimisation' of this element in planning. As many as 75 product groups were given such treatment in the period 1971–75.[104] Nevertheless 'the quality of schemes still does not meet contemporary requirements. In many of them the "point of departure" is not properly assessed, and the latest achievements of science and technology and other factors not taken into consideration . . . Multiple variants in terms of location and output levels, taking inter-sectoral links into account, are rare.'[105] Similar problems are reported for feasibility studies (TEOs), which under the pre-1981 system were supposed to represent 'documents bringing greater precision and detail into the schemes'.[106] In this connection:

the history of the creation of a [construction materials] base in Mirnyi, which was to serve as a lynch-pin for the erection of industrial and civil buildings and installations, is particularly instructive. Because of the absence of roads linking the town with the river Lena (Mirnyi is situated 267 km from the Lena) and a number of other things, the base was not completed on schedule, and the need for diamonds forced the producers to start production without the requisite infrastructure.

The long-planned Mirnyi construction materials base will now be completed only in 1965. The inadequate degree to which this whole project was thought out will inevitably tell: it is, after all, clear enough that the whole output of the new base will not find placement in Mirnyi, though, as a result of the lack of roads and the distance from river transport, consignment of output to other locations will be unprofitable.

Why is it that capital construction in this economic region is so badly implemented? The main reason, in our opinion, lies in the fact that design work for construction in Yakutia is assigned to a multitude of different design organisations, which have no knowledge of local conditions, and which do not take into account the unavoidable difficulties which the construction of every new industrial centre encounters. The inhospitable climate and permafrost-affected soils of Yakutia dictate the need for a special approach in design work on buildings, and of specialised design methods. It was no use assigning the design work on lightweight aggregate concrete panels and reinforced-concrete products for the Mirnyi complex to the Moscow institute Tsvetmetproekt [non-ferrous metallurgy design organisation], which knew nothing about, and indeed made no attempt at a preliminary study of, local conditions. The design organisation YakutNIIproalmaz [specialist diamond industry design organisation based in Yakutia], which was created just recently, has not yet had time to exert any significant influence on the construction of the Mirnyi complex.[107]

Another Soviet author is more explicit in tying this sort of thing in with lack of adequate feasibility studies.

Technico-economic feasibility studies frequently do not go beyond the appraisal of the advisability of construction of separate enterprises or projects, without account being taken of the development of complementary enterprises in allied sectors, necessary to guarantee projected capacities with raw material and energy resources, and with facilities for further processing of output.

For example, the 1965 plan envisaged the operationalisation of capacity for the production of the rubber 'neirit' at the Erevan synthetic rubber factory, although there are no guaranteed supplies of the basic raw material for the new line – acetylene.

At the Balakhna cellulose–paper combine the installation of paper-making machine No. 7 for the production of newsprint is just being completed, though there is no cellulose, technological steam or electrical energy for the machine to work on.

Serious errors were committed in connection with ensuring supplies of raw materials to the Astrakhan and Kzyl-Orda cellulose–cardboard combines, and the Kherson and Izmail cellulose factories.

All this happened because detailed technico-economic feasibility studies on the situation with respect to procurement of reeds were not done at the beginning of construction. If these studies had been done, it would have been established that the real possibilities for procurement of reeds for these four enterprises are significantly lower than what had been assumed, and the decision to build cellulose–cardboard combines in unafforested regions would scarcely have been taken. As it is, it will be necessary to bring in 600,000 m^3 of timber annually to utilise fully the new capacities.[108]

The problem of inadequate TEOs was one of the main themes of the colloquium on design work held in Moscow in May 1974,[109] and new regulations greatly increasing the stress on feasibility studies swiftly followed the recommendations of that colloquium.[110]

Now the reader should note that we are not talking here about externalities, nor about 'departmentalism' or 'localism' of one kind or another, but about straightforwardly poor work on the part of design organisations. This is not to say that the tendency for intermediate bodies to be indifferent to locational considerations may not rub off onto the design workers to some extent.[111] But there must be some more basic reason inherent in the organisation of design work itself. Sheer unfamiliarity with broad, locational problems will hardly do as an explanation, since design organisations are involved in the elaboration of the general schemes. The example from Yakutia does, however, give some indication of the basis of the problem. The 'atomisation without specialisation' pattern which has tended to characterise the general structure of the design organisation system means that (a) an appropriate specialised organisation may simply not exist in the case of a given project, and this will affect fundamental decisions more than it will the detailed working out of drawings etc., and (b) a large number of organisations may be working on the same project, which makes it very difficult for any one of them to cope adequately with general 'strategic' questions, and indeed may make it quite unclear who is responsible in this area. The clumsiness of the procedure for confirmation of TEOs tended to exacerbate this problem.[112] Thus we do come back to departmentalism indirectly.

Thematic plans are confirmed late and often changed. Ministries and departments chop and change the allocation of design projects, which makes stability in plans difficult . . . For example, the Ukrainian Ministry of Local Industry changed the thematic plan of Ukrgipromestprom [general local industry design organisation] on a number of occasions during 1974. The last 'reconfirmation' was on 28 December 1974 . . . Over the year 21 projects, worth 423,900 rubles, and forming 31 per cent of the annual volume of work of the institute, were excluded from the thematic plans. At the same time 49 additional pieces of work, worth 399,100 rubles, i.e. 24.8 per cent of the annual plan, were added.[113]

Another important factor has been the tendency for early-stage work to be undervalued, in terms of estimates of the total cost of a design, thus making it 'less advantageous'. 'Limits [i.e. on maximum expenditures – D.A.D.] for the compilation of technico-economic feasibility studies for development and location in some sectors of industry, and also with some large-scale construction projects are, for unknown reasons, very much on the low side, which is often one of the reasons why design work and construction of projects is carried on without adequate economic foundation.'[114] Now that feasibility studies are to become part of an upgraded system of 'schemes', one might suppose that this problem at least will be sorted out. A genuine improvement in the quality of pre-design assessment, such as is envisaged by the 1981 decree,[115] may have to await more radical organisational changes.

MONITORING OF DESIGN WORK

Before ending this chapter we must look briefly at the ways in which *proektnye organizatsii* are subject to elements of checking by the central authorities. The whole gist of the foregoing has been that the work of design organisations is in a number of important ways not the subject of effective *kontrol'*. But it would be dangerous to ignore completely the institutions which have the right to intervene in design work.

Normally a design assignment/technical design is confirmed by a republican government or ministry, or by a body chosen by them. As we have seen, these subordinate organisations cannot be expected to use their powers to eradicate elements of inefficiency which do not adversely effect their own success-indicators. They do, in addition, have their own 'axes to grind'. It is only in the case of 'the most important projects' (formerly defined as those worth more than 150 million rubles) that the design assignment/technical design is confirmed by the USSR Council of Ministers, and it is really only at this level that Gosstroi, which together with Gosplan presents the material to the Council of Ministers, is involved in detailed surveillance. As noted in Chapter 2, design assignments are normally subjected to examination by the organs of *ekspertiza* prior to formal confirmation. Evaluation of the project as such apart, *ekspertiza* is charged with '. . . the promulgation of standardised designs, seeing that financial accounts and estimates are correctly made up and that design-work norms are observed, and fulfilment of the instructions of the Party and government on reducing construction costs and raising the effectiveness of capital investments.'[116] Thus, for example, *ekspertiza* organs of Gosstroi Kazakhstan managed to cut estimates by 89 million rubles on 805 projects looked at in 1976.[117] The *proekt* for the reconstruction of the Kazakhsel'mash engineering factory was recently thrown out on the grounds of the obsolescence of the product lines to be installed.[118] But the general opinion of the effectiveness of *ekspertiza* in these matters seems to be fairly low, and criticisms of superficiality in their approach are common.[119] In addition, liaison between *ekspertiza* and Stroibank seems to leave quite a lot to be desired. 'Unfortunately, the organs of *ekspertiza* not only do not inform Stroibank about errors and miscalculations in designs, particularly in their economic sections, but frequently recommend for confirmation design assignments in which technico-economic questions are treated in a totally unsatisfactory way.'[120] The principle laid down in the 1981 decree is 'single-level checking', but it appears that in some cases examination of designs by *ekspertiza* may now be dispensed with.

Views on the work of Stroibank, the principal organisation concerned with the financial aspects of investment, are more positive. 'Enterprises, organisations and institutions present to the filials of Stroibank USSR a certificate confirming the existence of approved design-estimate documentation, and also of aggregated accounts and a report of expenditures.

'*The bank may demand the presentation of technical documentation for examination and the confirmation of the certificate.*' (Emphasis added – D.A.D.)[121] Detailed checks on the documentation and estimates of a particular project are done on a selective basis – clearly detailed checking of all projects would be out of the question. But the comparative effectiveness of the bank's work, within these essentially logistic limits, cannot be doubted.

Stroibank data indicate the growing effectiveness in recent years of checks by its filials on estimate documentation. In 1961, 7,472 million rubles' worth of aggregated financial estimate accounts and estimates, compiled on the basis of working drawings, were checked, and unnecessary extravagance and inflated estimates to the value of 52 million rubles, or 0.7 per cent of estimated value, revealed; in 1962 the same documents to the value of 9,210 million rubles, i.e. 23.3 per cent more than in 1961, were checked, and unnecessary extravagance and inflated estimates to the value of 106 million rubles (1.2 per cent) excised; in 1963 10,500 million rubles' worth of documents – 30 per cent more than in 1961 – were checked, and 140 million rubles' worth of economies made. Unnecessary extravagance and inflated estimates revealed in 1964 came to around 1 per cent of the estimated value of the projects checked.[122]

Contemporary sources indicate the continued vigour of Stroibank work in this field – in the case of the design for one reinforced-concrete plant the cost economy achieved was as much as 22 per cent.[123] It is clear that, in their work on project documentation, Stroibank have tended to concentrate on cost questions, rather than on problems of the quality of documentation, and this narrowness of approach has been a focus of criticism.[124] Stroibank workers themselves have pointed out the close relationship between the quality and cost factors.[125] Stroibank recommendations on cutting costs are in any case not always implemented with alacrity.[126] It is, furthermore, evident that the success-indicator régimes of Stroibank branches themselves are sometimes an obstacle to efficient checking work.[127]

Taken as a whole, then, the checking organisations do modify the picture to a definite degree. But not every project can be checked properly, and checks are usually of a partial nature. They introduce significant constraints on the tendencies discussed above, rather than change the behaviour pattern fundamentally. It seems that one of the aims lying behind the present policy of transferring design organisation onto credit financing is to rationalise and simplify information flows to Stroibank, thus facilitating *kontrol'*.[128] This may lead to some evolution of the rôle of the bank in the future.

It is, then, clear that fairly systematic elements of inefficiency are present in the work of design organisations. If inefficiency in the case of a given investment project takes the form of *raspylenie*, excessively high costs or incorrect locational and production profile, Factor D should always be borne in mind in seeking explanations. At the same time it should not be forgotten how frequently during this chapter phenomena appearing at first sight to relate to the operation of design organisations have turned out, on closer analysis, to be rather a function of the operation of other factors, particularly of C group factors. *Proektnye organizatsii* are not *powerful* organisations in the way that ministries are, and 'for many clients the *proekt* has become simply a document on the basis of which resources for construction can be obtained'.[129] It would be methodologically quite wrong to prejudge the question of the strength of different factors, but in instances where even detailed case-material does not permit a complete breakdown by factors we should be cautious about attributing any special weight to Factor D.

4

Specialised, subordinate executive bodies – the building industry

The civilian Soviet building industry is organised basically in the same way as other industrial sectors. (Note that in official terminology construction is classed as an *industriya*, but not as a *promyshlennost'*.) There are a number of specialist construction ministries, with subordinate main administrations (*glavki*), and actual building organisations of one kind or another at the bottom of the hierarchical scale. At the intermediate executive level, the Ministry for Heavy Industrial Construction (Mintyazhstroi) basically covers the coal and metallurgy industries, the Ministry of Industrial Construction (Minpromstroi) chemicals, oil-processing and petro-chemicals, and the Ministry of Construction (Minstroi) engineering, light industry, the food industry and other sectors. These three ministries are also to some extent specialised by region. Thus the Ministry for Heavy Industrial Construction does most of the 'bricks and mortar' work for all sectors in areas such as the Ukraine and South-west Siberia, which are traditionally dominated by ferrous metallurgy and coal-mining. The Ministry of Industrial Construction dominates in the same way in the oil-rich regions of the Volga–Urals, and Minstroi likewise has its 'own' territories. The work of all three is very much concentrated on the building rather than the equipment side of industrial construction. There is also a Ministry of Installation and Special Construction (Minmontazhspetsstroi), and a Ministry of Rural Construction. Minmontazhspetsstroi is the organisation which specialises in high-technology installation work, and its operations are of particular importance in relation to imported equipment. (For more detailed discussion, see the Appendix.)

All of these core construction ministries are union-republican organisations, though republican ministries do not exist for every republic for each ministry. Below the level of republic, the three bricks and mortar ministries are organised into territorially-based *glavki*. The organisational principle characterising Minmontazhspetsstroi is technological, rather than territorial. There are special all-union ministries for construction in the transport and oil and gas sectors. The latter – Minneftegazstroi – concentrates on the development of new fields in the eastern territories. Construction in the power industry is carried on by the union-republican Ministry of Power and Electrification.[1] (There was formerly a separate Ministry for Power-station Construction.) In 1975 these eight ministries accounted for 71.9 per cent of total contractual basis (see below for definition) construction and installation work.[2]

To add to the complexity, non-construction ministries usually have their own building enterprises, as have local soviets, and construction has always tended to be 'departmentalised' to an extent matched by few other sectors of the economy – but of this more later (see pp. 92–3). Military construction is carried on by a number of specialist ministries and other organisations, but no systematic information on their activity is available, and the succeeding discussion is limited to the civilian industry. During the *sovnarkhoz* period the majority of building organisations were handed over to those bodies.

BASIC MODE OF OPERATION

The most usual way in which actual construction organisations have been structured in the past is on the basis of trusts (*tresty*), or in residential construction combines (*kombinaty*), these having subdivisions called construction and installation administrations (*stroitel'no-montazhnye upravleniya*). On 1 January 1979 there were 25,968 administrations and 3,009 trusts in the industry.[3] Trusts are divided into four types – those specialising in construction for a specific sector of the economy, those carrying out general construction work in a particular area, those doing both specialised and general work and those working on only one site, usually that of a very large project.[4] Many trusts are quite small organisations – more than 20 per cent of the total number around 1979 had an annual turnover of less than 9 million rubles.[5]

Construction and installation administrations are classified as 'primary construction organisations' (*pervichnye stroitel'nye organizatsii*), but as a general rule the status of enterprise (*predpriyatie*) passed from administration to trust as part of the post-1965 reforms.[6] These terminological niceties reflect some genuine problems in the development of Soviet construction. In the early days of the industrialisation drive the trust tended to be very much an all-purpose organisation, embracing industrial subcontractors etc., and in this context the construction and installation administration enjoyed a real degree of independence. As the level of construction technology rose, the trust tended to become more specialised, and the administration progressively lost its independence, though the new position was never formalised.[7] It is perhaps for this reason that there is to this day a considerable degree of possible overlap between trust and administration with respect to planning and management functions, and it has been suggested that the situation should be rationalised by making either the trust or the administration the basic production unit in a given case.[8] But this specific issue has formed only part of an increasingly general controversy over the structure of management in construction. The chain of command may extend to as many as six links,[9] a high degree of specialisation by trust makes coordination on big projects almost impossible,[10] while specific aspects of the managerial structure hinder the general introduction of progressive forms of labour organisation, like the Zlobin brigade (see below).[11]

A few years ago there was, at least in the Ukraine, a movement towards the reorganisation of trusts into large-scale *kombinaty*, probably with dimensions nearer to those of a *glavk* than to those of a trust, though the experiment was not particularly successful.[12] In the mid-1970s the *ob"edinenie* was introduced into construction, following the pattern for industry proper. It appears, however, that this introduction was sometimes of a rather formal nature,[13] with Gosstroi giving little positive leadership, and the Ministry of Finance standing accused of outright hostility.[14] A decree of 12 October 1978 sought the elaboration of general schemes of management in construction which would reduce the maximum number of links to three.[15] Following on the planning decree of July 1979, a decree was published specifically nominating the production construction and installation *ob"edinenie* as henceforth the key unit, replacing the trust, in the management of construction.[16] The normal pattern of subordination would be ministry – *ob"edinenie* – construction and installation administration, with the last level having the status of enterprise only in exceptional cases.[17] There are clearly still a number of outstanding issues to be settled in relation to these changes – particularly concerning the status of territorial and sectoral principles.[18] In any case, whatever the future holds, purely organisational difficulties must form an important part of the background to the analysis of the construction sector in past and present.

Building organisations can be subdivided in another way – depending on whether they carry on their work on an 'in-house basis' (*khozyaistvennyi sposob*), or a 'contractual basis' (*podryadnyi sposob*). In-house basis organisations are, in principle, created for the purpose of doing a specific construction job, and normally cease to exist when that job is finished. Consequently, they tend to be small-scale, and relatively ill-equipped, in terms of both capital and skilled labour. Contractual basis organisations, on the other hand, are not created for a specific construction purpose, and their continued existence is not dependent on the continuation of work on a given project. Naturally, such organisations have greater scope to exploit economies of scale, and build up adequate stocks of equipment and skilled cadres.[19] In 1978 contractual basis organisations accounted for 90 per cent of total construction work, and in-house organisations the remaining 10 per cent. But the latter category had accounted for fully 67 per cent of the total 1933–38, and still as much as 18 per cent 1951–55.[20] Construction work carried on by authorities other than construction ministries is often on an in-house basis.

It is usual for a client to sign a general agreement with a trust operating as general contractor. The latter will then conclude separate subcontracting agreements for specialised work with specialised organisations. But a client may negotiate direct agreements with specialised organisations. In any case, whether on the basis of general agreement or of direct agreements, subcontracting organisations are taken on for periods of only one year at a time.[21]

PLANNING AND FINANCE

As is the case with design organisations, the traditional principal success-indicator in the building industry has been a variant of gross output. 'Gross volume of work' (*valovoi ob"em rabot*) is defined as the total value of work done, including unfinished work, plus the value of bought-in materials. During the period 1959–65 cost-reduction had the status of major success-indicator in construction, as in other industries. After 1965, following on the decisions of that year's September Plenum, a number of changes were introduced into the success-indicator system, though some only on an experimental basis. As with the design sector, profit seems to have been been brought in as a major success-indicator more or less immediately after the announcement of the reform. But it appears that it was initially calculated on the basis of the old output definition,[22] which also survived as a success-indicator in its own right. Most of the experimentation that has gone on since has centred round the problem of how to define work output, both as a direct measure of performance, and as a basis for calculating profit, labour productivity, etc. Preliminary experiments in this field did in fact start as early as 1963.[23] After 1965, however, a number of pilot schemes, involving a fairly large section of the industry, got under way. In Kiev, the Kievgorstroi No. 5 trust was put onto a system based on three major success-indicators – operationalisation of new capacity or stages of new capacity; rate of profit, calculated as the relationship between actual profit and estimated finished output (*gotovaya stroitel'naya produktsiya*); and total production, calculated on the basis of NSR (*normativnaya stoimost' rabot* – 'normed value of work').[24] NSR is, more or less, value added, but includes work in progress, and is defined on the basis of *proizvodstvo* ('production'), not *produktsiya* ('output'), though the quantitative distinction between the two concepts is not clear.[25] In the Moscow Glavmosstroi *glavk* experiments, sales (*realizatsiya*) was used directly as a success-indicator.[26] The use of sales as an indicator preserved a form of gross-output indicator in the Moscow experiment, but in other pilot schemes sales itself was calculated on the basis of NSR, with, apparently, no production target as such.[27] To make the picture even more complex, indicators in enterprises under the Glavsevkavstroi *glavk* were, around 1966, being calculated on the basis of SNT (*smetno-normativnaya trudoemkost'* – 'estimated normed labour-intensity'), presumably essentially a capital-labour ratio indicator.[28] More recently Glavsevkavstroi was involved in an experiment based on 'conventional-net output' (*uslovno-chistaya produktsiya*),[29] a forerunner of the 'normed net output' indicator (NNO) now in vogue. When general transition to the reform started in 1970, however, it was based on the Glavmosstroi experiment, with total marketed output (*ob"em realizuemoi produktsii*) being used in place of the old output indicator.[30] The status of NSR, conventional-net output, etc. was left ambiguous. They were not generally adopted, partly because of opposition from the ministries,[31] partly because of problems to which we shall return later, but were equally never officially rejected, so that the whole set-up continued to have a rather provisional flavour.

The third key indicator, and the one which sums up the whole emphasis of the new approach, was operationalisation (*vvod v deistvie*). As with profit, this was brought in as an indicator before the promulgation of the general reform.[32] In the Belorussian experiment, initially run in that republic's Ministries of Industrial Construction and Installation and Special Construction, and subsequently extended, operationalisation is the key indicator. Consistent with the general strategy of placing increased emphasis on completion, the procedure whereby the 'State Operationalisation Commission' (Gosudarstvennaya priemochnaya komissiya) carries on its work was tightened up in early 1966. Whereas previously the rule had been that 'enterprises are passed as being operational if production is possible on the installed equipment, irrespective of whether it has actually started',[33] only actually functioning enterprises would now be eligible to face the Commission.[34] In addition, building enterprises should get a share in the profits made in the 'extra' period of operation by an enterprise completed ahead of schedule.[35]

In construction, as in industry proper, changes in success-indicators were to be accompanied by changes in financial practice. Not only would operationalisation of new capacity now become crucial to bonus payments, it would also become the basis of payment for work done. The proportion of total construction for which accounts were settled on the basis of the completed project rose from 0.3 per cent in 1964 to 10.5 per cent in 1970.[36] By 1977 the figure had risen to 56.4 per cent,[37] and in 1978 it reached 60 per cent.[38] Under the Belorussian scheme all accounts are settled on this basis, and it is interesting to note that the Lithuanian Ministry of Construction was reporting 100 per cent payment by completed project before it even went onto the Belorussian system.[39] A further element in the new system was that work in progress should be financed out of credits or working capital. This arrangement would not be independent of the new principles governing investment finance discussed in Chapter 2. On the contrary, funds would be lent by Stroibank to contractors on the basis of funds deposited by clients (of contractors) with the bank. In case of these deposits being inadequate, the client would have to borrow money from the bank, at a rate of interest, to cover the difference.[40] But clients' advances still financed 85 per cent of total unfinished construction in 1979, with bank credit accounting for a modest 10 per cent.[41] This latter figure does, in fact, represent a slight drop from the 1978 figure of 11 per cent.[42] Indeed, a smaller proportion of contractual basis unfinished construction was being financed by bank credit in 1975 than in 1965.[43] But no less than 83.5 per cent of total unfinished construction was being financed by bank credit in the Belorussian Ministry for Industrial Construction at the beginning of 1979.[44]

Outside the house-building sector, where conversion of enterprises to some variant of the new system got under way fairly quickly,[45] progress with the general reform was rather slow. Mass transferral was originally supposed to get going in 1969,[46] but the first group of 40 enterprises was put onto the reform only in 1970.[47] By 1971 the number had risen to 227, and in 1972 about one-third of total construction work was being carried on by reformed enterprises.[48] By 1974 about one-half the total number of construction organisations were on the reform,[49] but the proportion did not subsequently rise a great deal, though by mid-1975 reformed enterprises were handling 70 per cent of total contractual basis work.[50]

As of the mid-1970s, then, a great deal of construction work was still being carried on on a traditional *val* basis. The situation with reformed enterprises may not in practice have been very different. The key here is the *ob"em realizuemoi produktsii* indicator. Obviously a gross indicator, it becomes in practice almost indistinguishable from *valovoi ob"em rabot* when calculated on the basis of stages which may be more or less arbitrarily defined (cf. discussion of stages in design work in Chapter 3). This is clearly the reason why, in the Belorussian experiment, stages are done away with for planning as well as financial purposes.[51] But 80 per cent of total construction work was still being planned on the basis of stages in 1976,[52] and a 1978 source confirms that the breakdown still tended to be done on the basis of types of construction work, rather than stage of projects as such.[53]

The financial side of the reform was particularly knotty. It is clear that the new planning arrangements could not work properly on the basis of the old system of advances from clients. Indeed the continued prevalence of this method of financing effectively neutralised the 'payment by completed project' principle, since advances are in practice indistinguishable from intermediate payments.[54] On the other hand, exclusive use of the completed project indicator demands some method of computing putative output and profit by the quarter, if only so that bonuses can be calculated and credit flows regulated.[55]

Finally, it became clear that as long as the annual plan, a key Soviet planning instrument, survived, scope for the introduction into construction of more sophisticated success-indicators and financial arrangements would be limited.[56] Under the Belorussian system, of course, two-year continuous planning plays a key operational rôle.

Managerial innovation during the 1970s was not restricted to reform of success-indicators. There was also a trend to the extension of the *khozraschet* principle upwards and downwards from the trust/construction administration level. The Belorussian Ministry of Industrial Construction was itself put on *khozraschet*, initially on the basis of *val*,[57] but subsequently using the same success-indicators as its subordinate organisations.[58] As far as the *khozraschet brigade* (work team) is concerned, some form of overall volume of work target and an upper limit on total wages and bonus payments are the only planning instruments used.[59]

The Zlobin method of brigade *khozraschet*, named after the man who originated it in 1970,[60] is thus basically an arrangement whereby the brigade is given a specific task, extending over three or more months, the requisite supplies, etc., and left to get on with it. In some cases *khozraschet* has been extended to even smaller units (*uchastok* – section, *zveno* – link).[61] Irrespective of specific success-indicator régimes, this sort of arrangement, like the *zveno* arrangement in Soviet agriculture, is likely to improve workers' morale and the level of on-site organisation. It certainly improves the quality of work,[62] and a survey covering 1,000 brigades reported a 17–20 per cent shortening of lead-times, and a 20–25 per cent improvement in productivity.[63] But its success has been constrained by an exogenous factor to which we shall return later in a more general context, namely supply uncertainty.[64] In addition, trusts and ministries are often somewhat resistant to introducing the system[65] – because it is too complicated (cf. earlier remarks about Zlobin and the traditional managerial structure) – so that it is not surprising that complaints of an inadequate level of general organisation for the method are heard.[66]

It may be partly for these reasons that introduction of brigade *khozraschet* has been largely limited to the residential construction sector, covering about 31,000 out of a total of 230,000 brigades in 1976,[67] and 70,000 brigades (41 per cent of total construction work) in 1979.[68] The method has been successfully introduced into industrial construction,[69] but the five-year plan itself envisaged that in 1980 just 25–30 per cent of total industrial construction would be carried on by

Zlobin brigades.[70] One wonders whether, quite apart from the problems discussed above, there may not be a more fundamental difficulty here, namely the problem of breaking up an industrial construction project into the kind of convenient 'building blocks' of which modern residential construction projects are usually made up. In any case, the present work is largely concerned with industrial construction, so there seems to be no need to bear the Zlobin method too strongly in mind in later analysis.

Given the rather unsatisfactory history of planning reform in the building industry in the 1970s, it was not surprising that the 1979 planning decree paid special attention to the sector. In many ways the history of the Kosygin reform in construction was one of ineffectuality at the general level, and interesting but unsystematised experiments, most of which ended in a blind alley, at the particular.[71] The 'mini-reform' of July 1979 was preceded by a *postanovlenie* on cadres in the industry in February of the same year, and followed by a number of more specific measures. This package sought to modify the situation systematically, and, in some respects, moderately radically. The model taken was the Belorussian system – the biggest and most sustained of the experiments of the post-1965 period. The results of that experiment had been encouraging, though not spectacular – over the period 1975–78 the Belorussian Ministry for Industrial Construction reduced average lead-times by 16 per cent, and the volume of unfinished construction by 4 per cent.[72] In any case the Plenum of the CC CPSU of October 1976 approved the general introduction of the system, and the measures of 1979 built further on this basis. At the risk of some over-simplification, we can list the most important of those measures, as they relate to the planning of the work of construction organisations, in the following terms:

(1) Full transition to accounts by finished project or stage by 1981.
(2) 'Self-financing' (*samookupaemost'*) to become a key financial principle.
(3) Further extension of the Zlobin system.
(4) Key success-indicators to be operationalisation, *tovarnaya produktsiya* (marketable output), profit (cost-reduction in planned loss-making enterprises), and labour productivity, measured in terms of NNO, or similar indicator.

A propos of (2) it is quite clear that self-financing means what it implies in relation to *working* capital. Unfinished construction is to be financed from own resources or from bank credit. It is not clear whether it extends into the sphere of fixed capital, on the model of the Ministry of Instrument-making (see Table 2.1). In relation to (4), experience with the Belorussian experiment has shown that clashes may occur between the demands of the operationalisation and *tovarnaya produktsiya* indicators. As noted in Chapter 3, *tovarnaya produktsiya* implies saleability, but not necessarily sale, so that in fact it is still very much a gross-volume-of-work-based indicator. A new ruling, however, stipulates that output can only be counted as *tovarnaya* once the capacities involved are actually in operation.[73] This effectively turns the *tovarnaya produktsiya* indicator into an alternative (quantitative) expression of the operationalisation indicator. A Gosstroi decree of early 1980 defined the concept of *normed conventional-net output* (*normativnaya uslovno-chistaya produktsiya*) as basically the normed wage bill plus the sectoral-average rate of planned accumulation, taken as a percentage of the wage bill – clearly an alternative to NNO which can be used with planned loss-making enterprises.

This package of measures is obviously likely to reproduce the results achieved experimentally under the Belorussian system in relation to lead-times etc., though it should be noted that some features of the experiment, for example continuous two-year planning, do not seem to be scheduled for universalisation. It presents a greatly improved array of success-indicators, though the continued high incidence of systematic loss-making in construction, affecting 25 per cent of the total number of building organisations in 1979,[74] has caused problems. More fundamentally, the proposed system is still partly command-based and strongly output-oriented. It is interesting that no statistics seem to have been published on the cost indicators of Belorussian experiment organisations. For our purposes, of course, the main significance of all this is to place in perspective just how little the post-1965 arrangements had moved away from the traditional system.

The system of remuneration in the building industry is similar to that found in design organisations. Managerial workers receive monthly salaries, plus bonuses for the fulfilment of success-indicators. As of around 1965 annual bonuses paid to managerial personnel could not exceed the equivalent of 4.8 monthly salaries, though on especially important projects the limit was the equivalent of 6 monthly salaries. About 85 per cent of workers were covered by piece-rate systems of one kind or another, but these rates were supplemented by bonuses (though only since 1960, apparently). Workers on time-rates also received bonuses. Around 40–50 per cent of total bonuses were going to workers.[75] There is no reason to believe that this overall picture has changed a great deal up to the present day. Despite the various changes in basic success-indicators discussed above, the total wage fund is still expressed as a percentage of the gross volume of construction work.[76] Around 1976, total bonus payments in organisations 'working on the new system' represented 12 per cent of total wage funds.[77]

As with design organisations, it has been normal for bonuses to be paid for fulfilment of tasks other than the principal success-indicators, but once again these do not seem to have generally affected behavioural patterns very much.[78] It has been noted that even labour productivity, which under the 1979 dispensation appears to have the status of a key success-indicator, still has no appreciable effect on the size of bonus funds.[79] Around 1977, bonuses paid for operationalisation accounted for just 21 per cent of total bonuses,[80] but post-1979 prescriptions have aimed to increase this proportion. A decree issued 11 September 1979 specified that a basic bonus representing 3 per cent of the estimated value of construction and installation work should be paid for on-time completion, provided the quality of the project were assessed by the State Operationalisation Commission as 'good'. If quality were assessed as only 'satisfactory', the bonus would be cut by 20 per cent, but 'excellent' quality would mean an extra 10 per cent. Projects completed 30 per cent ahead of schedule would attract a 50 per cent increment to the basic bonus, with 20 and 10 per cent lead-time cuts meaning, respectively, 25 and 10 per cent increments. A special increment of 25 per cent would be paid for on-time completion of projects involving large amounts of imported equipment. Overdue projects completed by the end of the year in which the planned completion date falls would still attract a bonus paid at a reduced rate of 75 per cent. As much as 20 per cent of the profit made in the 'extra' period of operation of projects completed ahead of schedule is to go into construction organisation incentive funds. Allocation of the funds thus accruing is subject to the rule that at least 50 per cent of total bonus payments must go to production workers.[81] We can expect that this highly ingenious system will probably result in an increase in the general weight of operationalisation bonuses.

Under the Zlobin system of brigade *khozraschet*, workers basically receive a terminal bonus at the end of 'the job',[82] but a good deal of scope is left for the payment of special bonuses for on-time or early completion, overfulfilment of physical indicators, cost-reduction, economy in the use of specific materials, etc.[83]

The general level of bonuses for management workers indicates the importance that fulfilment of the basic gross-output-type indicators has had in the past, while the prevalence of piece-rates among workers has strengthened the predominance of such indicators from below, though bonus systems as such have not been notably effective among workers in the industry.[84] Distribution to production workers has often in practice been extremely arbitrary,[85] while the effect of incentive payments on the basis of more sophisticated indicators in the 1970s has tended to be neutralised by the continued practice of giving socialist competition (*sotsialisticheskoe sorevnovanie*) prizes for performance in terms of straight 'gross volume of work'[86] terms. In any case, the old system of bonuses is not appropriate to the Zlobin system,[87] and a new statute on payment-by-results in construction (*Polozhenie ob akkordnoi oplate truda v stroitel' stve*) clearly aims to place the whole approach to incentive payments onto a higher, and more integrated level.[88]

DISTORTIONS INDUCED BY THE PLANNING AND MANAGEMENT RÉGIME

The system as described above, with its traditional emphasis on *val*, only marginally qualified by new developments in planning, has, of course, produced tendencies to low quality in work, disregard of customer needs, neglect of cost considerations and resistance to innovation, in the same way that similar systems have done in other sectors. We have seen that design organisations, ministries, etc. and enterprises can to some extent be blamed for inefficiencies which manifest themselves at the actual construction stage. But there is plenty of evidence of the direct operation of the success-indicator factor within the construction sector.

Instances of quality-lowering and/or specification-distortion to suit *val* can readily be found in the Soviet press. Irrigation work in the North Caucasus in the middle 1960s was vitiated by a number of characteristic faults: drainage pipes were laid only 10–15 cm below the surface, instead of the normal 70 cm, and the general standard of construction was so low that proper control over the system was not possible – backflows occurred, and sometimes too much water was supplied, so that land had subsequently to be drained.[89] It is, of course, perfectly clear that pipes are more quickly laid shallow than deep, which suits a target for metres of pipes laid. A report on the progress of the building of the Andizhan dam stressed the serious difficulties met with in trying to ensure adequate quality in concreting work, *despite continual pressure on building organisations by design workers and client*.[90] Quality problems are often particularly severe in the case of housing and infrastructure construction. In Azerbaidzhan 'completed' schools have been left without running water or window glass, with unpainted walls and unfinished classrooms.[91] New houses in Lithuania lack proper insulation, and the removal of a light switch can leave a hole in the wall right through to the next house.[92] It should be noted that finishing always tends to be particularly bad, because the later stages of building, being relatively more labour- and less materials-using, are less *val*-intensive than earlier stages. Thus gas pipeline builders in the Komi ASSR have neglected construction of compression stations in favour of maximising the length of actual pipe laid, as the easiest way to fulfil output targets (in this case unofficial output targets set at the ministerial level). Pipeline capacity in the absence of compression is only 30–35 per cent what it should be.[93] One of the most telling criticisms of the post-1965 system was, indeed, precisely that it continued to induce this particular distortion.

Because the indicator *tovarnaya produktsiya* basically consists of analogous indicators broken down by stages of work, its application orientates construction organisations primarily to intermediate production, and not to the operationalisation of completed projects. Tranches of construction work lose their identity with this indicator, and so contracting organisations can fulfil 'more advantageous' stages, in preference to 'less advantageous'.[94]

Violation of cost constraints occurs in much the same way as it does in other sectors, and the tendency is well documented with respect to wage costs. A number of specific facilitating factors are present here. Firstly, there is the peculiar rule, which was certainly in force up to the late 1960s, whereby the annual wages fund is based upon the previous year's actual wage expenditure, even if that was above plan.[95] Secondly, the system of tariffs which is supposed to keep piece-rate earnings more or less in line with a putative 'normal' wage for each grade of worker does not work properly. In 1979 the 'tariff' accounted for only 55–60 per cent of total earnings. This is apparently closely related to 'fiddling' on the estimated wage costs of auxiliary work.[96]

Thirdly, the complex system whereby supplementary payments can be made to workers to compensate for having to move around, or for poor living conditions and amenities, leaves plenty of scope for abuse.[97] Fourthly, there are, no doubt, special difficulties in controlling anything to do with the highly mobile, and indeed semi-casual, construction labour force. In any case, the extent to which workers can be overpaid for doing, for example, illegal overtime,[98] is quite staggering. 'Usually the foreman goes around the building site the day before the day off, and seductively rustles money in his pocket. He offers five, ten, or even twenty rubles to anyone willing to turn out for work on his law-given rest day. Some agree, but as a rule few take the money home. They drink it all away. What good is this to anyone?'[99] The fact that the average basic weekly wage of a building worker around 1970 was in the region of 30–35 rubles puts the significance of this 1969 report into perspective. To underline the point, *shabashniki* – 'lump' workers – make 2–4 times the 'normal' wage in Western Siberia.[100]

Aggregate overspending of the wages fund for all the construction ministries in 1975 was only 1.5 per cent, though it was over 3 per cent for some ministries.[101] Much higher figures are, naturally, reported for individual organisations.[102] But there is so much scope for *planned* wage fund to get out of step with the implications of other plans, that the significance of these figures should not be overstressed. Infringement of rules for the distribution of bonuses often takes the form of illegitimate payments to workers who would not properly be in line for bonuses.[103]

Lack of concern for cost constraints also manifests itself in terms of use of materials. A survey of 1,587 construction organisations undertaken in 1960 by Stroibank revealed the excess expenditures (in terms of established norms) shown in Table 4.1. These affected 1,189 organisations out of the total sample. Another Stroibank survey conducted around 1978 or 1979 found excessive material expenditures on 1,642 projects of 4.5 milliard rubles.[104] This confirms that there is still a problem, but in the absence of any figures on the total costs of the 1,642 projects we cannot make a direct comparison with the 1960 figures. Certainly the 'material-intensiveness' of Soviet construction, i.e. share of material costs in total costs, has remained virtually static over the past two decades – it was 56.3 per cent in 1960, 55.6 per cent in 1970, and 55.1 per cent in 1975.[105] New norms for material expenditures, to be worked out by Gosplan, Gosstroi and the ministries, were overdue in 1977.[106]

Table 4.1. *Excess material expenditures in construction*

Material	Unit of measurement	Normed utilisation	Actual utilisation	Actual as percentage of normed utilisation
Cement	tons	164,281	189,647	115.4
Timber	m^3	405,751	491,603	121.2
Concrete	m^3	768,382	840,321	109.4
Mortar	m^3	981,917	1,176,364	119.8
Reinforced concrete	m^3	263,351	287,881	109.3
Bricks	thousands of units	432,503	476,664	110.2
Glass	thousands of m^2	643.6	938.3	145.8
Nails	tons	463.2	602.4	130.0
Sand and gravel	m^3	102,362	128,023	125.1
Stone and road metal	m^3	180,656	218,236	120.8

Source: N. G. Kazhlaev, *Povyshenie Effektivnosti Kapital'nykh Vlozhenii*, Moscow, Ekonomizdat, 1963, pp. 174–5

Lastly, there is resistance to innovation. Apart from the general reluctance to spend time retooling etc., any innovation tending to reduce costs is looked upon with particular disfavour, because it goes directly against the nature of any output by value indicator. For example, the new and cheaper method of binding saline soil and shifting sand with bitumen and cement discovered by the Central Asian branch of the All-Union Road Research Institute was not brought into use for this very reason.[107] Pre-fabricated blocks are still little used in industrial construction, and this seems to be related to the fact that they raise the wage component in costs, presumably because of the need to employ more highly-skilled men, and because a number of material-intensive basic operations are cut out. Thus they are less 'gross-intensive'.[108]

On the other hand, introduction of advanced management methods has proceeded with some success, particularly at the brigade level. The Zlobin method of brigade *khozraschet* is frequently combined with the Orel system of continuous planning (*nepreryvka*), a form of applied critical path analysis.[109] The system is reported to yield a 1.5–1.7

times reduction in the number of projects simultaneously under way, a 15–20 per cent reduction in lead-times, and a 5–7 per cent reduction in building costs.[110] As with the Zlobin method, however, the application of the Orel *nepreryvka* has been limited largely to the residential construction sector.[111] Perhaps the major constraint on extension of the system has been the simple fact that superior organisations concerned primarily with 'assimilating' volume of construction work have by definition not been primarily concerned with continuity of operations. As one local planner put it, 'It's as if continuous planning didn't exist for Minstroi USSR.'[112] Electronics are also being brought into construction management, with 130 computer centres now serving the industry, though this network does not appear to be used with a high degree of efficiency.[113] Gosstroi USSR has been criticised for slowness in producing a standard information and coding system for use with the computerised calendar planning system developed by the research institute of Gosstroi Estonia.[114]

It is worth noting here that some of the experimental indicators mentioned earlier have run into special problems of their own. The NSR indicator, for example, does not, as it was hoped it would, excise the problem of 'advantageous' and 'disadvantageous' work.

Together with its positive characteristics, a number of defects in the NSR indicator may be noted . . . For example, earth-removing work gives a higher normative value if done by hand rather than on a mechanised basis. Under NSR repair-construction work is similarly 'advantageous'. (This was observed in finishing work, and in repair work on damaged electrical cables.) Overfulfilment of the plan for volume of production according to NSR cannot always be counted on as a positive factor.

Secondly, in some cases where the technology of production is changed and more progressive materials and structures utilised, with a corresponding increase in labour productivity in natural terms, the position is not always correctly reflected by NSR. For example, the use of ceiling panels with balcony extensions, instead of panels and balcony slabs, increases labour productivity in natural terms by 50 per cent, but reduces it, measured by NSR, by 37 per cent.[115]

The basic problem here is clear enough. Because NSR is a net, rather than a gross, indicator, it encourages excessive labour intensity – precisely the opposite distortion from that normally associated with *val*-type indicators. As noted in Chapter 2, the normed net output indicator should avoid this problem. To the extent, then, that NNO or similar indicators are introduced systematically into construction, at least some aspects of the classic success-indicator problem may be excised. But this is something very much for the future.

It is possible, then, to explain the contribution of the building industry to problems of quality, costs, etc. in success-indicator terms. But this is not to say that such an explanation would be an accurate reflection of reality. In fact, there are a number of other factors, in origin essentially external to the industry itself, which manifest themselves in actual construction activity and strengthen the tendencies discussed above. Without an understanding of these factors, we cannot fully comprehend how problems in construction activity contribute to *raspylenie* and other efficiency problems.

SUPPLY UNCERTAINTY

As was pointed out in Chapter 1, this is a perennial phenomenon in the Soviet economy, and can indeed be argued to be an inevitable characteristic of any centrally planned economy, given the present state of the arts. Some idea of the quantitative importance of the phenomenon in the present context is given by the results of a *sovnarkhoz* survey from the middle 1960s, which indicated that in 129 out of 824 cases of delayed completion supply deficiencies were to blame.[116] A source from the mid-1970s noted that 'in recent years the material needs of construction have been systematically left unsatisfied'.[117] The deputy minister of Minstroi USSR has stated that in 1979 the *plan* for deliveries of materials to the ministry was 150 million rubles short of requirements. Taking into account the fact that not all planned deliveries arrive, the total gap was 200 million rubles, representing 4 per cent of the requirements of the annual plan.[118] We must add considerably to this to take account of poor quality and misdirected deliveries, so that the overall picture of supply uncertainty in this particular case is very sharply delineated.

It has been remarked that building enterprises, despite the old proverb 'do not cut off the branch you are sitting on', seem to be particularly bad at building factories for the building materials industry.[119] This point is graphically underlined by the figures in Table 4.2. It is not surprising, then, that problems with supply of non-metal construction materials call forth continual complaints in the Soviet press.[120] And the issue is often outright deficiency, rather than just quality or specification. The network of establishments run by the Ministry for Building Materials itself is territorially extremely

Table 4.2. *Percentage fulfilment of plans for construction of enterprises producing non-metallic building materials*

	1976	1977	1978
Ministry for Heavy Industrial Construction USSR	22.8	46.2	73.9
Ministry of Industrial Construction USSR	92	83	99.2
Ministry of Construction USSR	84.2	69.3	67.8
Ministry of Transport Construction	57.2	89.6	84.2

Source: A. P. Lifatov, 'Uporyadochit' obespechenie stroek nerudnymi materialami', in *Ekonomika Stroitel'stva*, No. 4, 1980, p. 21

unevenly distributed, and the ministry has virtually nothing in north-western Siberia, the north-east, and some north-western *oblasti* of the RSFSR.[121] There are no less than 35,000 construction materials establishments in the Soviet Union,[122] and one might be tempted to cite excessively small scale as a cause of supply difficulties. The direction of causation does, in fact, tend to be in the opposite direction, with organisations building up their own 'dwarf-work-shops' as a hedge against supply uncertainty. The officially reported number of building materials associations and independent enterprises was just 3,864 in 1979.[123]

Similar problems have plagued the supply of steel and steel tubes.[124] Severe difficulties are also endemic with supply of construction equipment. Shortage of heavy earth-moving equipment has been a major problem in irrigation work in Uzbekistan.[125] But shortages have also been felt in the supply of the simpler kinds of equipment. 'A hand paint palette is a very primitive piece of equipment. But such articles are not produced by industry, and painters have to make their own. Spatulas are also not to be had. And the brush situation is particularly bad. We do not have a single brigade with a full complement of paint brushes.'[126] A 1975 *Pravda* editorial complains that construction ministries often have to make their own equipment in their own repair shops.[127]

Then there is the problem of supply of equipment for installation. Many completed projects are held up by lack of equipment, or by the unfinished state of equipment supplied.[128] In some cases the arrival of equipment is planned for a date later than the official operationalisation date. For instance, at the Lisichansk chemical combine, production of methanol was planned to start in the third quarter of 1966, but the necessary equipment was not planned to arrive until the first quarter of 1967.[129] An identical case occurred with the seventh coking battery of the Lipetsk metallurgical factory.[130] Building organisations respond by using a rule of thumb whereby installation work should not begin on a given project until at least 80 per cent of the equipment has arrived.[131] This naturally tends to extend lead-times.

On the other hand, equipment may also arrive early.

Practical experience shows that in a number of cases equipment is sent to building sites or operating enterprises before the required date, not as a result of production plan overfulfilment by suppliers, but because of inefficiency in the planning organs, in cases where there is simply nowhere to put the equipment. For example, equipment for the construction of building No. 3 at the Minsk motor-cycle factory was already starting to arrive in 1960. On 1 January 1961, 466,000 rubles' worth of it had accumulated there, including 343,000 rubles' worth of imported equipment, while the allocations for the construction of the actual building were not planned to go out until 1963. Or to take another example – equipment for the reconstruction of revolving cement furnaces at the Magnitogorsk cement factory was assigned in 1963, though the reconstruction itself is not planned to go through until 1966. Equipment has been arriving at the Magnitogorsk metallurgical combine for the department of cold metal rolling, presently under construction, since 1959, though the department is not planned to go into operation until 1965.[132]

Building enterprises are themselves sometimes to blame for this sort of thing, inasmuch as they order equipment too early.[133] But this is in itself no doubt a reaction to the prevailing situation of supply uncertainty, and a safeguard against the possibility of *late* arrival of equipment – disorganised supply engenders secondary tendencies which disorganise it further.

But supply uncertainty in the building industry is intensified beyond the normal level for Soviet industry as a whole by characteristic ministerial tendencies, already reviewed in Chapter 2. As we saw there, the drive to get as many projects going as possible sometimes extends as far as starting projects which are actually not in the plan. Thus the severe supply problems affecting the construction of the Soligorsk potassium combine in 1968 were hardly surprising given that many of the relevant orders were outside the plan.[134]

Some prospect for improvement in the construction supply situation may be offered by the 'supply by order' (*snabzhenie po zakazam*) system, which was experimentally introduced in six enterprises in 1970. This system seems to be based on a much higher degree of flexibility in supply arrangements than has been normal, and research done by the Scientific Research Institute for the Economics and Organisation of Material-Technical Supply indicates that it may yield a 20–25 per cent reduction in intra-shift delays due to irregularity in supply.[135] But by 1979 the system had been extended only to an additional 21 enterprises,[136] and one wonders whether the universalisation apparently envisaged by the 1979 planning decree is possible without a most radical revamp of the whole supply system, and, implicitly, of the whole planning system. Current policy trends specifically on supply to construction appear, in fact, to be anything but radical. An experimental system whereby equipment orders went through the appropriate design organisation was predictably unsuccessful,[137] while the most recent decree on equipment supply merely threatens heavier fines for errant suppliers.[138]

The most obvious way in which supply uncertainty contributes to inefficiencies in the building industry is in terms of quality and satisfaction of customers' needs, including completion dates. The built-in prejudice in favour of foundation work and against finishing work is strengthened inasmuch as 'all you need to move earth is a spade'.[139] But it also intensifies the cost problem. Poor quality and specification in supplies of gravel and sand result in a rate of above-normal utilisation of cement reaching 20 per cent.[140] Additional labour expenditures of 70 per cent above what is normal for fitting were required in construction administration No. 28, Mosstroi-6 trust, in order to excise defects in ceiling slabs.[141] Excessively early deliveries of equipment have an obvious cost in terms of the implicit rate of interest, but in the absence of adequate storage facilities the costs can be much greater, as veritable 'scrap-heaps' of valuable equipment accumulate on sites.[142]

OTHER KEY ASPECTS OF THE ORGANISATIONAL MILIEU

It was noted above that ministerial penchants represent one input into the supply uncertainty situation. Much more important is the simple and wholly to be expected fact that Factors C1 and C2 affect the construction industry in a general way as much as they do any other sector, and more than they do some. Thus ministerial over-bidding for investment resources tends to leave building organisations with a workload greater than they could reasonably be expected by the central authorities to be able to cope with.[143] Going back to

Minstroi USSR in 1979, the overall output target set the ministry was 5,903 million rubles' worth of work. But the implications of the annual plan as a whole represented 6,945 million rubles' worth of work for the ministry.[144]

Turning to the tendency to organisational autarky, it is common-sensical that an organisation which tries to safeguard its supplies of general components will also try to safeguard its supply of construction services, basically through in-house organisations – this, of course, is the only major way in which ministries can operate autarkically with respect to supplies for their own investment pro-grammes, since considerations of technology make the steel and machinery sectors unsuitable for that kind of treatment. One can hardly blame Minister for the Coal Industry, Bratchenko, complaining of delays in coal-mine construction, for believing that construction organisations run by the coal ministry itself might be more reliable.[145] But this sort of thing does lead to sacrifices of economies of scale and rational specialisation, hence lower productivity.

The Institute of Construction Economics estimates that the optimal size for primary building organisations corresponds to an annual value of work greater than 1.5 million rubles, and on this basis over 60 per cent of such organisations were of sub-optimal size in 1960.[146] That did, however, represent a considerable improvement over the position in 1955,[147] and one would expect that the geographically concentrated, multi-industry *sovnarkhozy* would have been able to build up construction capacity with less prejudice to optimal technical conditions. But Odessa correspondents of *Pravda* noted in 1969 that in the four years preceding – i.e. since the re-establishment of the ministerial system – the number of building and building-maintenance organisations in the city had grown four times, with all the organisations being under different departments.[148] Contemporary material suggests that the labour productivity lead of 'complex' construction associations over specialised (frequently departmental) trusts may be of the order of 100 per cent.[149]

It is worth noting that departmentalism affects construction on the housing, as well as on the industrial side. Because of the severe shortage of housing, coupled with the great difficulties involved in simply 'buying' accommodation, provision of housing by departments, enterprises, etc. is a very important determinant of labour supply. Not surprisingly, therefore, these organisations like to have their own housing construction departments. In 1965 only 1.5 per cent of state housing in Magnitogorsk was under the control of the local soviet,[150] while no less than 280 departments owned housing in Moscow.[151] Since then something has been done to reintegrate residential construction, and fragmentation has been eliminated in Moscow.[152] Overall, however, 60 per cent of housing remains outside the control of the municipalities.[153]

To the extent that departmental construction organisations are smaller than construction ministry ones, one would expect that they would use less capital-intensive methods. But the fact that departmental organisations are usually built up 'by hook or by crook' no doubt means that they may be *grossly* underequipped, even by Soviet standards, and taking their size into consideration.[154] In addition, smallness and lack of rational specialisation makes it difficult to apply modern techniques on the purely organisational side of construction – critical path analysis, network planning, etc. Not surprisingly, the Orel system of continuous planning can only work properly with residential construction when the traditional multiplicity of clients described above is replaced by a single OKS (capital investment department of the local executive committee – see p. 28).[155] Such rationalisation would clearly be much more difficult in industrial than in residential construction, and this may be one reason for the slowness with which the Orel *nepreryvka* is being introduced into industrial construction.

SOCIOLOGICAL FACTORS

The quality of labour in the construction industry is undoubtedly poor. For this there are a number of reasons. Historically, remuneration was relatively low, though measures were taken in 1969 which improved the situation.[156] The very low level of unemployment in the USSR means, of course, that there is little general pressure to go into low-paid sectors.[157] Living conditions, particularly in the developing eastern regions, are often very poor.[158] This not only strengthens the general disincentive to enter the industry as a worker, but means also that men who do so, though they may be perfectly competent workers, tend to alcoholism and rowdiness – only 'tough guys' are prepared to put up with the living conditions, and no doubt these conditions make them even tougher.[159] A survey of building organisations in Penza *oblast'* reported that 32.7 per cent of infringements of labour discipline were attributable to hard drinking and 8.1 per cent to 'social passivity'. Negative attitudes to work accounted for 19 per cent of the sample. But it is highly significant that it was the higher-paid workers who were most prone to infringements of discipline.[160] Now of course building workers all over the world manifest these tendencies to some degree, but special Soviet conditions seem to have created a problem serious enough to affect labour reliability, and hence efficiency, to a considerable extent. It is perhaps significant that it has been possible to introduce NOT (*nauchnaya organizatsiya truda*, scientific organisation of labour – a form of Taylorism widespread in the USSR) into only 12–20 per cent of construction work.[161] Lastly, it is through construction work that rural workers are often 'urbanised' in the Soviet Union.[162] There is, of course, nothing inefficient about this in general terms – the learning process must be accepted as legitimately bearing its own costs. But in terms of the activity of the building industry itself it must clearly result in below-average productivity.

The Soviet government has shown itself very much aware of these sociological problems in the last year or two, and measures have been announced which place stress on greater investment in infrastructure and training facilities. But they place equal stress on more socialist competition, a tougher line on discipline, etc.[163] The further development of brigade *khozraschet* must be the most promising basis for a general improvement in the quality of labour supply to construction; but, as noted earlier, there are systematic obstacles in the way of such a development.

THE TEMPORAL DIMENSION

The nature of Soviet planning, with its obligatory targets for definite, and often quite short, time periods, makes some unevenness in work tempi unavoidable. Even in market economies, the existence of deadlines in construction often results in 'storming'. But the various factors tending to create excessive work loads relative to the real capacity of the building industry can clearly be expected to increase the intensity of *shturmovshchina* tendencies. Over a period of twenty years (1953–73) residential construction was characterised by the following pattern of completions:

First quarter   8–11 per cent
Second quarter   19–21 per cent

Third quarter   20–22 per cent
Fourth quarter   46–49 per cent.[164]

Now storming cannot be dismissed as a purely negative phenomenon – it is in fact a way in which building organisations try to cope with problems which they can do little to solve directly. But *shturmovshchina* conditions must obviously accentuate the basic tendency to ignore considerations of cost and quality. Harking back to the last section, unevenness in completion schedules means that construction organisations have difficulty in finding work for stable cadres at the beginning of the year, but have to take on low-calibre workers at the end of the year. All this is bad for morale. During the *shturm* in the last quarter of the year productivity is reported to fall to 65–70 per cent of normal.[165]

We have already discussed the major problem of *raspylenie* in connection with intermediate bodies and design organisations. The foregoing analysis gives us a basis for assessing the contribution of the construction stage to this problem. Success-indicator distortions clearly play a major rôle, not only in terms of the obvious difficulties which clients might have in putting into operation a plant built badly, or to the wrong specifications, but also of the gross-output-induced disincentive to doing finishing work. Overloading of construction capacity must also contribute to the problem, as must supply deficiencies, both directly, and in terms of how building organisations react to it. The materials allocation organs try to cope with inadequate supplies by 'spreading around' available resources, but construction organisations tend to do the same thing. Krasovskii notes that builders themselves may try to start as many projects as possible, in order to be able to continue working on something, whatever the supply situation.[166] This tendency is strengthened by the fact that building organisations, like most other Soviet enterprises, often do not receive their annual plans until February or March. They are forced, therefore, to make a guess at what will be included in the plan. If the guess is wrong, the project involved may simply be abandoned.[167] It is not absolutely clear whether there is a formal rule, paralleling the one covering design organisations, to the effect that, when the time limit for the construction of a given project has run out, it should be abandoned in favour of the next one on the planned list. But this is certainly the way things seem to work out with lower-priority projects.

MONITORING OF CONSTRUCTION WORK

As is the case with design organisations, distortive tendencies in construction are subject to the constraint of the operation of various checking organs. Again as with design organisations, ministries, enterprises, etc. cannot, however, always be expected to have much interest in trying to excise elements of inefficiency in construction work, because of their own success-indicator systems, the ways in which they try to cope with supply uncertainty, etc.

As noted earlier (see p. 77), the State Operationalisation Commission had, prior to 1966, so very formal a remit that it had little chance to be effective. Since then, a consistent effort has been made to give more strength to the elbow of the Commission, without, it appears, a great deal of success. Complaints about its ineffectuality are still common,[168] and a recent *cause célèbre* reported in *Pravda* concerned the signing of an operationalisation certificate (*akt priemki*) for a factory that did not exist.[169] New legislation aims to tighten up procedure still further,[170] but purely procedural changes will surely continue to run up against a number of powerful factors tending to neutralise the *raison d'être* of the Commission. Firstly, although individual commissions are ultimately responsible to Gosstroi, they tend to be dominated in practice by local and departmental interests, certainly in relation to run-of-the-mill projects. Secondly, the traditional orientation of the Soviet economic system towards short-term output maximisation means that there is always pressure to pass a project, so that it can start to produce *something*. Lastly, formal operationalisation means a reduction in officially reported unfinished construction, which is, of course, pure virtue.[171]

The general impression of Gosstroi is that it is too busy planning and issuing building regulations to have much time for checking as such, but certain deficiencies in planning work have made control more difficult. Five years after the approval of guidelines for *normativy zadelov* (norms for uncompleted work) Gosstroi had by 1975 still not worked out a methodology for their application, so that 'monitoring of the correctness of plans for uncompleted construction . . . bears in the majority of cases an episodic character'.[172] Planning procedures do, indeed, continue to this day to evince a peculiar insensitivity to the monitoring of *raspylenie*. The key form 1-ks '*O vypolnenii plana podryad-nykh rabot*' ('On the fulfilment of the plan for contractual work'), which construction organisations have to fill in, contains about 400 indicators, but lead-time in months is not one of them. Only the quarter in which operationalisation is planned is shown. If this is postponed, as often happens, there is no way of directly tracing the reasons.[173] In general, as we saw also in connection with design organisations, coordination between Gosstroi and the banks seems to leave something to be desired.[174]

Be that as it may, Stroibank plays a rôle to be reckoned with in the implementation of construction plans. The bank's rôle as bursar for investment projects gives it at least the opportunity of controlling cost-inflationary tendencies in the implementation stage. We noted earlier how systematically Stroibank collects statistics on excess utilisation of materials. What is less clear is how much the bank is actually able to do about correcting the tendencies revealed.[175] One would expect this work to become increasingly important with the transition from investment grants to credits, though it should be noted that trends in financial procedures do tend to increase the workload of an already overburdened banking system.[176] The obligatory submission to the bank for approval of the annual intra-project (*vnutripostroechnyi*) *titul'nyi spisok*, 'makes it possible to supervise the proper inclusion in the construction plan of priority projects, to ensure that investments are concentrated on them in accordance with norms for gestation periods and that cost estimates and completion indicators for individual projects are observed, and to determine levels of advances required to bring working capital up to a level adequate to cover unfinished construction'.[177] In 1976 the Yaroslavl' branch of Stroibank proposed the exclusion of 67 new projects, worth a total for the year of 5.3 million rubles, from intra-project *titul'nye spiski*, on the grounds that the funds earmarked for these projects were below-norm. In the event, 35 projects, worth 2.9 million rubles for the year, were in fact excluded.[178]

It would appear, though the evidence is purely negative, that in the past Stroibank has concerned itself little with questions of the quality of construction. There are strong indications, however, that this situation is changing, and a 1975 report noted that the bank had withheld no less than 15 million rubles from Mintyazhstroi USSR on account of low quality of work.[179] A number of factors constrain this work of Stroibank. There are too many projects to check, and our conclusions on this point *vis-à-vis* the design stage must apply *a fortiori* to the construction stage. Perhaps more fundamental, so many of the problems of the construction are, with the best will in the world, beyond the strength of the industry to solve for itself. It is of little use to refuse extra finance to a building organisation which finds itself in difficulties because it has been let down by its suppliers!

This last point brings us nicely to some conclusions on the construction industry. Like design organisations, construction organisations are not powerful, though some construction ministries may be. On the other hand, construction organisations are peculiarly open to the effects of all the general inefficiency elements in the Soviet economic system. Thus when we make reference to Factor E we are not necessarily attaching 'blame' to the construction industry, and indeed we are frequently simply talking about special cases of the operation of C group factors. But systematic elements of inefficiency are present in the work of building organisations. Apart from general considerations of quality, any specific case of escalation of cost estimates or *raspylenie* demands a study of the actual process of construction.

5

Official state doctrine

The official *Weltanschauung* of the Soviet state is Marxism-Leninism. There are current in the Soviet Union a number of more or less officially endorsed normative propositions touching on economic matters which are, in the main part, based on some section or other of the Marxist-Leninist classics. It is not the aim of this chapter to enter into any discussion of the correctness or otherwise of the derivation of these various propositions, but simply to evaluate to what extent observance of the propositions could be expected to result in deviations from the yardstick.

Before going on to an examination of the propositions it is necessary to clarify which instances in the decision-making process we can expect to be influenced by them. The strongest *a priori* case can be made out for the central authorities who are, after all, the proponents, or the successors of the proponents, of the propositions. In a number of cases, however, for instance in that of investment appraisal criteria, the propositions, if implemented at all, are implemented by lower-level organisations – ministries, design organisations, etc. But no bonuses are awarded for observation of the propositions, and we have already seen that subordinate organisations usually have enough troubles without getting involved with things which do not directly affect their income levels. On the other hand, observance of the propositions would not, in most cases, go against the material interests of subordinate organisations, nor would it usually involve them in much additional work. It is quite possible that, for example, a design which is not based on the standard coefficient of relative effectiveness (CRE) procedure (see below, pp. 103–9) is automatically rejected by the central authorities, where they are the approving authorities, though no evidence on this is available. But what about

99

the many instances where the approval function is carried out at a
lower level? It is, in fact, difficult to make out a strong *a priori* case that
the propositions are observed at all by subordinate organisations, and
in cases where observance would be prejudicial to their material
interests the *a priori* case must surely be against their observance. The
empirical evidence on this issue is, furthermore, fairly scrappy, as we
shall see in a moment, so that the *a priori* reasoning must take more
weight than one would perhaps ideally wish. While, then, we try to
indicate the kind of systematic deviations which observance of the
propositions could induce, we must remain sceptical about the
'operationality' of this factor, except in the context of large-scale
projects involving central approval, not only of *titul'nye spiski*, but also
of design assignments, or where reliable positive empirical evidence is
available.

THE 'GENERAL LAWS' OF SOCIALISM

The 'Basic Economic Law of Socialism' postulates the 'steady
expansion and improvement of production on the basis of advanced
technique, with the aim of the fullest satisfaction of the steadily
increasing requirements and the many-sided development of the
members of society'. In addition, there is the 'Law of the Planned
(Proportional) Development of the National Economy'. 'The predominance of socialist, and within that of all-people's ownership of
the means of production conditions the coordinated management
[*vedenie*] of the whole national economy as a unified whole, on the basis
of the upholding [*podderzhanie*] of the proportions between different
types of production corresponding to social needs.'[1] Berliner is surely
correct in arguing that neither of these propositions can be accepted
as true laws, of either a causal or teleological nature, but are only
meaningful as statements of aims,[2] and indeed contemporary Soviet
works on the subject are also fairly clear on this point. The 1968
Politicheskaya Ekonomiya (political economy textbook) states the fundamental law of socialism as unequivocally an aim, albeit an objectively
conditioned one, while it notes, *à propos* of planned, proportional
development, that '... one should not, however, equate what is
possible with what is. To turn possibility into actuality, to plan and
manage the economy correctly, requires the study and the mastering
of the law of planned, proportional development, and of how to apply
it with a full understanding of the matter.'[3] Even as statements of

aims, however, these dicta are so broad in their formulation as to be of dubious semantic value. What meaning they have seems to run in terms of some kind of crude optimality concept, so that there seems to be no reason to expect that their observance would, *per se*, lead to any deviations from the yardstick.

The case of the other principal 'general law', the Law of Value, is somewhat more complex. During the Stalin period, indeed, the entire question of the status of the Law of Value under socialism was in confusion,[4] and only comparatively recently has the view been accepted that it does, in some sense, operate under post-revolutionary conditions. Once again it can reasonably be argued that the idea of commodity prices corresponding, in some way, to labour inputs, can only have the status of a desideratum under conditions of Soviet socialism, except where the private, and possibly also the collective, sectors are involved.[5] The content of the 'law' is, however, in this case somewhat more definite, and its observance could clearly be expected to lead to the emergence of deviations from the yardstick. Investment decision-making would be distorted to the extent that (a) equipment, materials and final goods prices would not correspond to efficiency prices; (b) rent considerations would not be taken into account; (c) no rate of interest would be imputed. We consider these three headings in turn in the following three sections.

PRICING AND THE LAW OF VALUE

It is not in fact clear that any important practical considerations are involved here, and this for two reasons. Firstly, it has never satisfactorily been made clear how the labour theory of value should, or even could, be used as a basis for an operational theory of planned price formation.[6] Secondly, the level of computer technology is only now reaching a level where it can cope with the scale of operations involved in highly centralised price planning,[7] and Soviet hardware is not the most advanced in the world.[8] In any case, for most of the post-1930 period computers have not been available at all to the Soviets, so that it is clearly nonsensical to speak of prices being formed in the past on any scientific principles. The fact that Soviet prices have been, and continue to be under reform conditions, formed more or less on a cost-plus basis could be tied in with the labour theory of value in its cruder forms, but could equally well be explained as virtually the only practical possibility.[9] Though profitability is now an officially endorsed indicator of 'general economic effectiveness', it is in any case still not clear that Soviet planners consistently use list prices as planning parameters. There is, then, neither any great need nor good reason to resort to the state-doctrinal factor in explaining deviations which result from faults in the general price structure. And because these faults are, in fact, rather random and unsystematic, the price system simply tends to fuzz up perception of efficiency (see discussion in Chapter 1), rather than producing readily identifiable deviations.

Rent and interest imputations are, of course, involved in the calculation of general structures of efficiency prices, but they are also directly involved in investment appraisal. And here we must give more attention to official practices, simply because the technological constraints limiting the possibility of working out comprehensive shadow-price systems certainly do not apply to interest imputations, and do not apply to the same extent to questions of land valuation.

THE IMPUTATION OF RENT

As we have seen, it has not been usual for rental charges to be levied on executive organisations in the post-1930 period, or even in the post-1965 period. The question here, however, is whether the central authorities make allowances for rent in their own decision-making, and in their instructions to other decision-making bodies. Direct evidence on this is not easy to come by, but Probst argues that they frequently have not, or at least have done so to a grossly inadequate extent. He cites the example of the Lower Ob' hydro-electric scheme, where 145,000 km^2 of submersion zone were valued at only 0.1 rubles per hectare, despite the fact that the land contains rich deposits of oil and natural gas.[10] 'If the design workers had correctly valued the economic losses from submersion and partial submersion (*podtoplenie*), they would not have come to the conclusion that it was "economically optimal" to build a HES of capacity 7 million kW on the Lower Ob', and would probably have decided that it was economically ineffective.'[11] Such a large project would obviously have come into the above-limit category with respect to design assignment as well as *titul'nyi spisok*, so it is no use blaming the ministry. Purely technical deficiencies in valuation procedures may have had something to do with it, but the indication here, as with other cases, is that there has been some systematic tendency to undervalue natural resources which is correctly imputed to the state-doctrinal factor, rather than to the institutional features discussed in Chapter 2. There is clearly at the present time a growing consciousness on the part of the political leadership of the importance of proper land valuation,[12] but this only serves to confirm the tenor of our general conclusion.

THE COEFFICIENT OF RELATIVE EFFECTIVENESS

As far as interest imputation is concerned, the situation up to about the middle 1950s, or perhaps even later, is unclear. Interest costs were probably not imputed in many sectors, but do seem to have been in power generation and transport construction[13] – very highly capital-intensive sectors, but with significant variations in the degree of that capital-intensity, depending on the exact techniques used. It is certainly in these sectors that the procedures for interest valuation now officially blessed were originally developed.[14]

In 1958 an all-union conference on 'problems of determining the economic effectiveness of capital investment and new technology' was held, and two years later a *Standard Methodology for Determining the Economic Effectiveness of Capital Investment and New Technology in the National Economy of the USSR* was published.[15] Revised versions of the *Standard Methodology* appeared in 1969 and 1981.[16] We must take these documents as reflecting the official position on interest valuation, though their exact status is not completely clear. The 1960 document was not made obligatory for design organisations,[17] and one of the authors of the 1969 version noted at the time that 'much work remains to be done before these principles can be transformed into working instructions for each sector, ministry, department and their subordinate institutions. It is necessary to finish this work quickly, so that instructions for the different sectors can be properly confirmed this year.'[18] No confirmation that this work was carried through satisfactorily has come to hand. The 1981 *Methodology* has not been vouchsafed the epithet *Standard*, and its preface emphasises its provisional status. We are, then, left in some doubt as to the exact nature of the operationality of the documents.

The approach to project evaluation espoused in the *Standard Methodologies* is the recoupment period/coefficient of relative effectiveness method. The basic mathematical formulation of this method is:

$$t = \frac{K_1 - K_2}{C_2 - C_1},$$

(1)

or:

$$e = \frac{C_2 - C_1}{K_1 - K_2},\qquad(2)$$

where K is capital expenditures, C is running costs, including depreciation, and subscripts denote projects with identical output characteristics to be compared. The subscript $_1$ is used for the more capital-intensive, and the subscript $_2$ for the less capital-intensive variant. The more capital-intensive variant is considered preferable if t is less than a normative T, or e greater than a normative E. It will be noted that t is in fact a kind of marginal recoupment period – the time it takes a more capital-intensive variant to pay off the extra capital costs with running cost economies, and that e, the coefficient of relative effectiveness, or CRE, is simply the reciprocal of t.[19]

A more general formulation, permitting comparison of more than two projects, and facilitating comparison with orthodox theory, is:

$$C + EK = \text{minimum.[20]}\qquad(3)$$

Bearing in mind the discussion on pp. 7–8 of Chapter 1, it is clear that the relevant criterion from western allocational theory to which this expression should be compared is that of Present Value. In mathematical terms, this criterion can be formulated as a cost-minimisation test thus:

$$\sum_{n=0}^{N} [K_n + V_n][1 + i]^{-n} = \text{minimum,[21]}\qquad(4)$$

where K is capital costs, V is running costs *not including depreciation*, the n subscript denotes the time period in which the given expenditure is made, and n is the life of the project. The symbol i denotes a rate of interest such as would bring the supply and demand for capital into equilibrium.

Let us proceed for the moment on the assumption that E is set at the clearing level. (See definitional discussion below.) It is clear from a comparison of (3) and (4) that the former has three deficiencies. Firstly, it ignores the possibility of capital expenditures occurring in more than one time period. Secondly, it ignores the possibility of variation in running costs over time. Thirdly, it incorrectly includes depreciation in running costs. In fact, however, this last deficiency works out as an advantage in the case of projects which do have once-and-for-all capital outlays and constant operating costs, and brings the CRE criterion more or less into correspondence with the Present Value test. In such a case the Present Value criterion reduces to:

$$\frac{-\Delta V}{\Delta K} = i + \frac{i}{(1 + i)^N - 1}. \tag{5}$$

What this means is that the rate of annual cost economy from a marginal investment must equal the rate of interest plus a sum which, when compounded at a rate i, will accumulate after N years to a unit value. In other words, the annual cost economy must cover not only imputed interest charges, but also the replacement cost of the capital at the end of N years. Where projects have the same service life, the requirement reduces quite simply to an equivalence of the annual cost economy per unit of capital for all projects.

Turning now to the CRE criterion, we can deduce from (3) the requirement:

$$\Delta C + E\Delta K = 0. \tag{6}$$

Reformulating this in terms of V, and rearranging slightly, we get:

$$\frac{-\Delta V}{\Delta K} = E + \frac{\Delta D}{\Delta K}, \tag{7}$$

where ΔD is the difference between the depreciation charges of the projects being compared. Given that depreciation charges are normally worked out on a 'straight-line' basis in the Soviet Union, $\Delta D/\Delta K$ will normally be the same for all projects with identical service lives. Thus the CRE criterion reduces, in this case, to exactly the same requirement as the Present Value criterion – that annual cost economy per unit of capital must be identical for all projects.

Where service lives are not identical, some divergence does occur between the requirements of the two criteria, and Durgin shows that, in principle, the CRE method discriminates against projects with longer lives, in the case of very long-lived projects quite sharply.[22] But Bergson points out that if we take actual Soviet depreciation procedures into consideration, which would mean that the clearing level of E would be lower than the corresponding one of i, there may, paradoxically, be an opposite tendency to favour longer-lived projects unduly, though the tendency would not be a very powerful one.[23]

Where capital expenditures occur over a number of years, and/or where operating costs vary, (3) would clearly be a rather inaccurate guide to efficient investment decision-making. Capital projects with long gestation periods are probably usually also long-lived projects, so that use of (3) would tend, *ceteris paribus*, to discriminate unduly against such projects, if all capital expenditures were assumed by planners to be made in the initial period. If non-initial capital expenditures were simply ignored, the distortion would be in the opposite direction, and could be of serious proportions. To the extent that running costs tend to rise progressively with short-lived, more than with long-lived projects, the latter would be discriminated against if operating costs were assumed to continue at their initial level. If, however, operating costs were taken as an average of estimated costs over the life of the project, the opposite would be the case, since the higher, later costs would be taken account of in an undiscounted way.

The *Standard Methodologies* do give a variant of the CRE criterion which takes into account these complications. The 1960 version recommends use of a coefficient K_{pr}, equal to $(1 + E)^T$, T being here simply the number of years in the discounting period, for reducing the value of future investment flows into terms of present investment flows.[24] In 1969 and 1981 the formulation was V equal to $1/(1 + E_{NP})^t$.[25] Ignoring small changes in terminology, it is clear that V is simply the reciprocal of K_{pr}, bearing the same relationship to the latter as T to E in our standard terminology. But the new formulation was recommended for use in cases affected by the second as well as the first complication. Bergson quotes a formulation:

$$\sum_{t=0}^{T} (C_t + K_t)(1 + E)^{-t} = \text{minimum} \quad [26] \tag{8}$$

which demonstrates that the K_{pr}/V equation is formally identical with the Present Value criterion. It is, however, stated in terms of C, not V, and this double-counting of capital expenditures would distort results derived from its use. Since C overstates, *ceteris paribus*, the value of V by a greater amount in the case of short-lived than in the case of long-lived projects, use of (8) would tend unduly to favour the latter. But C equally overstates the value of V by a greater amount in the case of capital-intensive than in that of non-capital-intensive projects, other things being equal. Thus if long-lived projects tend also to be capital-intensive projects (8) may involve few substantial dangers of misranking projects. It is in any case quite unclear to what extent this version of the criterion is in actual use, and it may be quite reasonable to treat it as having marginal importance in terms of study of specific cases.

We must now relax the assumptions made about the value of E. In practice E has varied very considerably between sectors, and has tended, at least until very recently, to be below clearing-level values, i.e. below the level which would bring the aggregate volume of investment for the economy as a whole or a specific sector down to the planned level, if E were operating as a quasi-rate-of-interest. In the light of the difficulties created by the priority principle, as discussed in Chapter 1, we must conceive this level to be a grey band rather than a black line. The 1960 *Standard Methodology* gave an upper limit for E of 0.3, and a normal lower limit of 0.15. But for some sectors, for example transport and power, a figure as low as 0.1 was quoted.[27] Alternative sources from the same period confirm that E equal to 0.1 was being used in power construction at the time,[28] and a 1965 source indicates a range of at least 0.33 to 0.1.[29] In the more distant past, however, E seems to have sometimes been set at lower levels. In 1958, for example, it appears to have been 0.06 in power.[30] In addition, use of a lower E (normally 0.08) in calculations of K_{pr} or V, where that refinement is introduced, appears to have been recommended on the grounds that not all of the economy in capital outlays thus accruing would in fact be invested in 'productive' sectors.[31] One of the innovations of the 1969 *Standard Methodology* was the introduction of a general lower limit to the value of E of 0.12. Even here, however, so many possible grounds for making an exception are spelled out that one wonders how big a change there may really have been at the policy level.[32] By 1977 the lower limit had been pushed down to 0.1, while the general range had been narrowed to 0.2–0.1,[33] equalling 0.14 for metallurgy, 0.17 in construction and construction materials and 0.2 in the coal, oil, gas and timber industries.[34] For chemicals, light industry and engineering, however, it could still go as high as 0.33. The 1981 *Methodology* predicates a norm for the whole economy during the period 1981–85 of 0.12, with a maximum of 0.25 and a minimum of 0.08. Estimates of the marginal product of capital, which would approximate the clearing level of E, always bearing in mind the 'Bergson effect' discussed on p. 105, vary. The one most frequently met with is 0.15,[35] but Kantorovich and Vainshtein have calculated it to be as high as 0.2–0.25.[36] Clearly, then, E has generally been set too low for clearing in the past, and this may still be the case, if not to such an extent.

What are the implications of all this? Firstly, on sub-clearing-level values for E: there is a difficulty here, inasmuch as the CRE is a coefficient of *relative* effectiveness, whose job is to choose between different ways of doing a particular thing, rather than to determine whether the thing is worth doing in the first place. There is also a concept of general or absolute effectiveness, which is defined in terms of increment in National Income, value added or NNO against investment ($\Delta Y/\Delta K$, or, if you like, the incremental output-capital ratio) for the economy as a whole, branches thereof or republics; and in terms of increment in profit or cost reduction against investment for associations, enterprises, etc. In the past there has been no systematic statement of any kind of 'normal' level of absolute effectiveness.[37] Now, however, the 1981 *Methodology* has laid down norms for levels of absolute effectiveness which are to operate as 'gateways' through which blocks of investment projects should have to pass. The principle on which this norm is set out for the whole economy for each five-year period is 'not lower than the average actual ratio for the previous five-year period'. In practice, for the period 1981–85, the reported aggregate relationship for 1976–80 – 0.14 – has been applied more or less unmodified. Sectoral norms for the same period vary widely – 0.16 for industry, 0.07 for agriculture, 0.05 for transport and communications, 0.22 for construction and 0.25 for internal trade, material-technical supply, etc.[38] The average, aggregate nature of this indicator, at least as applied above the enterprise level, means, of course, that it cannot operate as a general criterion for specific investment projects. Rather it simply provides a check on whether the economy as a whole, a specific sector or association, etc., is holding to the policy aims of the authorities in relation to the overall incremental capital-output ratio. It cannot by itself provide a guide to action in cases where a divergence from those aims is indeed diagnosed.

In fact, however, there is no reason in principle, *pace* Wiles,[39] why the CRE method should not be used as a gateway criterion. The CRE equation takes no account of the values of final outputs, but this would only matter if one were concerned with welfare considerations. As long as we are just concerned with efficiency, so that the final bundle of goods etc. is given, it need not be an insuperable obstacle. I intend, then, to follow Bergson in treating the CRE method as a general investment criterion. On this basis, sub-clearing-level values for E obviously mean rationing, which necessitates bringing in other criteria for deciding which projects should be taken in what order. There is no *a priori* basis for knowing what these other criteria might be. Variation of E by sector should presumably be taken to *reflect* consideration of other factors.[40] In other words, we might come to the conclusion that neither of these two 'irregularities' need necessarily involve state-doctrinal deviations at all, though they open the way for other deviations to appear. In fact, however, there are other aspects to the situation which can reasonably be tied in directly with the state-doctrinal factor. Sub-clearing-level values for E mean not only rationing – they also mean that a higher degree of capital intensity than corresponds to efficiency considerations will be permitted, i.e. that the investment project 'mix' may be skewed towards excessive capital intensity. If we look at the particular way in which E has varied inter-sectorally, we find a parallel phenomenon. It is in the heavy-industrial, highly capital-intensive sectors that E has normally been set at a relatively low level. We have seen that there is some tendency, under certain conditions, for the internal mathematics of the CRE formula unduly to favour long-lived, and therefore probably capital-intensive, projects. The fact that E has usually been below clearing level must have strengthened the Bergson effect, though use of a specially low normative coefficient for calculation of K_{pr} or V must, as Durgin points out,[41] discriminate against projects with long gestation periods, which we have assumed may tend also to be long-lived projects. Both directly and indirectly, then, it is the value of E, as it affects the key issue of capital intensity, that is the really important aspect of the whole CRE question. Is it possible to tie in this essentially 'external' characteristic of Soviet investment appraisal methods with state doctrine? To answer this question we must examine Soviet doctrine on rates of growth of the A and B sectors of industry, and of subdivisions A1 and A2.

THE 'LAWS OF INDUSTRIAL STRUCTURE'

It was until circa 1970 the official Soviet position that the production of producer goods (department A) must grow faster than the production of consumer goods (department B).[42] In addition, it has been postulated, though less categorically, that within department A production of producer goods for the producer goods sector (subdivision A1) should grow faster than the production of producer goods for the consumer goods sector (subdivision A2). These 'laws' are based on certain statements made by Marx,[43] though contemporary critics argue, with some justice, that Marx was talking about laws of capitalism, not laws of socialism. But irrespective of the necessity of such trends, there can be no doubt that A has grown faster than B. The share of A in total industrial production grew from 39.5 per cent in 1928 to 71.8 per cent in 1959.[44] Now in fact the two 'laws' hold no necessary implications for investment, because the categories involved are defined as gross, i.e., for example, department A includes not only investment goods, but also intermediate goods. A rise in the degree of vertical disintegration, with the investment ratio held constant, would ensure the observance of the first 'law'. In addition, the coverage of the two departments is limited to industry. But discussion of the 'laws' has usually centred around the investment component in National Income, and the industrial sector is clearly the predominant contributor to that component. We shall, then, proceed on the basis that any serious defence of this particular part of state doctrine must involve the argument that investment goods production necessarily grows faster than consumer goods production, and that investment in the investment goods sector (second-order investment) necessarily grows faster than investment in the consumer goods sector (first-order investment).

What, then, is the real content of these latter propositions? Wiles has argued in detail that the propositions basically reflect no more than simply the input-output implications of a high savings/investment rate, as a condition for a high rate of growth.[45] A high rate of abstinence is meaningless unless it can be embodied in physical investment equipment, and in the absence of the desire for and/or the possibility of large-scale imports of capital goods, as in the Soviet case, it necessarily involves a high rate of production of investment goods. Thus any rise in the rate of abstinence will necessarily involve a rise in the rate of production of investment goods (or, to look at it from the other side, a fall in the rate of production of consumption goods). But investment goods cannot be produced without equipment suitable for their production, so that any decision to raise the rate of investment must necessarily involve raising the rate of second-order investment, and by a more than proportionate amount, on familiar 'accelerator' principles. Looked upon from the other direction, enforcement of a higher rate of growth of production of investment goods will necessarily mean a higher rate of abstinence, and enforcement of a higher rate of growth of production for second-order investment goods will necessarily involve a higher rate of growth of production for investment goods as a whole, and consequently a higher rate of abstinence. Most fundamentally, then, implementation of these propositions should be seen as a roundabout way of stating the aim of a high rate of savings/investment, as a means of raising the rate of growth, or, if you like, simply as reflecting a low social rate of discount. As such, they do not affect considerations of efficiency at all.

But there is another aspect to the investment/consumption goods, first-order/second-order issue. The above analysis was conducted on the assumption of constant capital-output and capital-labour ratios. If these ratios change, then changes in inter-sectoral proportions can be expected, if a given rate of growth is to be maintained. If the capital-output ratio in general tends to rise, then production of investment goods will have to grow faster than production of consumer goods, otherwise a more or less immediate downturn in growth rates will ensue. If capital-output ratios rise more in second-order than in first-order sectors, then investment in the former will have to grow faster than investment in the latter, if a slowdown in the rate of growth of production of investment goods, and, *ceteris paribus*, an eventual slowdown in the overall rate of growth, is to be avoided. Such a rise in the capital-output ratio might be conditioned by the need to raise the capital-labour ratio, as labour reserves became exhausted. On the other hand if, with technical progress, the capital-labour ratio rises, but with the capital-output ratio remaining constant or falling, adjustments would have to be made if full employment were to be maintained and maximum production potential attained, though this would have the corollary, not only of a higher savings/investment rate, but also of a higher rate of growth. Note also that there can be no danger of 'break-down' here, as there is in the first case. Soviet theorists have, in fact, tried, however illogically, to combine these two aspects.

The higher rate of growth of production of the means of production under socialism is necessary because socialist production is large-scale mechanised production, constantly developing and being perfected on the basis of higher technology . . . Technical progress under socialism consists in the intensification of mechanisation and automation in the sphere of material production . . . workers are better and better equipped with up-to-date tools . . . and the tools themselves become ever better . . . A swifter rate of growth of production of the means of production is necessary because society needs more and more means of production by virtue of technical progress in the production of every article of consumption . . . At the present stage of technical development there can be no technical progress, no kind of significant growth in the productivity of social labour, without a faster rate of growth of production of the means of production.[46]

Again:

socialist society cannot increase national income per head to a significant extent and satisfy growing material, cultural and spiritual needs on the basis of growth in the labour-time fund [*fond rabochego vremeni*] alone. It is the economising of living labour that permits society continually to push production beyond the limits of that fund, and at given stages to reduce the absolute quantities of working time used up in material production. In this context increased labour productivity makes it possible not only to economise the labour of workers already employed in the sphere of material production, but also to compensate for any inadequacy in their numbers.[47]

Now we have already seen how Soviet 'laws' tend to take on the character of statements of aims. It is surely not unreasonable to suggest that what starts off as an objective prediction that there will be a tendency towards greater capital-intensity may end up as a policy of encouraging capital-intensity for its own sake. And such a policy could clearly affect the allocation of investment with a given savings/ investment rate, as well as that rate itself.

The extent to which one can tie up investment appraisal criteria with the propositions just discussed is obviously a matter for speculation. But it is interesting that the movement towards higher average CREs, and the controversy over, and eventual 'repeal' of the A/B, A1/A2 'laws' did happen at around the same time. It seems to me that there is some basis for arguing that the way in which CREs have been used has reflected a state-doctrinal preference for capital-intensity connected with the A/B, A1/A2 propositions. This preference has weakened in the most recent period, though it should be noted that from 1975 the prominence of department A has been *de facto*, though not *de jure*, re-established.[48]

The argument so far, then, is that both the form of the CRE and the way it has been used have tended to excessive capital intensity, and that these tendencies may be correctly interpreted as reflecting the operation of the state-doctrinal factor, though with respect to the former there is no need to argue that the specific intentions of the central authorities on matters of factor proportions are involved as such. To round off the discussion we must just mention three points, the first two of which strengthen, and the last of which may modify, the above argument. Firstly, to the extent that in some sectors during the Stalin period no form of imputed interest charge may have been used at all, there was presumably an almost complete absence of constraint on tendencies to excessive capital-intensity. Secondly, expenditures on scientific-research and general design are not, according to the 1960 and 1969 *Standard Methodologies*, correctly included in estimates of total capital costs,[49] though this recommendation was heavily criticised by some Soviet writers,[50] and appears now to have been reversed in the 1981 *Methodology*. Quite apart from the obvious resultant danger of wasteful use of resources in such activity, this could have resulted in under-estimation of the relative cost of most highly capital-intensive projects, to the extent that they tend to involve greater initial research expenditures. The third point, which must be taken to modify the above, is that in a situation of declining productivity of capital, long-lived projects (in most cases highly capital-intensive projects) which involve extended gestation periods may correctly be given preferential treatment in terms of the current rate of interest, since some of the capital expenditures will be made in later years, when the equilibrium rate of interest may have fallen.[51] It is true that there has been a tendency for the marginal productivity of capital to fall in the Soviet Union, most markedly in the late 1950s and early 1960s, and again in the 1970s.[52] The tendency in the earlier period was probably largely a function of the kind of implementational problems discussed in preceding chapters, and perhaps of the state-doctrinal factors just discussed, rather than of objective technological factors. In the case of the current period the widening scope of exploitation of raw material resources in Siberia – large-scale and highly capital-intensive – has clearly been a major factor, as has the big investment effort devoted to a stubborn agriculture. It is, then, not clear that we are dealing here with a secular, technologically-conditioned trend, though the Siberian developments may have a dominating influence for a decade or so. There certainly seems to be no general tendency for the marginal productivity of capital to decline in advanced industrial economies.[53] There is, therefore, no need to place great stress on this point.

LOCATIONAL PRINCIPLES

The last main element in Soviet official state doctrine affecting investment matters is the list of 'principles of location of productive forces'. These run as follows:

(a) Location of enterprises as near as possible to raw material sources and centres of consumption.

(b) Even distribution of economic activity throughout the country.

(c) Rational division of labour between economic regions, and complex development of the economy of each region.

(d) Raising of the economic and cultural level of all backward national areas to that of the most advanced.

(e) Elimination of the distinction (*razlichie*) between town and country.

(f) Strengthening of the defence potential of the country.

(g) International division of labour within the socialist bloc.[54]

The two main sources for this set of principles is Engels' *Anti-Dühring* and Lenin's 'Draft plan of scientific and technical work'. In the former, having noted that 'the first great division of labour, the separation of town and country, condemned the rural population to thousands of years of mental torpidity, and the people of the towns to subjection, each to his own individual trade',[55] Engels goes on to argue that:

only a society which makes it possible for its productive forces to dovetail harmoniously into each other on the basis of one single vast plan can permit industry to be distributed over the whole country in the way best adapted to its own development, and to the maintenance and development of the other elements of production.

Thus abolition of the antithesis between town and country is not merely possible. It has become a direct necessity of industrial production itself, just as it has become a necessity of agricultural production, and, besides, of public health. The poisoning of the air, water and land that is going on now can be stopped only by a fusion of town and country; and only such a fusion will change the situation of the masses now languishing in the towns, and enable their excrement to be used for the production of plants instead of for the production of disease.[56]

He concludes that 'the abolition of the separation of town and country is therefore not utopian, in so far as it is conditioned by the most equal distribution possible of modern industry over the whole country'.[57]

Lenin's piece is very short, and is worth quoting in full.

The Supreme Council of National Economy must immediately give the following instruction to the Academy of Sciences, which has just started a systematic study and investigation of the natural productive forces of Russia:

to form a group of specialist commissions for the compilation, in as short a time as possible, of a plan for the reorganisation of industry and the economic advancement of Russia.

In this plan should be included:

A rational *location pattern* for industry in Russia from the point of view of nearness to raw materials, and possibilities of minimising the amount of labour tied up in the transfer process between raw-material processing and all subsequent stages of manufacture of semi-finished goods, right up to production of the finished article.

The rational amalgamation and concentration of production lines in a few very big enterprises, from the point of view of the most modern, large-scale industry, especially trusts.

Making sure that the present Russian Soviet Republic (excluding the Ukraine and the *oblasti* occupied by the Germans) can, as far as possible, independently supply itself with *all* main forms of raw materials and industrial production.

The devotion of special attention to the electrification of industry and transport, and the application of electricity in agriculture. Utilisation of second-grade fuels (peat, low-grade coal) for the production of electrical energy with minimal expenditures on the extraction and transport of fuel.

Water power and windmills in general, and in their application to agriculture.[58]

It is clear that principles (b) and (e) are based largely on Engels, though the Lenin material does have some indirect bearing upon them. The remaining principles, apart from (d) and (g), find their inspiration in the 'Draft plan', although there is no explicit reference in that document to regional complex development. Principle (d) covers a conception which, though not mentioned in the 'Draft plan', is obviously Leninist.[59] Principle (g) was, for reasons that need no explanation, added only after World War II.

What is the real content of the principles? Though Wiles is undoubtedly formally correct in arguing that principles (a) and (c) are, in their standard Soviet formulation, internally contradictory,[60] I am inclined to interpret this as linguistic clumsiness rather than illogicality, and to agree with Kistanov's criticism of the substance of Wiles' point.[61] Principle (a) should surely simply be understood as meaning 'the conditional minimisation of transport costs' (a phrase, by the way, which is very difficult to translate into Russian). Principle (c) is stated in terms, not of 'division of labour', but of 'rational division of labour', which surely denotes a consciousness that division of labour between regions must be limited to the extent that there is scope for *rational complex* development, i.e. regional self-sufficiency.

On the basis of this interpretation of these slightly dubious formulations of principles (a) and (c), we can proceed to a consideration of whether observation of the principles could be expected to lead to deviations from the yardstick *in any way not covered by other factors in the A and B groups.* In other words, we are concerned to see whether these state-doctrinal propositions may have affected the policies of the central authorities in directions which *a priori* considerations of the likely scope of government interests would not incline us to think probable.

There is no reason to believe that observation of principles (a) and (g) would result in any deviations. Principle (c) clearly implies the need to take into consideration differences in resource endowment between regions, which is perfectly orthodox, but also that long-term-planning-horizon considerations may (must?) be given priority over medium- or short-term in matters of regional development. This could result in deviations, but not in any way not covered by Factor A1. The content of principle (f) is obviously covered by Factor B1. This leaves us with the rather more difficult principles (b), (d) and (e).

On (d), Probst, the late doyen of Soviet locationists, has said that 'the implementation of the Leninist nationalities policy of the Communist Party, the priority given to the industrialisation of national areas and "their swifter rate of economic and cultural development" (Programme of the CPSU) in no way violates the specific laws of location of socialist economic activity. Nationalities policy affects only the sequence of the practical realisation of these laws.'[62] If we take this as the official position, which is highly likely, then there is no reason to expect that the observation of principle (d) would result in any deviations not covered under Factor A1.

Principle (b) has always been a troublesome one for Soviet writers, and it seems to have been consigned to quiet retirement in recent years. Troshev states that 'under equal conditions of economic effectiveness of location of enterprises in various regions, in the interests of full utilisation of labour resources in all regions and the prevention of excessive concentration of production in large cities, it is necessary to put into effect the principle of the greatest possible evenness of distribution of productive forces throughout the country'.[63] This seems to imply (i) that the existing distribution of population should, at least to some extent, be taken as a datum in making location decisions; (ii) either a value judgement against big cities, or a recognition of the possibility of serious external diseconomies in large conurbations, or both. However, the stated condition that these considerations should only be taken into account in the event of narrowly economic considerations giving no grounds for preference, and the watering-down of 'evenness of distribution' to 'greatest possible evenness of distribution', must leave some doubts as to the real content of the statement. More recent sources are less equivocal. A Soviet textbook on industrial economics from the mid-1960s states that 'minimisation of the distance between socialist industry and sources of raw materials on the one hand, and centres of consumption on the other, guarantees the even distribution of industrial production throughout the territory of the country'.[64] Here principle (b) is taken as being simply a derivative of principle (a), and loses all independent significance. Probst, in a late work,[65] also virtually dismisses the principle, as does Zakirov in a book published in the early 1970s.[66]

It is clear, then, that the concept of 'evenness of distribution' has not, over the last 15 years or so, been taken very seriously. What the situation was in the Stalin period is impossible to say, because of the lack of published comment, but it is quite possible that the contemporary explicit attitude reflects what has always been implicitly held. There are, then, grounds for simply ignoring principle (b). Now it is quite clear that for Engels the ideas of 'even distribution of industry' and 'abolition of the distinction between town and country' were essentially just different ways of looking at the same thing, and such an attitude would seem to be a commonsensical one. Nevertheless, the controversy over principle (b) has not been accompanied by any references to principle (e), so we must presume that the latter has been, rather incongruously, left to stand, perhaps because it is so vague by itself as to be virtually meaningless, and therefore harmless. It seems reasonable, while recognising that the observance of principle (e) could in theory lead to the emergence of deviations (indeed, of almost any conceivable deviation!), to dismiss it as a likely factor in decision-making.

There is one last element in official Soviet theory on locational matters, centring round the concept of the 'territorial-production complex' (*territorial'no-proizvodstvennyi kompleks*).[67] But the significance of this concept is rather in terms of how it brings together the separate principles discussed above than in any distinct element within it, so that there is no need, in the present context, to analyse it separately.

Our conclusions on the state-doctrinal factor are, then, as follows:

(a) There may be a state-doctrine-based tendency to 'under-shadow-price' natural resources.

(b) There is reason to believe that there is a definite state-doctrinal preference for excessive capital-intensity, and any deviation involving such a factor mix demands consideration in terms of this factor.

(c) There is no strong argument that the observance of any of the official location principles, as they have been interpreted, would lead to the emergence of any deviations not covered by the A and B factors already discussed.

6

Some case studies

The purpose of these case studies is to illustrate in greater detail the operation of the various factors discussed in previous chapters, and in particular to introduce a greater degree of realism on the empirical side by demonstrating how, in many cases, a number of factors may operate simultaneously. All the cases cited display fairly clear-cut deviations from the yardstick, though to greatly differing extents. Some of them, in addition, draw attention to certain aspects of the investment process which have been left out of account by the more or less conventional static approach of Chapters 2–5, but which were mentioned in Chapter 1 and will be expanded upon in the last chapter. Case study 1, the Bratsk hydro-electric station, fulfils a special rôle, in addition to those listed above. The publication of a bulky, two-volume set of documents (*Sbornik Dokumentov*) on that project[1] has made available the basis for reconstructing an almost day-to-day account of its progress, so that we have a unique opportunity to follow through the full process of a single, large Soviet investment project. This is of immense illustrative value, quite apart from any specific analytical points that may emerge.

CASE STUDY 1: THE BRATSK HYDRO-ELECTRIC STATION

(Note: although many of the items in the *Sbornik Dokumentov* were originally published elsewhere, references are made only to the secondary source.)

Description
The hydro-electric potential of the Angara was mentioned as early as 1920, in a report to the Congress of Soviets by the GOELRO

119

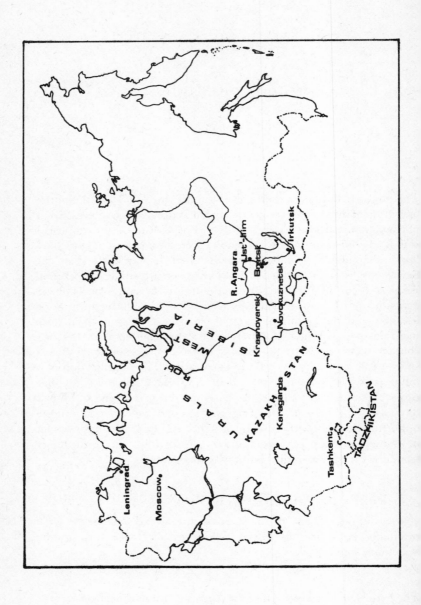

Commission.[2] Serious discussion of actual projects did not, however, start until after World War II. Design work on the Bratsk station, which was entrusted to the Moscow section of the Gidroenergoproekt design organisation (under the jurisdiction of the USSR Ministry for Power), seems to have started around 1950–51. According to the preliminary estimates, Bratsk was to have a capacity of 2.5 million kW, an average annual output of 17 milliard kWh, while production costs (*sebestoimost'*) were to be less than 1 kopeck per kWh.[3] The construction of such a huge dam in the virgin wastes of Eastern Siberia was, of course, very much a pioneering effort, and this must be borne in mind in assessing the implementation of the project.

It was recognised in 1951 that the submersion zone of the reservoir would cover an area including 130 settlements, with 7,000 households, and also 100 kilometres of the Taishet–Lena railway line, including a railway bridge over the Angara. But the economic significance of this was reckoned to be small, compared with the energy effect of the hydro-electric station (hereafter HES).[4] It is clear that, right from the beginning, the idea was to use the energy locally, and Gidroenergo-proekt Moscow was entrusted with the design work for the entire Bratsk industrial complex, though that institution was to receive help from design organisations subordinate to the ministries covering the industrial sectors involved. The total cost of the whole complex was estimated in 1951 at 35–40 milliard rubles (1961 prices).[5] The 'schematic design' (*skhematicheskii proekt* – presumably a form of TEO – see Chapter 3) was to be completed by October 1952, but fears about the on-time completion of design work were already being expressed in 1951.[6]

By 1955 work on the HES had started, with Nizhneangargesstroi, a construction trust presumably specially created for the job (see Chapter 4), running the operation.[7] By this time estimates of the capacity of the dam had risen to 3.2 million kW, with annual output fixed at 22 milliard kWh.[8] Earliest reports from the construction sites mention 'significant difficulties', and the need to improve working conditions.[9] There was probably also a labour shortage, no doubt to some extent caused by the bad working conditions, and it was decided in late 1955 to 'draft in' 1,500 communists and *komsomols*.[10] Plans were also being laid around this time for the construction of a 220 kV transmission line of length 650 km from Irkutsk to Bratsk, to supply *Bratsk* with power, and one wonders whether this planning should not have been done earlier.

Other difficulties arose almost immediately in connection with turbines and building materials. The Leningrad *Order of Lenin* metal factory, which seems to have been entrusted with the design work on the turbines, made an official recommendation in July 1955 to the effect that, in view of the technical difficulties involved in constructing such large turbines, special research work should be undertaken, and a special scientific-research institute for hydro-turbine construction set up.[11] Plans were being discussed for the development of a 2–2.5 milliard ruble construction/construction materials base, but it was reckoned that building materials would have to be brought in from elsewhere up to 1957.[12] The Ministry for the Building Materials Industry was to start construction of a cement factory at Bratsk in 1956.[13] Again, one wonders whether this might not have been done earlier.

An interesting article by the Minister for Power Station Construction, published in *Pravda* in November 1955, gives the first details of the work to be done in connection with the dam itself by other ministries. The Ministries of Transport and Transport Construction were to lay a railway line on the left bank of the Angara (to replace the one which would be submerged?), while the Forestry Ministry was to see to the clearing of about 38 million m^3 of timber from the submersion zone. The tasks of the Ministry of Communications, in terms of laying telephone lines Bratsk HES–Irkutsk–Moscow, were also spelled out. The Ministry of Automobile Transport and Trunk Roads was criticised for slowness in constructing a road alongside the Irkutsk–Bratsk transmission line. The Power Minister also made an interesting plea for greater on-the-spot control, not only of the actual construction work, but also of the design work.[14]

By early 1956 estimates of the capacity of the HES had once again been modified, and now stood at 3.2–3.5 million kW, with annual output to be 20–25 milliard kWh. In his report to the Irkutsk Party conference in January 1956, Naimushin, the general director (*nachal'nik*) of the construction site, gave some interesting information on plan fulfilment for 1955. The plan for construction work by Nizhneangargesstroi had been overfulfilled by 12.5 per cent, but plans for work by subcontracting organizations of other departments had been only 40 per cent fulfilled. Some ministries had not, in fact, started work at all.

In his speech Naimushin laid stress on the problem of accommodation for workers – more than 1,000 workers, some with families, were living in tents. He noted also that tendencies to inflation of wage payments had appeared. Lastly, he complained of delays in delivery of design documentation, noted that Giprogor (a specialist town planning PO) had not yet decided on the question of the location of the town of Bratsk, a task which had presumably been 'subcontracted' out to them by Gidroenergoproekt, and repeated the request that design work should be transferred from Moscow to Bratsk.[15]

Work proceeded fairly successfully in 1956, with the plan for construction work by Nizhneangargesstroi overfulfilled by 13.3 per cent, though overfulfilment for all forms of work was by only 7.5 per cent, suggesting continued problems with the work of 'other' departments.[16] Severe problems certainly did exist with respect to the work of the Forestry Ministry. The plans for capital construction in the submersion zone had not been fulfilled, adequate information on the number of trees in the zone had not been collected, no work had been done on norms for timber clearing (*lesoochistka*), no tapping of pine trees had taken place, and special equipment for felling and clearing had not been procured. This last difficulty may, of course, have been the fault of suppliers rather than of the Forestry Ministry, and it is certainly true that many forestry problems must be attributed to delays on the part of Giprolestrans (timber transport design organisation), who were doing the design work, and low quality in the design documentation which was received.[17] It is in any case clear that the Forestry Ministry was at this time a particularly weak ministry. As noted on p. 40, it always tends to be decimated by the forces of departmentalism, but in 1957, on the eve of the *sovnarkhoz* reform, only 386 out of a total of 15,000 sawmills were under its control.[18]

Work on the dam itself was hampered by delays on the design side. The design assignment was only finally confirmed by the Council of Ministers on 11 August 1956, and the technical designs for the dam itself and the turbine generators had at that time still not been completed, nor indeed had a final decision been taken on the exact type of dam to be used.[19] A statement by the Minister for Power issued a week later gave 1 July 1957 as the date for the completion of the technical design on the 'basic installations' of the dam, and 1 March 1957 as the deadline for settling the question of the type of dam.[20] In the light of this situation, it is not surprising that complaints about lack of design documentation were common.[21]

Supply shortages affected construction of the dam itself (which clearly cannot have passed beyond the foundation stage at this point),[22] but seem to have been more serious with the Irkutsk–Bratsk transmission line, where work was going very badly. Labour shortages were also a major factor in this latter case.[23] By July 1956, the majority of workers' families had been transferred from tents to apartments,[24] but general living conditions remained poor, with a number of workers still living in tents in November.[25] It would be surprising, then, if only the transmission line had been suffering from labour shortages in that year.

The confirmation of the design assignment revealed that there had been a further increase in the estimated capacity of the dam, which now stood at 3.6 million kW – 21.5 milliard kWh per annum. (Note the tendency for the estimate of annual production capacity to become more modest in relation to that of installed capacity.) The total cost of the dam was given as 11,020 million rubles in 1950 prices.[26]

March 1957 saw the preliminary damming (*perekrytie*) of the right bank of the Angara, by means of a 'storm' lasting 9 hours 30 minutes,[27] while the technical design of the turbines was recommended for confirmation in the same month. A final decision to construct a dam of the gravitation, concrete type, with broadened joints (*rasshirennye shvy*) was taken in July.[28] But lack of technical documentation remained a problem,[29] and other problems typical of 1956 survived into 1957 – poor amenities,[30] and delays in developing the construction materials base.[31] In addition complaints about the level of organisation on the dam site and about low quality and escalating costs began to appear. A *postanovlenie* of the Irkutsk *obkom* (provincial Party committee) dating from June 1957 did not paint a very rosy picture of progress on the dam.

The bureau of the *obkom* CPSU notes that as a whole the construction of the Bratsk HES is behind schedule . . .

The bureau of the *obkom* CPSU considers that the basic reasons for existing deficiencies consist in a lack of systematic approach in operational production management, the absence of clear, operational planning, and lack of coordination of the activities of sub-units and of day-to-day supervision (*kontrol'*) over the fulfilment of assignments . . .

In the course of 1956 the cost of site work was 24,090 thousand rubles (6.6 per cent against planned value of work) more than it should have been. Inflation of costs was particularly serious on the construction of the transmission line . . . – 21.5 per cent of the general volume of fulfilled work, and in the Padunskii administration . . . – 18.2 per cent . . .

Many construction workers on the Bratsk HES continue to find themselves in poor living and amenity conditions . . .

There are delays in the construction of bakeries, meat combines, the sausage works, the non-alcoholic drinks factory, hospitals, clubs, playing fields, and other amenity enterprises.

The Party committee of the Bratsk HES site and the Bratsk *gorkom* CPSU (city Party committee) pay insufficient attention to the organisation of work and the conditions of the workers. They do not struggle hard enough against primitive, small-scale methods of work and *raspylenie*. They do not sufficiently focus the efforts of the collective on the introduction of industrial methods and the speeding-up of the operationalisation of construction materials projects. They are not sufficiently demanding *vis-à-vis* management workers, fail to carry on continuous organisational and political work in the brigades, and are weak in the organisation of socialist competition between brigades for economy in the use of equipment and materials and improvement in the quality of work.[32]

It is not clear whether plans for 1957 were fulfilled or not – the silence of the *Sbornik* on this point might be taken as an indication that they were not. But 1957 did end with a victory. On 8 December the Irkutsk–Bratsk transmission line went into operation.[33]

The year 1957 saw a major organisational change in the Soviet economy – the replacement of most of the ministries by *sovnarkhozy*. This did not, of course, affect the dam itself, since power was one sector which, for obvious reasons, retained an all-union organisation. Other aspects of the complex were, however, affected. It is quite clear that the Irkutsk *sovnarkhoz* was, by 1958, in charge of timber-clearing operations.[34] The construction of the Bratsk timber-industrial complex (whose operations were clearly to survive the filling of the reservoir), the Novo-Chunskii timber-processing combine and the Korshunovskii ore-concentrating combine did, however, remain under the direction of Bratskgesstroi (presumably the successor organisation to Nizhneangargesstroi), i.e. ultimately under that of the Ministry for Power.[35] Complaints were voiced at the end of 1958 about delays in the construction of the former two of these.[36] Little else of interest emerges from a study of events in 1958, though it may be noted that amenity problems remained serious throughout that year.[37]

In March 1959 the capacity of the HES was again raised, this time to 4.05 million kW.[38] It was also announced at the XXI Congress of the CPSU that production of electricity would start in 1961.[39] The left channel of the Angara was dammed (*perekrytie*) on 18 June 1959.[40] By August 1959 the construction materials base already consisted of three concrete factories, factories of inert materials, reinforced-concrete factories, and sawmills and wood-processing factories.[41] But familiar problems were still cropping up. Severe delays in the construction of the gravel-sorting factory on the right bank were reported.[42] Research and design organisations were criticised for *still* not having solved some 'cardinal problems of hydro-electric construction'![43] Serious delays in accommodation and amenities construction continued to occur, and the relevant plans for the first half of 1959 were underfulfilled.[44] Complaints were also voiced about organisational techniques in construction, about *raspylenie*, and about bad finishing in completed enterprises.[45] The June Plenum of the CC CPSU expressed concern about costs and work tempi. In fact, however, by the end of the year construction costs (*sebestoimost'*) had been reduced by 11.7 million rubles more than planned. (The reader should bear in mind that cost-reduction had been generally introduced as a major success-indicator in 1959.) The year ended with the capacity of the dam being upped once again, this time to 4.5 million kW.[46]

The foundation of the building which would house the turbines etc. of the HES was laid in April 1960,[47] and construction costs reduced by 3 million rubles more than planned in the first nine months of 1960.[48] Around this time the final completion date for the project was set for 1963, though this was a 'socialist obligation', rather than an element in the plan proper.[49] But familiar difficulties continued to make themselves felt. Amenities were still a problem,[50] as was organisation of building work.[51] Poor organisation of work and problems with cement supply in June and July held up cement laying in the HES building, and seriously threatened the schedule for the whole year.[52] This was also the year of preparations for the filling of the reservoir, which was due to begin on 1 July 1961.[53] It is clear, however, that these preparations were not going well. The tenth session of the Bratsk city soviet, held in September, instructed that 'it should be brought to the notice of the executive committee of the provincial soviet of workers' and peasants' deputies [i.e. provincial government] that an extremely serious situation has arisen in enterprises subordinate to the Irkutsk *sovnarkhoz*, in connection with the evacuation of personnel and preparation for the first stage of submersion, which could lead to the "drowning" of enterprises and the wastage of already prepared timber.'[54] The soviet recommended that 'the provincial executive committee and the Irkutsk *sovnarkhoz* reconsider the *proekt* for the plan of work of the Bratskles [Bratsk timber] combine for 1961, with a view to reducing the volume of timber procurements, and establish as the priority task for the combine the carrying out of timber clearing, and the relocation of settlements outside the submersion zone'.[55]

The following year, 1961, was the year of the final stage of submersion, and attention was largely focussed on the problem of evacuation. We have already seen that preparations for this operation had been carried out rather unsatisfactorily, and it is hardly surprising that the implementation of the job left a great deal to be desired. An Irkutsk provincial executive committee decision of 13 July 1961 read as follows:

noting that work on the preparation of the bed of the reservoir, and in particular the evacuation of the population by enterprises of the *sovnarkhoz*, is going ahead very slowly, the provincial executive committee admonishes the heads of the forestry industry administration and the meat and dairy industry administration, . . . and instructs them to take additional measures for the intensification of work on the resettlement of people, and the relocation of enterprises and evacuation of material assets.[56]

A month later a similar statement (in the form of a *postanovlenie*) by the Irkutsk *obkom* appeared.[57] After expressing concern that the completion of the first stage of the reservoir and operationalisation of the first aggregates of the dam might not be achieved by the fourth quarter of 1961, as planned, the statement went on to note that as of 15 August 1961 5,312 people were still living in the submersion zone, while 1,309 buildings and installations had not been evacuated. No less than 1,350 hectares of timber remained to be cleared. Delays in the construction of roads, railway lines, telephone communications, water and electricity supply networks and housing and amenities construction in the resettlement areas were also criticised. The interesting point emerges that timber-clearing work and housing and amenities construction were at this time being shared between three organisations – Bratskgesstroi, Bratskles, the biggest of the timber combines, and Bratskstroi, the local general construction organisation. The latter two were presumably both under the jurisdiction of the *sovnarkhoz*, but we may have evidence here of the confusion of 'creeping reministerialisation' as *sovnarkhozy* progressively lost jurisdiction to various State Production Committees in the early 1960s. Another *obkom postanovlenie* of the same date called for urgent measures for the evacuation of the Bratskgesstroi work-force from the submersion zone, and instructed various organisations to 'ensure normal living conditions for the population evacuated from the submersion zone, and not to permit the dispersion of people in wagons, tents and other unsuitable forms of accommodation'.[58] Filling of the reservoir started on 1 September 1961,[59] but evacuation work had not been completed, and it is clear that the situation at this time approached crisis proportions.[60]

The construction of the actual dam continued to be affected by problems of work organisation and supply,[61] and, as in the previous year, cement laying got into particular difficulties. 'Cementing of joints was in an unsatisfactory state. Work plans were badly worked out, and there was not always a proper "work front". Many joints were covered in muck, and on many sections cement work was ruined through bad regulation of temperature, caused by the absence of a refrigeration installation.'[62] Despite this, and despite the fears of the *obkom*, however, a trial switch-on of the first set of turbines (*agregat*) took place on 27 October 1961.[63] Construction of the timber and aluminium works, which were planned as important consumers of Bratsk power, also seems to have got under way in 1961.[64] At the XXII Congress of the CPSU, in October 1961, Naimushin gave assurances that the HES would be completed by 1963.[65] In the same month Gidroenergoproekt announced that, on the basis of a number of improvements made in the *proekt*, permitting economy in earth-removing and cement work, estimates for total capital expenditures had been reduced, as also had estimates for running costs. Table 6.1 gives an indication of how planned indicators changed over the 1956–61 period.

The year 1962 started off well, with the second quarter plan for volume of construction work by Bratskgesstroi overfulfilled by 18.4 per cent, and for all construction work by 19.6 per cent – perhaps an indication that priority was now being shifted off the dam itself. Even the plan for operationalisation of housing construction was fulfilled in this quarter, and the cost-reduction plan overfulfilled by 6 per cent.[66] As the year progressed, however, the picture became less favourable – for the first three quarters of the year overfulfilment of the plan for all construction work was down to 7.5 per cent,[67] and for the whole year the plan was only just fulfilled.[68] The annual plan for construction work on the HES itself, however, was overfulfilled by 24.2 per cent.[69] Though the usual problems of inflation of costs, bad organisation of labour and uncertain supply, particularly of cement, continued to be mentioned,[70] it seems, in fact, that work on the dam went well,

Table 6.1. *Technical indicators for the Bratsk hydro-electric station*

Indicator	Unit of measurement	Estimates 1956	Estimates 1961
Installed capacity	million kilowatts	3.6	4.5
Average annual output	milliards of kilowatt-hours	21.5	22.6
Guaranteed minimum output	milliards of kilowatt-hours	20.3	21.2
Excavations	millions of m^3	5.8	3.4
Embankments etc.	millions of m^3	16.6	9.6
Concrete and reinforced concrete	millions of m^3	7.3	4.8
Total estimated cost (*stoimost'*) in 1955 prices, with 1961 price weights	millions of rubles	1020.8	816.6
Capital investment per kilowatt	rubles	214.0	142.0
Capital investment per kilowatt-hour of average annual output	kopecks	3.6	2.8
Cost (*sebestoimost'*) of electricity per kilowatt-hour	kopecks	0.045	0.038

Source: V. F. Mal'tsev (ed.), *Bratskaya GES. Sbornik Dokumentov i Materialov*, vol. I, Irkutsk, Vostochno-Sibirskoe Knizhnoe izdatel'stvo, 1964, p. 431

and by the end of the year nine sets of turbines were in operation.[71] What is clear, however, is that work on the timber complex was not going well at all,[72] and that is presumably the reason why total construction-work indices for the year were so much lower than the corresponding indices for work on the dam alone.

The following year, 1963, was another good year for the HES itself. The annual volume of construction work plan for Bratskgesstroi was overfulfilled by 5 per cent,[73] and another seven sets of turbines started work – bringing the station near to completion.[74] In addition, the Bratsk–Taishet transmission line went into operation on 24 November 1963,[75] making Bratsk energy available in a westwards direction, including to Chunskii. The line to Krasnoyarsk was also completed.[76] The construction of the Bratsk industrial complex itself was, however, proceeding with mixed success. Work on the timber complex was seriously behind schedule, partly due to supply difficulties.[77] At a plenum of the Bratsk *gorkom*, held in early 1964, the director of the complex noted that, 'while the overall plan for construction work on the production side was fulfilled, construction ran into serious difficulties in crucial departments like the block of sulphate-cellulose factories, where the plan was only 51 per cent fulfilled, the cardboard-drying factory block, where the corresponding figure was 57 per cent, and the block for activation and regeneration of lime, where the figure was 28 per cent.'[78]

Work on evacuation from the submersion zone was still going on in 1963, and a *reshenie* (decision, decree) of the Irkutsk rural provincial executive committee stated that the work had been 'largely completed'.[79] As many as 109,400 people, 8,673 buildings and installations of state organisations and 14,783 private dwelling houses had been evacuated, while 13,980 dwelling houses and 4,299 collective farm and state farm buildings and installations had been constructed or reassembled in the resettlement areas. But serious deficiencies in the work of evacuation were noted. 'Basic technical demands in connection with the completion of all the work on the bed of the reservoir for the period of six months before submersion (to a depth of 382.8 metres on 1 April 1964) are not being met satisfactorily by some *raion* executive committees and economic organisations.'[80] A great deal of equipment, particularly agricultural and food-processing, remained unevacuated, while some local consumer cooperatives had still not moved out the contents of their shops and warehouses. Individuals, particularly elderly, were not being afforded the necessary help in evacuating. A number of organisations were criticised for failing to dispose of dung, scrap metal, and other polluting agents.

But the problems of evacuation were made much more serious than they might have been by deficiencies in the planning of the Bratsk industrial complex. 'Simply as a result of the absence of a preliminary complex lay-out plan for the Bratsk energy–industrial region, and of lack of coordination between different departments, it was subsequently necessary to demolish many thousands of square metres of dwelling space, evacuate from the submersion zone a section of railway, build duplicate communications, etc.'[81] In fact, as much as 300 km of the Taishet–Lena railway, and a new bridge over the Angara, ended up under water.[82] The final balance-sheet of the submersion operation, published a number of years after the completion of the HES, was as follows: 5,410 km^2 under water, including 1,723 km^2 of farmland and 3,120 km^2 of forest; a total of 249 settlements flooded, and 68,100 people resettled.[83] Thus almost twice the originally estimated number of settlements were in fact flooded (249 as compared to 130). It is interesting to note, however, that the above figure for number of people resettled is considerably lower than the figure reported by the Irkutsk rural provincial executive committee in 1963 for number of people *evacuated* (109,400). This may suggest that there was significant net emigration from the area at the time of the submersion operation.

With the HES virtually completed, and the reservoir, for better or worse, filled, priority shifted in 1964 and 1965 to the construction of the Bratsk industrial area. The capacity of the station had initially been only 20–30 per cent utilised, because of lack of customers, though the opening of the transmission line to Krasnoyarsk raised this to 50–60 per cent,[84] presumably on the basis of consumption by the Krasnoyarsk aluminium factory. That started work in 1964,[85] though it was not completed until 1970 at the earliest.[86] The construction of the timber complex continued to present problems, but the failure to install the boiler on time seems to have been the fault of suppliers rather than builders.[87] A landmark was passed in March 1965, when the first stage of the Korshunovskii ore-concentrating (presumably bauxite) combine went into production.[88] Around the same time, on the other hand, construction of Bratsk city seems to have been going very badly, owing to lack of design documentation, low quality of work, supply problems, particularly with plastic materials, and financial difficulties. Plan fulfilment was felt to be in danger. Interestingly, an instruction to Gosstroi to create a local Giprogor (town planning) group in Bratsk had not been carried out.[89] In December 1965 the cellulose department of the timber complex finally went into operation,[90] and in July 1966 the first stages of the aluminium factory started work.[91] But construction of the city was still running into problems in mid-1966, and it is clear that plans were not being fulfilled.[92] Completion of the timber complex and aluminium factory took in the end almost 10 years. By the time they were completed the output of the Bratsk HES had been fully allocated to other uses, and it seems that adequate electricity supplies to those projects had to await the completion, at the end of 1977, of the Ust'-Ilim HES.[93]

Analysis

In evaluating the Bratsk case there are two quite separate issues to be discussed. Firstly, did the siting of a giant HES on the Angara in itself represent a deviation from the yardstick? Secondly, what were the principal elements of inefficiency in the actual implementation of the project? To start with the first question: though it is impossible to prove anything conclusively about such huge undertakings, at least in the absence of reliable efficiency price data, it is quite possible that the construction of the hydro-station did not represent a medium-term least-cost solution to Union-wide problems of power supply. On the other hand, the project was conceived right from the beginning as a complex project, involving the building up of power-intensive industry in Eastern Siberia, and it seems fairly clear that Factor A1, l-t-p-h considerations, was of importance. Strategic considerations (Factor B1) may also have been involved to some extent, as may state-doctrinal considerations (Factor F). In view of the fact that the population of Eastern Siberia is small and largely non-ethnic, Factors B2–B5 are unlikely to have been of much importance. C factors can be ignored in this connection, since the design assignment was centrally confirmed.

The question of the implementation of the project is more complex and interesting. Despite perennial problems of the C1, D and E types, the dam was completed and was able to start functioning efficiently more or less on time, and this part of the project may incline us to look with greater sympathy on Soviet 'storming' methods. Estimates of HES costs, far from showing any general tendency to inflation, actually fell somewhat over the construction period, though this may be partly due to 'windfall' improvements in the design introduced around 1961. One way or another, the learning process showed a quite clear 'profit' in relation to the dam itself, never mind lessons for other dam-builders. Serious problems did, however, occur in the coordination of the dam project itself with general infrastructural work. Ministries other than those concerned directly with power were clearly reluctant to attach priority to tasks whose fulfilment would provide few internal benefits, and when tasks were implemented they were often implemented in a way which engendered high external costs (Factor C3).

But the major losses suffered in the implementation of the project were probably caused by the lateness with which the energy-using enterprises were completed. This is a difficult issue to analyse, because it involves consideration of the whole strategy of Soviet development. Here we will be content with a fairly pedestrian analysis, leaving any attempts at a higher degree of generalisation to the concluding chapter. It is clear that Factors C1, D and E affected the construction of the energy-using enterprises more than they did that of the dam itself, and we could just leave it at that. But it is interesting to speculate why these factors had a more serious effect in the 'secondary' sector. Can this be put down to the operation of taut planning and the priority principle (see Chapter 1)? The argument would run that the Soviet planners had reasoned thus: there are insufficient material and human resources to ensure normal working conditions on all sectors of the project simultaneously: setting of 'impossible' targets may, however, pull out something extra, and, failing this, resources can be pulled back onto the 'king-pin' of the project – the dam itself. The point is, of course, that the 'secondary elements' in the project cannot be seen realistically as non-priority sectors, because of their close input-output and locational connection with the dam, so that there was no real way of avoiding serious costs in the event of excessive tautness.

Another possible argument in relation to the bad coordination of the complex project would run in terms of Factor C3. As we have seen, the Bratsk timber complex, the Novo-Chunskii timber combine and the Korshunovskii ore-concentrating combine were all built by Bratskgesstroi itself, an organisation subordinate, at different times, to the USSR Ministry for Power-Station Construction and the USSR Ministry of Power and Electrification. It is clear that the benefits which would eventually accrue from that project, in terms of output etc., would not accrue to those ministries, but to a *sovnarkhoz* or other ministry, so that in terms of the interests of the power ministries, these projects were of secondary importance.

CASE STUDY 2: PIT DEVELOPMENT IN THE KARAGANDA BASIN

The Karaganda Basin in one of the most important centres for the extraction of coking coal in the Soviet Union. Development started during the first five-year plan period, and in 1932 the field produced 739,000 tons of coal.[94] By 1965 Karaganda was producing 11,004,000 tons of coking coal annually, 7.9 per cent of total Soviet production of coking coal.[95] Fully confirmed reserves of coal in the field total 36,100,000,000 tons.[96] Karaganda is an important supplier of coking coal to the metallurgy plants of the Urals, though ferrous metallurgy within Kazakhstan itself is of increasing importance, with the development of the Karaganda metallurgical combine.[97]

The unique characteristic of coal-mining is, of course, that construction and exploitation cannot be clearly separated as they can in

other sectors. The construction of a pit inevitably involves extraction
of some coal, and the pit by definition expands and changes its nature
as full-scale extraction proceeds. This by itself makes coal-mining
interesting to students of the investment process. In the present
context, however, the most important factor in the choice of
Karaganda as a case study was the existence and availability of a
highly detailed discussion of problems of development in the
Karaganda field written by G. E. Khrapkov.[98] The following description is based wholly on his work.

The nature of the problem
Delays in achieving full production capacity in Karaganda pits
during the late 1950s and early 1960s were excessive. Figure 6.2
indicates the extent to which excessive gestation periods – on average

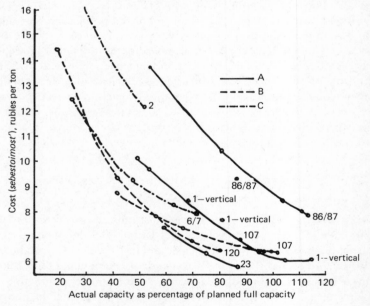

Figure 6.2 Costs and levels of capacity utilisation in Karaganda coal mines.
　　　　　A – 'Industrial' Sector shafts;
　　　　　B – Saran' Sector shafts;
　　　　　C – Churubai-Nurinskii Region shafts.
Numbers on graph refer to individual pits.
Source: G. E. Khrapkov, *Ekonomicheskaya Effecktivnost' Kapital'nykh Vlozhenii v
Razvitie Karagandinskogo Basseina*, Alma-Ata, Nauka, 1965, p. 162

seven years – raised current costs (*sebestoimost'*), quite apart from any consideration of notional rate of interest.

Terminology and variables

The total amount of coal extracted from a given pit consists of that coming from stopes (*ochistnoi zaboi* – working face), and that coming from development faces (*podgotovitel'nyi zaboi*). The percentage relationship of the latter quantity to the total should be 6–10 per cent in the first two years of exploitation and 2–7 per cent thereafter. Degree of utilisation of planned capacity does, then, depend secondarily on this relationship, but primarily on the rate of extraction from stopes. This in turn depends on the length of the stope and its unit load (*udel'naya nagruzka*), i.e. the quantity of coal extracted from one linear metre of coal face per standard period. Going one step further, unit load is the productivity of a square metre of face multiplied by the rate of advance of face. Designs include planned rates of growth in the length of face for each shaft, and corresponding changes in the level of unit load. Obviously this rate of growth is much greater in the first stage – the development stage – than in the stage of full-scale exploitation, and rates of advance slow down markedly towards the end of the development stage. As a general principle, rate of advance of face – and hence also unit load – varies inversely with length of face, and directly with the level of mechanisation in the removal of hewn coal, as well as with qualitative and quantitative personnel factors. It is important to note that planned levels of shaft production capacity may be achieved where planned unit load is not, simply by exceeding planned length of shaft.

After a shaft has gone into production, stope and development work can proceed simultaneously, but this creates difficulties for the latter type of work in terms of material supply and transport. On the basis of 1962 data the rate of implementation of foundation work in shafts under construction is 1.35–1.7 times greater than in shafts already in operation, and the same relationship holds, *ceteris paribus*, with relative speeds of development of advance lines. In addition, tunnelling work can be carried on simultaneously on a greater number of faces during the construction stage than in the post-operationalisation stage. Clearly, then, it is advisable to prepare the maximum possible length of stope during the construction stage. Taking Karaganda Basin data, 0.5–1.0 years is the additional period required to complete development of stope advance lines before operationalisation, and this

permits reduction in the time needed after operationalisation to reach
full capacity from 7 to 1.5–2.0 years. Using a methodology of the type
described on pp. 106–7, the economy in capital expenditures works
out at 22 per cent, even with a full additional year on the construction
period.

The development work schedule

In practice the bulk of development work has been done in the
post-operationalisation period. *Proekty* for Karaganda shafts have, as
a general rule, aimed at the development of 30–70 per cent of stope
line of advance during the construction stage. In a number of cases
where speedy operationalisation has been required, however, the
percentage has been arbitrarily reduced to 8–12 per cent. This has
obviously meant that proportions of total extraction coming from
development faces have tended to be excessive.

Delays in the development of advance lines have occurred partly for
reasons internal to pit organisation, partly because of factors over
which mining enterprises have little control. On the first count,
coordination of stope and development work, and the organisation of
the latter, have often left something to be desired. The key variable
here is the success-indicator/incentive scheme system, which places
primary emphasis on extraction work. In the case of Pit No. 1 –
vertical ('Industrial' Sector), where 4,357 and 6,991 linear metres of
work on increasing the size of the stope was done in 1955 and 1956
respectively, as compared with projected 7,620 and 8,440 respectively, straightforward implementation problems of this type were
of paramount importance. Such problems have, indeed, been of
particular importance throughout the old-established 'Industrial'
Sector.

The second group of factors – those essentially external to pit-face
work as such – have been of relatively minor importance in the
'Industrial' Sector, where geological and mining conditions are most
favourable, but of primary importance in the Saran' Sector and
Churubai-Nurinskii Region, where conditions are more difficult. The
crux of the matter here is unreliable survey material. The preliminary
proekt for Churubai-Nurinskii Pit No. 1, for example, reckoned on the
development of 1,064 out of a total of 1,657 metres of stope before
operationalisation. Just before the pit was due to go into production,
however, it was discovered that it was technically not feasible to work
seams K_{16-17} and K^2_{18}. Planned initial extent of stope was accordingly

reduced to 790 metres. The actual amount of work done was in fact only 216 metres, or 13 per cent of the original projected figure. The slow growth of production capacity in the succeeding four years was caused by the fact that they were operating only one wing of the pit – because the other had not been properly surveyed.

In many cases underfulfilment of set tasks on particular seams has had a cumulative effect. In Pit No. 121, for example, 1,140 instead of the projected 1,300 linear metres of work was done on seam K_{13} prior to operationalisation. The subsequent termination of work on this seam effectively halved the extent of developed stope in the pit as a whole, however, and excluded the possibility of any rapid expansion in the future. Over a period of five years the stope grew, in fact, by only 200 metres, i.e. by 30 per cent. As a result, the length of operational stope in 1962 was only 50 per cent, and the rate of extraction only 67 per cent, of planned.

As far as the newer Sectors are concerned, then, the basic reason for delays in the development of stopes has been low-quality geological survey work. To make matters worse, however, no systematic efforts have been made to work out ways of increasing the length of stope when this kind of problem has supervened.

Other aspects of pit construction

Development work has not been the only field where delays in completion or non-completion have been a recurring problem. Sometimes much more fundamental operations have been involved. Extended construction periods and unsafe rock at the sides of seams have meant that shoring-up is frequently necessary. This kind of work should obviously be done before operationalisation, but in Pit No. 4, for example, 30,000 rubles' worth remained to be done at time of operationalisation. For Pit No. 2 the corresponding figure was 325,000 rubles. This meant that only 331 tons per 24-hour period could be extracted in the first year of exploitation, as against planned 1,100. In Pit No. 22 degasification work, without which exploitation of seams K_{10} and K_{12} is practically impossible, was not done before operationalisation.

Serious cases of work uncompleted at time of operationalisation have also occurred with surface installations. These have involved construction of waste heap facilities, skip complexes, emergency coal warehouses and mechanised timber warehouses.

Responsibility for this category of problem is attributed primarily to poor organisation in construction, hampered, as it has been, by shortages of qualified manpower. Deficiencies in design work may often have lain behind these organisational difficulties.

Levels of unit load

In the case of a number of pits, delay in reaching planned production capacity has been related to a degree of underfulfilment of planned level of unit load that has persisted throughout the life of the pit. It is of great importance to bear in mind here that the degree of mechanisation is a major variable affecting the rate of advance of face, which in turn affects the level of unit load, and that the behaviour of this variable depends to a great extent on geological conditions. Rates of advance of face in new pits of the Karaganda Basin do in fact vary from 18 to 34 metres per month, and it is significant that the fastest rates, 26–34 metres per month, are found in the 'Industrial' Sector, where geological conditions are easiest. This is clearly related to the higher degree of mechanisation of stope work possible in these seams. Despite these variations, however, *proekty* for all pits envisage the use of the Donbass and UKMG coal-cutting combines, and fix rates of advance per day at 1.2–1.4 metres, irrespective of length of face or geological conditions.

As was noted earlier, rate of advance of face varies inversely with length of face. Where geological conditions permit, pits may tend to increase length of face even if this means a drop in the rate of advance of face. At Pit No. 1-vertical ('Industrial' Sector), for example, with a projected average length of face of 175 metres, average actual length in 1962 was as much as 218 metres, while rate of advance of face was only 85 per cent of what it was supposed to be. In contrast, average actual length of face in Pits Nos. 120 and 121 of the Saran' Sector, where geological conditions militate against extended faces, has been 1.5–2 times shorter than projected. The rate of advance, consequently, has been well above the planned level. There is an optimal length of face which balances these considerations – 200 to 300 metres in the 'Industrial' Sector. Differences between actual and planned rates of advance have resulted, to a great extent, from the fact that designs have not been based on any conception of optimal length of face. Under such conditions the key planning indicators of rate of advance and unit load tend to lose their operational significance, with inevitable deleterious effects on implementational efficiency.

More recent reports indicate that the post-1965 changes have not succeeded in modifying to any great extent the perennial problems of pit development in the Karaganda Basin. The director of Karagandagiproshakht (pit design organisation) himself, B. Kurdyaev, complained in 1971 of inadequate preliminary investigations, excessive capital and production costs, delays in reaching planned capacities and low levels of labour productivity.[99]

Analysis

It is clear, then, that this particular case is to be explained largely in terms of Factor D, with a subsidiary rôle being played by Factor E. In an odd sort of way Factor C2 may also have been involved, inasmuch as in 1957–58 the Karaganda *sovnarkhoz* apparently switched tens of millions of rubles from the Karaganda metallurgical factory and the coal mines of the Karaganda Basin on to the construction of a theatre, circus, holiday centre, *sovnarkhoz* building, swimming pool and other local projects.[100] The problems under discussion have survived the demise of the *sovnarkhoz* system, however, so that there is no question of this being a major element.

To return to Factors D and E: the only point deserving special note in connection with the latter is that we must here be talking about the success-indicator régimes etc. affecting miners themselves as well as construction workers. The design organisations, however, hold the centre of the stage, and a number of particular points are worthy of mention. We have an excellent example of the neglect of preliminary survey work, which we discussed as a general tendency in Chapter 3, and the tenaciousness of the problem is indicated by its persistence in a sector where general geological conditions are as obviously of primary importance as is conceivable. What may be of even greater importance is the extent to which design organisations have been prepared to try to reduce pit development planning to an oversimplified stereotype, quite apart from the quality of survey work – and this in a sector where, as was noted in our opening remarks, the relationship between the various stages of construction and actual operation are by definition very close, and in the fairly unusual situation of a unified, specialised, local design organisation. But we must exercise a little caution in our ascriptions here, with respect to Factor E as well as Factor D. The early years of the seven-year plan, i.e. the late 1950s, witnessed a virtual cessation of construction of new pits in the Donbass, the main Soviet coal field. When the error of this decision was discovered necessary levels of coal output could only be attained on the basis of storming tactics, i.e. the overloading of existing pits. Successful in the short run, these tactics were by the middle 1960s having their ultimately inevitable deleterious effects on plan fulfilment. Preparatory work and pit planning had obviously been neglected, and rates of productivity did, indeed, begin to fall.[101] No direct evidence on how this affected the Karaganda Basin is to hand, but it would be surprising if some of the pressure did not filter through. Thus policy error at the highest level may be a necessary element in a full explanation of case study 2. This element does not figure in our list of factors because it cannot reasonably be argued that there is a strong *a priori* reason for it to exist at all. But its possible importance in individual cases cannot be denied.

CASE STUDY 3: THE NUREK HYDRO-ELECTRIC STATION

Description: the dam itself
Though the possibility of utilising the vast hydro-electric potential of Tadzhikistan was discussed in the 1930s,[102] nothing was done until the late 1950s, except for the construction of a few small stations. It was in 1959 that the idea of building a giant HES at Nurek, a small township a few miles from Dushanbe (see Fig. 6.3), began to take concrete shape.[103] In the same year SAOGIDEP (Sredneaziatskoe otdelenie Gidroenergoproekta – Central Asian HES design organisation) was given the all-clear to go ahead with the *proekt* for the HES,[104] and construction began in 1961.[105] It was originally estimated that capital costs of the 5 million kilowatt HES would be 68.7 rubles per kilowatt (1.57 kopecks per kilowatt-hour) and running costs 0.027 kopecks per kilowatt-hour.[106] The first stage of the station was to go into operation in 1965,[107] and the whole project was to be finished in 1967.[108] However, the project soon ran into fairly serious problems, and cost estimates started to rise sharply. Revised estimates as of 1967 put capital costs at 205 rubles per kilowatt (4.84 kopecks per kilowatt-hour) and running costs at 0.071 kopecks per kilowatt-hour.[109] By then the projected capacity of the dam had been reduced to 2.7 million kilowatts,[110] and it is quite possible that this is closely connected with the rise in projected unit capital costs. It was reckoned in 1968 that the first stage of the dam would go into production in 1971.[111] This did not in fact happen until autumn 1972–spring 1973, with the operationalisation of two sets of turbines.[112] By August 1974,

the dam itself had been built to half its projected height,[113] and by January 1976 the third set of turbines was in production.[114] The fourth set of turbines went into production in early 1977,[115] and the fifth in September 1977.[116] The ninth set was operationalised in September 1977,[117] and the tenth and last was to be completed for the XXVI Congress of the Party.[118] These further delays in completion must imply some further escalation of capital costs, quite apart from any notional imputation of interest. It is interesting to note that when completion was announced in 1977 (though the tenth set of turbines was not yet in operation), it was reported as fifteen months ahead of schedule.[119]

Organisational problems on the building site seem to have played some rôle in the escalation of costs.[120] These may have been exacerbated by the fact that the initial construction work was divided between three organisations – Gidroelektromontazh and Gidromontazh, both presumably subordinate to the Power Ministry, and Gidrospetsstroi, which sounds like a Minmontazhspetsstroi organisation. In fact, the predecessor of Minmontazhspetsstroi, the State Production Committee for Installation and Special Construction Work, was not created until 1963. Labour force difficulties have also made themselves felt, and an effort was made in the early 1970s – with some success, it seems – to 'ginger up' workers through a combination of closer *kontrol'* and greater financial incentives.[121] Supply problems have been prominently discussed in the local press, and have clearly been exacerbated by the isolated location of the project. A special kind of socialist competition involving dam-builders and suppliers called *rabochaya estafeta* was organised in 1971, and this may have contributed to some improvement in the supply situation, although reports are conflicting.[122]

But these more or less 'normal' elements do not provide any kind of complete explanation of the degree of escalation of cost and completion date estimates. It is only when we turn to the design stage that a clear picture of the nature of the problem begins to appear.

As is well known, the design assignment for the HES was not underpinned by exact technico-economic calculations, engineering research work, or data on natural conditions in the construction area.

As a result, it turned out that the type of dam would have to be changed, while the cost of many overflow [*vodosbrosnyi*] installations rose sharply. The 40- to 50-ton dumpers and other forms of modern technology which the designers were counting on cannot in fact be used in a number of cases because of the cramped mountain conditions [and] narrow work front . . .[123]

The difficulties of the Nurek project did not, however, end with the rise in generation costs.

SAOGIDEP envisaged that Nurek would transmit energy to the North, and participate in the covering of electricity loads and the fulfilment of reserve functions in the Central Asian integrated power grid, initially to the extent of 70 per cent, and eventually to that of the whole of its capacity. However, this is not economically effective because of the sharp rise in the cost [*sebestoimost'*] of electricity c.i.f. the user caused by the additional expenditures necessary for the construction of a double transmission line in mountainous conditions.[124]

In fact, capital costs of building a high-tension line from Nurek to the Tashkent grid were estimated in the middle 1960s at 134.6 million rubles, with running costs of transmission at a level of 0.068 kopecks per kilowatt-hour.[125] Estimates from the same period for large-capacity thermal-condensation stations working on gas in the Tashkent region are as follows: capital costs of 50–55 rubles per kilowatt (0.7–0.8 kopecks per kilowatt-hour) and running costs of 0.12–0.13 kopecks per kilowatt-hour.[126] Thus on the basis of the 1967 estimates the current cost of Nurek electricity c.i.f. the Tashkent grid would have slightly exceeded that of thermal stations situated in the Tashkent area, while capital costs per kilowatt of the former would have exceeded by about 5 times those of the latter. It has been argued that the long-run marginal cost of gas-based thermal generation in Central Asia may be very much higher than the average,[127] because of the uniqueness of deposits, and this is a point to which we shall return later. There is no evidence, however, that the long run has, in this particular respect, yet been reached.

There is some indication that the problem of transmitting Nurek energy to the Tashkent area, over the Turkestan mountains, was never properly considered at the time when the *proekt* for the dam itself was being done, for even if the f.o.b. cost of Nurek energy had not risen as it did, it does not appear that Nurek energy c.i.f. the Tashkent grid would have been the preferred variant on the basis of the ten-year pay-off period [normative CRE of 0.1] then in use in electricity generation in the Soviet Union. In any case, there cannot be the slightest doubt that on the basis of the revised Nurek estimates the Tashkent grid could get cheaper electricity from 'home' thermal stations than it could from Nurek. In the light of this the authorities considered abandoning the whole project around 1963–64.[128] It was finally decided, however, to carry on with construction of the dam, but to change the scheme for utilisation of the energy. Only a single transmission line would now be built from Nurek to the Tashkent grid. The line would have a reversive character, that is current would move both ways, to cover peaks as they arose either in the Tashkent area or in south Tadzhikistan.[129] It appears that construction of the transmission line had been completed by 1974.[130] The greater part of Nurek energy would, however, now be used in south Tadzhikistan itself. To this end it was decided to build an electro-chemical combine at Yavan, and an aluminium factory at Regar, subsequently renamed Tursunzade (both chemical and aluminium production are power-intensive).[131] It was probably about this time also that it was decided to build the dam of earth and rubble (*nasypnoi*), on a concrete base, rather than wholly of concrete. This is a safeguard against the highly seismic conditions of the area. Earth tremors are, indeed, supposed to make earth and rubble dams stronger.[132]

Description: the complementary projects

The evidence on the prehistory of the Yavan chemical combine is rather confused, and any interpretation must be fairly tentative. 'Three or four years ago, when the first contours of the future electro-chemical combine were being mapped out, in connection with the preliminary search for the most rational scheme for the use of the energy of the projected Nurek HES, the idea of creating a large-scale chemical complex was met by many with doubts, and was the subject of fierce discussion.'[133] Since the book from which this quotation is taken was published in 1964, the discussion referred to must have been in 1960–61, or even earlier, allowing for some time-lag between writing and publication. Now the author does give the impression that it had already been decided in principle at that time to build a chemical combine, but this is in clear contradiction to what Klopov and Ryl'skii, writing in 1966 or 1967, say (as quoted above p. 142). It seems reasonable to suppose that what in fact happened was that the idea of building a chemical combine was initially rejected as being uneconomic (presumably on the basis of the original f.o.b. cost estimates for the Nurek HES), but was brought up again when it was discovered, after the construction of the dam had started, that transmission of the bulk of Nurek energy to the Tashkent grid would involve very high costs. Even then, however, doubts about the advisability of the project lingered on. V. P. Bondar', writing in 1966 or 1967, pointed out that:

it must be borne in mind that impressive figures for current costs and capital expenditure on (chemical) production in Tadzhikistan, though of undoubted importance, are not by themselves a sufficient condition of the economic advisability of locating the chemical industry in this region. The economic effectiveness, from a national point of view, of the various possible locations can be correctly determined only on the basis of a comparison of total costs of production and of transport to the user. It is particularly important to take the transport factor into consideration in the case of location of chemical production in south Tadzhikistan, which occupies a peripheral geographical position, and is extremely isolated both from the basic users of chemicals in Central Asia and from the industrial centres of the other economic regions of the country.[134]

As mentioned in Chapter 2, another author noted in 1966 that the Yavan valley is specially suitable for growing high-quality cotton, and that the chemical combine would inevitably have deleterious effects on the cotton. He also noted that the site chosen has a seismic coefficient of 8–9, and was – as of the middle 1960s – 275 km from the nearest railway line.[135] These factors were all no doubt discussed in the early 1960s, and must have contributed to the misgivings felt by economists and planners.

Construction of the Yavan electro-chemical combine seems to have started around the middle of the 1971–75 plan period,[136] and it was scheduled to go into operation during the 1976–80 period.[137] By 1976 218 km of the Termez–Kurgan-Tyube–Yavan railway line had been completed,[138] and this development is presumably related to the transport needs of the chemical combine. However, by the end of 1976 only 15 per cent of planned capital expenditures on the combine had been implemented. Annual expenditures, which were running at a level of 6–7 million rubles during the ninth five-year plan (1971–75), were due to rise to 16 million rubles in 1976 and 41 million in 1977. It seemed likely, however, that this acceleration might run into serious problems of labour supply.[139] Further delays reported in 1980 were, however, blamed on late delivery of equipment and design-documentation.[140]

It is not clear when construction of the aluminium factory began, but it was probably in the early years of the ninth five-year plan. It is interesting that the building of the enterprise has been primarily the responsibility of the Ministry for Power[141] – the main contractor on the project is Tadzhikgidroproenergostroi (at some point renamed Tadzhikgidroenergostroi – a specialist energy construction organisation, but not involved in the construction of the HES itself).[142] By late

1974 the buildings of the factory had been largely completed (by Minpromstroi organisations), but no equipment had been installed – because none had been delivered.[143] The year 1975 witnessed a big effort on the aluminium factory, with planned expenditures fixed at 61 million rubles,[144] and on 31 March of the same year the first ton of aluminium was produced.[145] By autumn 1975 the first stage of the factory was in full production,[146] and it was scheduled to be 'basically' completed by the end of 1980.[147] As of 1979, however, more than 100 million rubles' worth of unfinished construction was outstanding on the project.[148] That year did, nevertheless, see completion of the first stage of the prebaked anodes (*obozhzhennyi anod*) department.[149] The final stage of the department was finished in October 1980.[150]

It is clear that supply problems have played a key rôle in delays in the construction of the aluminium factory. As late as 1976 deliveries of structural steel (*metallokonstruktsii*) were running at a rate of less than 30 per cent of planned, while supplies of reinforcement (*armatura*) for reinforced concrete were in permanent deficit.[151] Labour supply has been a problem, as with the electro-chemical combine, and this appears to be related to problems of accommodation,[152] and to an inadequate level of regional wage coefficient – just 30 per cent.[153] Interestingly, irregularity in the provision of funds was mentioned as a focal issue as late as 1979.[154]

Another major difficulty in relation to the aluminium factory is that of raw material supplies. Kaolin is extracted along with the coal at Angren, but not in quantities sufficient for the needs of the new factory.[155] As a result, raw materials will have to be brought initially from the Urals and Transcaucasia.[156] Later on the large local deposits of nepheline at Turpi will be used,[157] though their location is somewhat inaccessible.[158] The problem of transporting finished production will presumably affect the aluminium factory as much as the electro-chemical combine. Again as with the Yavan project, the externalities issue with respect to agriculture rears its head. The opportunity cost of taking over irrigated land for construction purposes in the area of the town of Tursunzade is estimated at 2,000 rubles per hectare annually, but this was not taken account of in the planning of the town.[159]

The Yavan and Regar/Tursunzade projects have, then, now become major bottlenecks in relation to the development of the South Tadzhikistan power-industry complex. One source does, indeed, suggest that the HES itself could have been finished by 1976, but that work had to be slowed down because the two main customers were not ready to use the electricity.[160] In 1979, with full capacity more or less reached, the HES was operating at only 50 per cent of that capacity, because of the delays in construction of the complex. Department-alism must obviously be a major element in any comprehensive explanation of these persistent hold-ups as far as the aluminium factory is concerned. The three ministries involved – Minpromstroi, the Power Ministry and the Ministry for Non-ferrous Metallurgy – have not worked well together. But even the last-mentioned stands accused of adopting attitudes unlikely to further the interests of either the enterprise or the national economy as a whole. After the comple-tion of the first stage of the prebaked anodes department, which was adequate to provide for the needs of the factory at its then capacity, the ministry wanted to reconstruct the department, presumably with a view to supplying other plants under its jurisdiction. The point of view of the factory management was that, if this were done, the department would just have to be 'reconstructed back' once full capacity had been reached. What the ministry ought to have been doing was getting on with finishing the factory (cf. the question of financial hold-ups discussed on p. 145).[161] It is not clear how this argument was finally settled.

The water-regulation and irrigation side of the Nurek project was given little prominence initially, but has been increasingly emphasised since the late 1960s. Some of the construction delays of the late 1970s on the HES itself were related to the building of a fourth tunnel, which would, it was claimed, make the irrigation side of the project more efficient.[162] With a reservoir capacity of 10.5 milliard m^3, Nurek will irrigate more than 500,000 hectares of cotton-growing lands in Tadzhikistan, Uzbekistan and Turkmeniya,[163] and one recent report portrays the dam as primarily an irrigation project.[164] Here again, however, the environmental issue complicates the picture. It has been argued that the clean, controlled water supply which Nurek provides is much less useful than the old natural supply of muddy water. The silt contained in that water represented the Vakhsh valley's most valuable fertiliser input, and that input cur-rently has to be replaced by artificial fertiliser. Now that there are no more flash floods, expensive drainage systems are having to be built to wash out acid soils, and the new conditions have also increased the vigour of insect pests. That means more DDT, and the contaminatory effects of this are felt as far as the Aral Sea. Finally, the silt is clogging up the reservoir capacity of the dam itself. All but 6 out of the 18 million m^3 of capacity of the 'home' reservoir (*vodokhranilishche pri Golovnoi GES*) are affected by silting-up.[165] These points are not uncontroversial, but must clearly be taken into account in any final totting-up of the balance sheet.

Analysis

It is not possible, on the basis of the evidence adduced, to say definitely whether the decision to build the electro-chemical combine and the aluminium factory, *given the fact of the prior existence of the Nurek HES*, does or does not fulfil the requirements of the m-t-p-h efficiency condition, though the manner of implementation of these two projects has been manifestly inefficient by any standards. It seems fairly clear that the original decision to build the HES could not be justified on the basis of that criterion. The fact that the original plan for utilisation was abandoned is fairly strong evidence to this effect. Nevertheless, had there been an obvious, good alternative way of using the energy, the possibility does exist that the modified scheme might still fulfil the m-t-p-h efficiency condition. Given, however, the cost of the single transmission line, and the transport and externality problems of the two factories, it seems reasonable to rule out this possibility. Clearly the water-regulation and irrigation side has helped, to some extent, to 'save' the project, though one might wish to reserve judgement on the more extreme assertions published recently in this connection, particularly in view of the environmental complications it involves. It is claimed that the dam had paid off its costs by 1980, taking increased cotton production related to irrigation into account.[166] Given that it has taken 19 years to build, however, and whatever the exact pattern over time of the investment expenditures, even this could hardly represent a CRE anywhere near 0.10.

As with the Regar/Tursunzade and Yavan projects, the building of the HES has been characterised by many elements of operational inefficiency, often conditioned by supply problems. More generally, there has been a lamentable lack of coordination between the basic project and the two main potential customers. Thus we can distinguish clearly between two questions in our analysis of the Nurek project – the question of *conception* and the question of *implementation*. The former relates exclusively to the dam itself, while the latter touches every aspect of the development of the south Tadzhikistan power-industry complex.

There is, as has been indicated, plenty of evidence that the *proekt* for Nurek was very poorly done. Some of the initial rise in capital cost estimates may be attributable to inconsistencies and internal errors in the *proekt*, but it is quite clear that a more careful evaluation of the project would have resulted in a much less optimistic set of cost estimates – current and capital. It would be easy enough, then, to cite Factor D as a major factor here. But why was everyone so keen to get started on such a gigantic project on the basis of what must have quite obviously been inadequate evidence on costs? As far as the transmission line to the Tashkent grid is concerned, no proper design work seems to have been done at all until after construction of the dam had started. Bearing in mind what was said in Chapter 3 about the 'strength' of design organisations, one cannot help suspecting that considerations of economic efficiency on any basis were simply not in the forefront of attention when the decision to go ahead with Nurek was taken. What considerations, then, could have been involved? It is difficult to see any strategic significance in Nurek. The state-doctrinal priority granted to scale and capital-intensity is obviously potentially relevant here, though it can hardly have been of decisive importance – there were surely plenty of other possible big projects around at the time. What about Factor C2? One is tempted to try to establish some link between Nurek and the *sovnarkhoz* system, for it was during the period when the latter was in use that the project was first suggested and subsequently started. However, it is clear that the project as originally conceived, with the bulk of the energy going to the Tashkent area, would in no way have increased the degree of self-sufficiency of Tadzhikistan, which was the territorial unit of the relevant *sovnarkhoz* at the time when the vital decisions were being made. (The unified Central Asian *sovnarkhoz* was not created until 1962.) Thus there seems to be no direct link in terms of the organisational autarky factor. Nor, indeed, is this a surprising conclusion, for it is difficult to conceive of the *sovnarkhoz* 'slipping through' such a huge project. Even on the basis of the initial cost estimates the project was easily big enough to have its design assignment confirmed by the Council of Ministers. What about factors B2–B5? Obviously a hydro-electric station could not possibly have any connection with the 'labour intensity' deviation. On the other hand, the undertaking of the Nurek project did correspond to an increase in the percentage ratio of the amount of investment funds going to Tadzhikistan to total investment for the whole Soviet Union (0.7 in 1960, 0.8 in 1964 and 0.9 in

1965),[167] so that Nurek could perhaps be seen as some kind of 'bribe' to the Tadzhiks, or as a move in foreign policy. But there were alternative ways of using 'extra' funds in Tadzhikistan (e.g. on improvement of transport facilities, textile manufacture, non-ferrous ore extraction, agriculture). Why were such alternatives rejected?

It seems very difficult to explain Nurek completely in terms of any of the 'legitimate' factors enumerated in Chapter 1, so that one feels compelled to fall back on investment good fetishism. In the light of his famous speech on the importance of the time factor in making choices between hydro- and thermal-generation,[168] it seems unlikely that Khrushchev himself fetishised hydro-electric stations. The most plausible hypothesis is that it was the local Tadzhik leaders who were indulging their preference for 'energy-giants', though they may have received support from the 'hydro faction' within the power establishment, which was at this time notoriously divided between hydro and thermal partisans, to such an extent, it seems, as to prejudice rational comparisons.[169] Going back to the Tadzhik leaders, this seems to be the only way in which a connection can be established between Nurek and the *sovnarkhoz* system, since the latter did undoubtedly represent an increase in the power of local political leaders, as well as a change in the organisational structure of industry. It is interesting to note, in the light of the sharp criticism which the Nurek project came in for in the early middle 1960s, that there was an almost complete clean-out of the Tadzhik Party leadership at the VII Plenum of the Central Committee of the Tadzhik Party, held in April 1961, following allegations of 'fiddling' of agricultural production returns, nepotism, etc.[170]

Turning to implementational questions, we shall not pause over details which add nothing to the general picture of implementational problems already presented. Rather we shall concentrate on the issue of the coordination of the development of the different components of the south Tadzhikistan power-industry complex, related as this is to the question of delays in completion. It does seem extraordinary that after the exhaustive discussions and heart-searchings of the middle 1960s the 'retrieval' operation should have been so botched. There may, however, be a fairly systematic reason for this. Supply problems, labour problems, financial problems – the incidence of complaints about these, above all in relation to Yavan and Regar/Tursunzade but also in relation to the dam itself, suggests some basic lack of priority. Having peaked in 1965, Tadzhikistan's share in total USSR investment fell back to the 1964 level in 1970, and to the 1961 level in 1975.[171] In 1974 the aluminium factory was receiving only a quarter of planned deliveries of steel *from the ministry actually building it*.[172] Of course, that ministry was the Power Ministry, for which aluminium production presumably contributes nothing to reported aggregate output (though it helps to keep up electricity output!). The case of the Yavan electro-chemical combine is in some ways even more telling. Built by Minstroi organisations and under the jurisdiction of the Chemicals Ministry, the combine should have been immune from the most obvious forms of departmentalism. In fact, poor work by Minstroi Tadzhikistan is blamed for many of the problems on this site.[173] The Chemicals Ministry has kept finance flowing, but one feels again that if the Ministry were heavily committed to the project they would surely be able to pull a republican bricks and mortar ministry into line.

It is, of course, not difficult to find individual examples of non-priority projects, even within priority sectors. Perhaps the special feature of the Nurek case, and the reason why, in the end of the day, so many resources have been wasted, is that here a project which had originally been top-priority, which had turned out to be misconceived, was subsequently saved when it could have been abandoned, but without priority being attached to the salvage job.

CASE STUDY 4: THE ENGINEERING INDUSTRY IN TADZHIKISTAN

Description
Engineering in the Tadzhik republic is fairly small beer – certainly by comparison with our other case studies. It accounted in the late 1960s for just 7.6 per cent of gross industrial production in the republic, but 10.6 per cent of industrial fixed assets and 16.5 per cent of the industrial work force.[174] As of the same period there were no less than 18 factories in all, though the seven largest of these accounted for more than three-quarters of total gross output.[175] These basic statistics suggest low levels of productivity, and this impression is confirmed by the figures presented in Table 6.2.

Following on from this, it should be emphasised that there is really no 'project' as such involved here as there is with the other case studies. The very purpose, indeed, of introducing this particular case study is to provide some counterpoint to the 'grand projects' which

Table 6.2. *Productivity in the Tadzhik engineering industry*

	Average annual gross output per ruble of fixed productive capital	Average annual gross output per worker (*rabotayushchii*)
Chemical and oil machine building		
Ordzhonikidze factory (Tadzhikistan)	1.7	15–28% lower than at other Central Asian factories in this sector
USSR average for *armaturostroenie* (plating and reinforcement) factories	2.15	n.a.
Transformer production		
Kurgan-Tyube factory (Tadzhikistan)	1.06	41% lower than at the Chirchik factory
Chirchik factory (Uzbekistan)	3.93	n.a.
Namangan factory (Uzbekistan)	2.58	n.a.
Best (*peredovoi*) transformer factories in the USSR	n.a.	40–80% higher than at the Chirchik factory
Cable production		
Tadzhikkabel'	3.1	n.a.
Tashkentkabel' (Uzbekistan)	6.06	n.a.
Kirgizkabel'	3.56	n.a.
Turkmenkabel'	4.03	n.a.
Vehicle spare parts production		
Avtozapchast' (Tadzhikistan)	n.a.	More than 300% lower than at Tashavtomash (Uzbekistan)

Note: All data are for 1963, except data on average annual gross output per worker in chemical and oil machine building and transformer production, undated, but probably also for 1963

Source: I. K. Narzikulov (ed.), *Problemy Razvitiya i Razmeshcheniya Proizvoditel'nykh Sil Tadzhikskoi SSR*, Dushanbe, Donish, 1967, pp. 72 and 74

otherwise dominate the case material, to take a look at how a particular sector in a particular region 'just growed', but to attempt to give some analytical breakdown of that process of 'just growing'. Locational aspects are wholly dominant here (Fig. 6.3), and the case study may help in addition to give perspective on the locational problem *per se* in the Soviet system.

The two main characteristics of the actual pattern of location of the sector within Tadzhikistan have been a strong prevalence of the dwarf-workshop syndrome and an almost complete lack of any complementarity either within the sector or between it and other sectors in the region, despite the fact that Tadzhikistan has no obvious comparative advantage in any particular branch of engineering. It is clear that this pattern gelled during the first ministerial period, when the various factories seem to have been distributed among a number of ministries.

The engineering industry of Tadzhikistan started to develop with the organisation of small-scale enterprises, serving the needs of the republic in small batches of easily produced items. Productive capacities in these enterprises gradually grew *in the course of continuous expansion and reconstruction.* [Emphasis added – D.A.D.] All the factories are full-cycle (from production to assembly). As a result engineering in contemporary Tadzhikistan is represented by a collection of enterprises with virtually no mutual production links.[176]

As is so often the case, castings production is strongly concentrated in dwarf workshops – 15 in all, with an average annual level of production of 900–1,000 tons,[177] but nevertheless with considerable reserves of underutilised capacity.[178] A similar situation prevails with respect to the production of tools (*instrument*) and general metal goods (*metizy*).

At the present time almost every engineering enterprise is engaged on their manufacture. They meet their own needs on a cottage-industry basis, using non-specialised tools and an outdated technology. It is impossible to use fully progressive types of equipment . . . and, consequently, to reach acceptable technico-economic indicators in the production of these. As a result, the cost of production of tools and nuts and bolts in the enterprises of the republic is several times higher even than wholesale prices.[179]

Moving back to the question of complementarity, or rather the lack of it, the prevailing situation has meant that in many cases factories send most of their finished production outside Tadzhikistan, and even outside Central Asia.[180] Table 6.3 shows the percentages of the production of two factories which went to the various regions of the

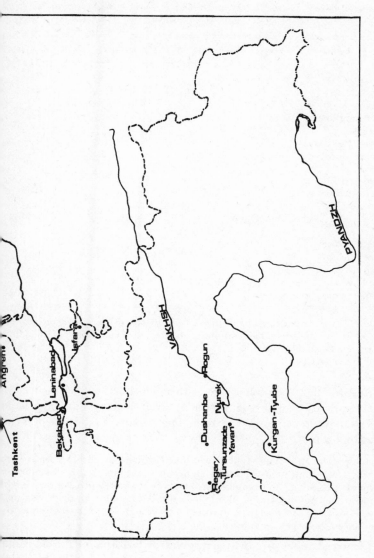

Figure 6.3 Tadzhikistan.

Table 6.3. *Percentage breakdown of deliveries of goods produced at the Traktorodetal'
and Avtozapchast' factories to the various economic regions of the USSR in 1962 (on the
basis of gross output)*

	Traktorodetal'	Avtozapchast'
North-west	2.36	0.98
Centre	4.44	3.62
Volga–Vyatka	1.59	1.01
Central Black Earth	2.26	0.57
Volga	2.86	6.35
North Caucasus	11.04	1.74
Transcaucasia	0.11	3.35
Urals	10.22	6.11
Western Siberia	14.69	10.52
Eastern Siberia	9.69	7.00
Far East	8.25	1.39
South, South-west, Don, Dnepr	3.29	0.27
West	0.31	—
Central Asia	11.30	33.11
Kazakhstan	14.20	20.90
Belorussia	0.80	—
Moldavia	0.25	—
Other (export, reserve, etc.)	2.34	3.08

Source: I. V. Chirgadze, *Mashinostroenie Tadzhikistana i Osnovnye Napravleniya ego
Razvitiya*, unpublished dissertation for the degree of Candidate of Economic
Sciences, Dushanbe, 1965, p. 135

USSR in 1962. The other side of this coin is, of course, that large
quantities of engineering products, even of everyday household
goods, have to be brought in from other regions. In the case of north
Tadzhikistan:

at the present time household articles like earthenware dishes, iron stoves,
ovens, aluminium utensils, knives and even coal tongs, all of which are in
general use among the population, are brought in from other regions of
Central Asia and the Union (from the Baltic, Transcaucasia, Belorussia and
the Ukraine). Transport expenditures on bringing in these goods frequently
amount to 10–30 per cent of their value.[181]

Changes in the production profiles of factories in the Tadzhik
engineering sector seem to have been fairly frequent. In 1965 the
Isfara electro-mechanical factory, the Karikachum hardware factory,
and the Kurgan-Tyube transformer factory were using only 35–40 per
cent of their capacity to make 'name' production.[182] How important

this has been in the present context is confirmed by the history of the Ordzhonikidze factory. Originally established in 1933 as a small-scale repair station, it was taken over in 1942 by the Ministry for the Oil Industry, and switched over to the production of heavy fittings (*armatura*) for the oil industry, despite the fact that demand for such production in the virtually oil-less Tadzhikistan is insignificant.[183] More recently the works has extended its profile to cover similar fittings for the chemical and gas industries,[184] this possibly corresponding to a transfer of subordination to the Ministry for Chemical and Oil Machine Building, created in 1965. There is, however, no evidence of supplies going to, for example, the Yavan electro-chemical works, supply problems affecting which were discussed in the previous case study.

In the period 1957–65, when the ministries were replaced by *sovnarkhozy*, something was done to correct these distortions. Unfortunately, new problems arose in the course of this correction process.

During the past few years a significant degree of progress has been made in engineering enterprises in connection with concentration and specialisation. However, this has been effected within the boundaries of each republic, with no account taken of the existence of analogous engineering enterprises in the other republics of Central Asia, or of the needs of the whole Central Asian region in this or that product. This has led to the creation in each republic of duplicating enterprises which produce identical goods. In many cases specialised enterprises have been created with capacity sufficient only to meet the needs of the republic, which has often meant the creation of small-scale, unprofitable enterprises, with a low level of technology.[185]

As noted in Chapter 2, the outstanding case of this was in cable and general metal goods manufacture, but the tendency was also noticeable in the production of high- and low-voltage apparatus, and of some kinds of equipment for light industry.[186] It is not difficult to understand these developments, given, for example, that it was 'impossible to place orders for the production of *osnastki* (types of fittings) outside the republic'.[187] Nevertheless they were particularly harmful, because of the small size and tortuous, economico-geographically arbitrary boundaries of the republic/*sovnarkhoz*, as indeed of the neighbouring republics/*sovnarkhozy*. A contemporary author emphasises that 'the engineering industry of north Tadzhikistan should be considered in terms of the formation of a single engineering complex not only for the Tadzhik republic, but also for the whole of Central Asia'.[188] This was clearly a major consideration (not just in connection with engineering) in the creation of the Central

Asian *sovnarkhoz* in 1962, though by then the *sovnarkhoz* system had already been seriously encroached upon by 'creeping re-ministeriali-sation'. We saw in Chapter 2 that formal re-establishment of the ministerial system in 1965 was followed by some development in the direction of a stronger element of regional planning than had been present before 1957, but it is clear that *vedomstvennost'* of a very old-fashioned type soon began to show itself again. Traktorodetal' simply stopped sending supplies of cast-iron couplings to the Bekabad cement factory in 1966, and the latter had to switch to supplies from the Volokolamsk castings factory, subordinate to the Ministry for the Building Materials Industry, but located in Moscow *oblast'*.[189] Production in the republic of gas rings and cylinders ceased, and as of 1968 these were being brought in from other centres as far distant as Saratov. Production of furnace castings for local use ceased at the Torgmash factory after the setting of an extremely demanding target for the production of electric hotplates – admittedly the main production line of the factory – by the Ministry of Light Machine Building.[190] A request for the construction of a centralised fittings factory, directed to the Ministry for the Machine Tool and Tool Industry sometime in the late 1960s, was categorically rejected by the Ministry on the grounds that the projected factory would be too small.[191] As of 1969 it was planned to build a new castings shop with an annual production capacity of 20,000 tons at the Tadzhik-tekstil'mash factory. This shop would be able to supply the needs of the whole southern area of the republic in castings.[192] No information on the progress of this project has come to hand.

Analysis

Two questions arise in connection with the foregoing material. Firstly, is the existence of an engineering sector in Tadzhikistan compatible with the m-t-p-h efficiency condition? Secondly, taking the existence of the sector in the republic as given, to which factors can we attribute specific distortions in locational patterns, production profiles, etc? Factor productivity is very low, but one of the reasons for this is the presence of these specific distortions. Assuming optimal location, production profiles, supply arrangements, would the sac-rifices in economies of scale which would nevertheless clearly always be involved in a Tadzhik engineering industry be more than accounted for by economies in transport costs? The Ministry for the Machine Tool and Tool Industry seems to have thought not, but given the ministerial tendency to be insensitive to transport costs, this is hardly conclusive evidence. It is, in any case, possible that the authorities in Moscow have attached considerable importance to the *educational* rôle of the development of engineering in this formerly most backward area of the Soviet Union – the technological complexity but relatively high level of labour intensity of the sector make it particularly suitable for the formation of a proletariat. However the economies of scale/transport costs equation works out, then, there may have been an element, though not necessarily a decisive element, of long-term economic policy involved. Factors B2 and B3 could also have some relevance here. Finally, though this is something that is difficult to fit into our system of factors, it could be argued that engineering establishments primarily oriented to the needs of a particular area in terms of repair and maintenance, and the supply of special types of equipment, for example for cotton-growing in given agricultural conditions, need to be physically located in the area, simply so that communications be at an adequate level. The system has, of course, shown itself to be singularly incapable of exploiting such potential gains.

This brings us to specific locational etc. distortions, and it is clear that Factor C2, the tendency to organisational autarky, is primarily involved here. The dwarf-workshops, the 'transport-intensiveness' of the location pattern as it emerged from the first ministerial period, the countervailing tendency to build 'duplicating capacities' in the *sovnarkhoz* period, the subsequent disruption of local supply links after 1965, are textbook examples of the autarkical tendency at work. Clearly the ease with which the production profile of engineering factories can be changed (cf., for example, power stations or coal mines) has played an important part in facilitating the operation of the tendency. There is a strong impression, however, that distortions are more serious in Tadzhikistan than they are in more central areas of the Soviet Union, and this impression is confirmed by material from other peripheral areas.[193] Thus we are presented with strong confirmation in the case of engineering of the general point made in Chapter 2 – namely that ministries tend to use small plants in outlying areas as 'dwarf-workshops writ large'.

CASE STUDY 5: WEST SIBERIAN OIL AND GAS

Basic history and geography
The need to start systematic prospecting for oil on the eastern slopes of the Urals was noted by the Academy of Sciences as early as 1932.

The presence of oil was confirmed in 1934. Prospecting was interrupted by the war, however, and it was not until 1948 that the first drilling rig was erected. The first major gas strike was made at Berezovo in 1953, and the first major oil strike in 1959. Commercial exploitation of gas started in 1963, and of oil in 1964.[194] The Megion well, the first commercial well at the giant Samotlor oil field, was sunk in 1968,[195] and production started in 1969.[196] In the same year a major decision of party and government gave special priority to the development of West Siberian oil and gas. Table 6.4 gives a picture of production trends in recent years. More than 50 milliard rubles were spent on investment in Western Siberia between 1976 and 1980[197] as against a planned figure of 35 milliard.[198]

Table 6.4. *Production of oil and gas in Western Siberia*

| | Oil (millions of tons) | | Gas (milliards of m^3) | |
	Plan	Actual	Plan	Actual
1976		181.7		44.2
1977	214.5	215	63.1	72
1978	250	almost 246	100	90
1979	280	274+	125	111
1980	310 (303.5)*	312+	150 (162.6)*	156

* Modified targets published in 1980
Sources: 'Zapadnaya Sibir' – glavnaya', in *Ekonomicheskaya Gazeta*, No. 16, 1977, pp. 12–13; *Economic Survey of Europe in 1977*, Part I, New York, United Nations, 1978, pp. 128–9; 'Toplivnyi kompleks', in *Pravda*, 31/1/79, p. 1; 'Zapadnaya Sibir' – glavnaya toplivnaya baza strany', in *Trud*, 6/5/80, p. 2; BBC monitoring reports; 'Razvitie neftyanoi promyshlennosti', in *Ek. Gaz.*, No. 14, 1981, p. 2; 'Razvitie gazovoi promyshlennosti', in *Ek. Gaz.*, No. 13, 1981, p. 2

Around 1975 total confirmed gas reserves in the region stood at about 14,000 milliard m^3 (63 per cent of Soviet total),[199] while potential reserves were estimated at 70,000 milliard m^3.[200] No comparable estimates for oil deposits are available, but on the basis of statistics on, for example, drilling, there can be no doubt of their massive extent.[201] Important fuels often found in conjunction with these deposits are accessory gas (found with oil) and condensate (found with gas). The latter is a highly useful form of liquid fuel which is used, unprocessed, by the oil and gas prospectors themselves to run tractors, automobiles and drilling engines.[202] West Siberia is a sparsely populated and unevenly developed area, and many of the

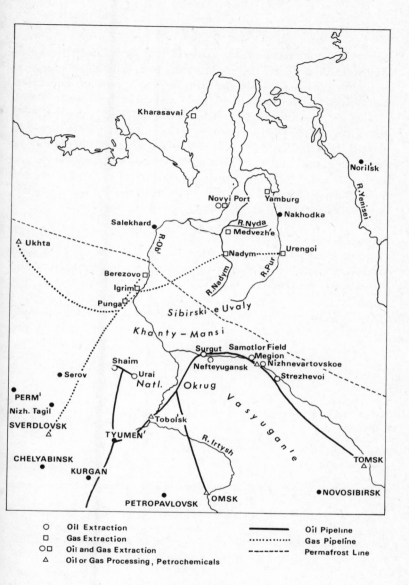

Figure 6.4 Western Siberia.

Note: An oil pipeline Surgut–Perm'–Gor'kii–Polotsk was completed in 1981.
A gas pipeline Urengoi–Chelyabinsk was due to be finished in 1980, and
another, going from Urengoi, through Peregrebnoe and Nizhnyaya Tura, to
Petrovsk, was due to be finished in 1982. No evidence on the precise routing
of these pipelines has come to hand

most valuable locations, particularly of gas, are in areas previously
wholly virgin, often characterised by the most difficult geographical
conditions – permafrost below a certain depth, long frozen winters
and short, wet, boggy summers. The question of the extent to which
oil and gas should be processed locally has been a controversial
strategic issue, to which we shall return later. But it has never been in
dispute that the bulk of West Siberian oil and gas should be
transported south and west. This, in addition to the vast distances and
accentuated 'roadlessness' which are features of the area itself, has
made transport a key issue in development strategy. Figure 6.4 gives
a general picture of the spatial dimension of the complex.

The question of costs
The cost characteristics of Tyumen' oil and gas are the subject of some
controversy. Table 6.5 presents comparative estimates for capital and
current costs as of early and late 1970s.

Table 6.5. *Economic indicators of fuel extraction (in rubles per ton of conventional fuel)*

| | Unit capital costs | | Current costs | |
	1971	1977	1971	1977
Tyumen' gas	10.0	29.7	0.9	2.8
Tyumen' oil	24.8		2.4	
Kansk-Achinsk coal	6.2	16.4	1.0	3.0
Ekibastuz coal	8.9	17.3	1.3	1.8
Kuzbass coal	30.8	22.1*	6.8	4.8*
Mangyshlak oil	31.7		3.1	
Central Asian gas	25.0	17.6	1.3	3.1
Orenburg gas		22.3		2.7

* Open cast
Sources: A. Probst, 'Puti razvitiya toplivnogo khozyaistva SSSR', in *Voprosy
Ekonomiki*, No. 6, 1971, p. 52; Ya. Mazover, 'Razmeshchenie toplivodobyvayushchei promyshlennosti', in *Planovoe Khozyaistvo*, No. 11, 1977,
p. 142

It is a pity that no recent estimates of oil-extraction costs seem to be
available, but it is clear that even in the early 1970s Tyumen' oil had
no clear cost advantage over other major Soviet energy sources with a
big potential for long-term expansion. Gas estimates have risen
sharply, and Table 6.6 confirms that the bulk of the escalation in

Table 6.6. *Output-capital ratio (fondootdacha) in the extraction of gas (in m³ per ruble)*

	1970	1971	1972	1973
USSR	163.5	144.4	118.8	97.4
Komi ASSR	143.8	110.0	95.9	66.9
Kuibyshev and Orenburg provinces	44.8	67.2	57.5	30.0
Krasnodar province	136.8	115.0	74.8	54.5
Stavropol' province	228.3	180.6	150.1	115.3
Tyumen' province	117.5	111.1	81.7	63.2
Khar'kov province	260.6	220.1	180.7	150.3
L'vov province	126.5	118.2	99.4	146.7
Ivano-Frankovsk province	116.4	102.1	103.1	85.1
Uzbek SSR	373.2	359.9	296.3	196.6
Turkmen SSR	391.9	325.8	276.1	201.3

Source: G. Z. Khaskin *et al.*, *Osnovnye Fondy Gazovoi Promyshlennosti*, Moscow, Nedra, 1975, p. 40

capital costs occurred in the early 1970s, as gas pioneers began to move north of the permafrost line.

There is plenty of other evidence to support the thesis that capital costs in the pioneer areas of the north and east tend to be very high, whatever the sector involved. Labour productivity on Siberian building sites is only half the Soviet average, projects take 2–3 times as long to complete as in the central regions of the USSR, and actual construction costs of projects constructed on the basis of standard designs exceed planned by 30–40 per cent. Permafrost conditions push up basic construction costs by at least 20 per cent, reduce the life-span of installations and demand maintenance expenditures reaching 50 per cent and more of initial capital costs. Local supplies of building materials are usually inadequate, and have to be supplemented, at high cost in terms of transport, by 'imported'. The level of wages in Siberia is 15–70 per cent higher than in the European part of the USSR, and labour costs in the north are 2–3 times greater than in settled regions.[203] As noted in Chapter 4, *shabashniki* make 2–4 times the wage 'norm' in Western Siberia. Some of these characteristics are partially related to organisational and technological factors to which we shall return later. But clearly capital costs would always tend to be somewhat higher in Siberian than in more normal conditions, short of the technological millenium, quite apart from considerations of infrastructural investment. Probst calculates, on the basis of imputed total costs (*privedennye zatraty*, calculated, presumably, on the basis of the methodology described on p. 106), that c.i.f. costs of Tyumen' gas are roughly double f.o.b. costs over 1,000 kilometres, and treble f.o.b. over 2,000 kilometres.[204] As a result, for example, Komi or Archangel gas is cheaper in Leningrad or Moscow than Tyumen' gas.[205] Piping of oil is much less expensive, but even here transport pushes up costs by 14 per cent when distances of over 2,000 kilometres are involved. (To put this into perspective, the Samotlor oil field is just about 2,000 kilometres from Moscow as the crow flies.) Even more striking are the figures on general infrastructural investment. On average for the oil-bearing regions of Western Siberia 6,000–7,000 rubles' worth of new investment in the non-material sphere (i.e. services, education, housing) is required for each new arrival.[206] In the Middle Ob' area the figure is 20,000 rubles, and in the extreme north of West Siberia around 40,000 rubles.[207] The comparable figure for the central regions of the Soviet Union is 3,000–3,500 rubles.[208]

We do not have an adequate basis for any kind of comprehensive cost-benefit calculation on the development of West Siberia, even on the most simplified assumptions. There is a very real sense, however, in which this is a side issue as far as present purposes are concerned. The decision to go for rapid development of West Siberian power resources was directly related to the power needs of Soviet industry. Given the Soviet determination to maintain a high degree of self-sufficiency in power and fuel, a subject to which we shall return, it was necessary to open up new resources. It is not at all clear, on the basis of our fragmentary data, that Tyumen' oil and gas is marginal (Aganbegyan says that the pay-off period is only about one year),[209] though individual deposits in the Far North may be. Even if it were, however, there would be, given the constraints, nothing in standard allocation theory against its exploitation, except the existence of other, less marginal, unexploited possibilities. Looking round the Soviet Union, the obvious alternative option is Eastern Siberian coal, but in the context of the costliness of transporting coal, particularly low-calory brown coal, such as is found in the unique Kansk-Achinsk field (see Table 6.5), and pending the solution of the problem of transmitting electricity over distances greater than 3,000 kilometres, Eastern Siberia cannot provide solutions to problems of the total Soviet energy balance.[210]

The question of overall conception

Certain key strategic elements in West Siberian development remain less than wholly clarified. As we have seen, basic considerations of transport costs make the 'export'/home consumption balance a most sensitive variable, and there are other factors to complicate the issue. It is only economical to transport gas over long distances as long as the pressure in the seam being exploited remains above a certain level. Low-pressure gas simply needs an impossible number of compression stations. In addition, there are technical limits to the diameter of gas pipelines.[211] Most surprisingly, but most interestingly, a limit is placed on the *number* of pipelines by environmental factors, even in the vast expanses of West Siberia. 'The Siberian taiga and tundra is already criss-crossed by "corridors" of pipelines. Their construction destroys most valuable timber resources, and harms reindeer pastures and hunting grounds. In a word – every new line represents more damage to the fauna and flora. Where is the solution?'[212] The solution, as this author proceeds to point out, is in the development of local processing, particularly of petrochemicals, and Figure 6.4 shows that a good deal is being done in this direction. But it appears that it is considered, at least by scientists, to be inadequate. The possibility of constructing ammonia and methanol plants at Surgut and Sergina has apparently been under examination for some time now, but the projects were until recently still at the stage of *tekhniko-ekonomicheskie obosnovaniya*. Construction of the key Tobol'sk petrochemical combine, due for completion in 1979, effectively ceased in 1978 because Gosstroi USSR and the local planners were unable to settle a fundamental disagreement, involving a factor of nearly two, about required capacity.[213] Even more fundamental, the bulk of energy-intensive developments in the period 1976–80 for the Soviet Union as a whole were west of the Urals.[214]

Clearly these are issues which may only become crucial in the future, as the oil and gas fields attain, and pass, maturity. But a certain lack of long-term perspective planning is suggested, and this suggestion is fully confirmed by other evidence. Two sources from 1967 complain of the lack of any long-term plan of development for West Siberia.[215] In an interview given in 1972 N. Lebedinskii, deputy chairman of Gosplan, referred to a programme that had been worked out for the development of the West Siberian oilfields,[216] but sources from 1975 and 1977 make it quite clear that this programme, however meritorious it may have been *per se*, has been given no organisational identity at all. There seems now to exist a more general Gosplan scheme for the development of the whole region, but it still has gaps, and its figures have been criticised for being 'insufficiently firmly based'. More fundamentally, the scheme still lacks an implementational dimension.[217] Indeed, no kind of special authority charged with coordination of the different sides of West Siberian development exists at all.[218] The Siberian filial of the Academy of Sciences is working out a long-term regional programme entitled 'The oil and gas of Western Siberia', as part of the 'Siberia' complex programme,[219] but this is clearly just a background research project. As far as Far North gas is concerned, there appears to be still no specific developmental scheme of any kind.[220] This has left ample scope for disagreement between Gas Ministry and local gas-men on the optimal sequence of development of Far North gasfields – with the Ministry inevitably being largely concerned with medium-term maximisation of output.[221] Against this background of uncertainty on basic strategic options, and of vacuum at the level of regional planning, we can proceed to look at the organisational problems which have been encountered in the course of the formation of the Tyumen' fuel complex.

Implementational problems

Perhaps the outstanding single issue that has cropped up at the implementation stage is that of transport and communications within the region. In 1967 *Ekonomicheskaya Gazeta* correspondents asked: 'What is the point of the drive on the part of some leaders to force the pace of extraction of oil in the West Siberian basin at any price? Construction of roads to oil sites . . . , cheap methods of transporting oil . . . and other things are forgotten about, and the failure to solve these problems will cost the state a pretty penny!'[222] As late as 1981 the Soviets had still not developed an operational air-cushion vehicle for transport across swamps.[223]

Moving back to 1975, we find another interesting case of interaction of transport and technology problems. The utilisation of special prefabricated building techniques is obviously of crucial importance in the context of unique natural conditions, labour shortages, etc. Introduction of these has, however, been hampered by the inadequacy of facilities to transport the giant 'building blocks'.[224] River transport is the most obvious way to move bulky loads of this kind, and there is certainly no shortage of waterways in the region. But the navigation season is very brief, and utilisation of waterway potential has been hampered by under-development of loading and unloading facilities. It is clear, in fact, that the optimal transport pattern for the region must be based on a well coordinated combination of overland and water transport. Even at the present time, however, such a pattern is far from being realised. At the now relatively old-established Samotlor oil field a highly rationalised transport construction system has, indeed, been developed. 'The idea of production "corridors" was born, and its implementation fully confirmed the estimates of the specialists. Priority was given to the construction of main trunk routes, which pulled in all the small approach roads, communications and installations. Alongside the basic roads were laid gas pipes, pressurised oil pipes, power transmission lines and telephone cables. This kind of communications corridor, not much more than fifty metres wide, is always accessible for repair work, and incurs sharply reduced running costs.'[225]

In the more northerly, pioneering areas, however, the situation is much less satisfactory. 'The lagging behind of transport construction in relation to rates of construction of oil and gas wells creates a situation whereby oil-men, geologists and gas-men have to build up huge reserves of materials. It is not unusual for equipment to arrive in Tyumen' in the autumn, and reach the northern areas only the following spring. But its journey does not end even there. Having been taken by water to the port nearest its destination, it has to wait for the winter, so that it can be taken over frozen bogland to the assembly point.'[226]

Turning to the current focal point of gas development in the Far North – Urengoi – a 1977 report noted that:

the most important issue in the current stage in the development of North Tyumen' is the absence of a reliable transport network. Last year it was planned that materials and equipment for the Urengoi deposit should be taken down the river Pur during the navigation season and unloaded at the Urengoi settlement. From there it was to be taken by *zimnik* [temporary winter road built over frozen bog, lake, river, etc.] to the main development base – the Yagel' settlement. But the Pur unexpectedly became shallower, and the barges had to turn back to Nadym . . . the loading/unloading service . . . was not coping well. This is not surprising – there is still no river port in the town . . . The Tyumen' gas-men made an attempt to solve the problem – so crucial for the whole new fuel complex. On their instructions . . . designs were done for mooring berths with loading bases at Labytnangi and Nadym. However, the organ of *ekspertiza* of the USSR Ministry for the Gas Industry cut this out of the *titul'nyi spisok* for construction . . . The first commercial train departure from Surgut to Urengoi will reach the north – despite great efforts on the part of the builders – only in 1980. But the first deliveries of commercial gas from this deposit are supposed to reach consumers as early as next year [i.e. 1978]. In trying to 'economise' on the construction of mooring berths, the Gas Ministry has put its own extraction organisations in a most difficult position . . . The RSFSR River Transport Ministry is still unprepared for the growing volume of work on the northern rivers. For some reason they do everything to avoid even deliveries of goods via the Pur to the Urengoi settlement. The ministry has simply refused to have anything to do with the transport, by tanker, of methanol and diethylene glycol. But without these important chemical agents, necessary for the drying of the gas, there can be no question of working these deposits.

To facilitate the transport of goods from Nadym to Medvezh'e and Urengoi the USSR Ministry for the Construction of Enterprises in the Oil and Gas Industries (Minneftegazstroi) was given the job of extending the local railway line . . . to Yagel'. At the beginning it was planned that the first train should reach Yagel' in the summer of 1977. But Minneftegazstroi did not release a sufficient quantity of rails and other supplies last year, so that the opening of the line has been delayed . . . It took the gas-men four years to convince the USSR Ministry of Transport Construction of the need for a bridge over the Great Kheta. Now the same story is being repeated with the bridge over the Little Kheta . . . The chief of the organ of *ekspertiza* of the USSR Ministry for the Gas Industry, A. Efimova, deleted a bridge across the river Nyda from a design for a service road at the Medvezh'e deposit, on the basis, it would seem, of the idea that in the north winter lasts eight months, and the river can be crossed by ice.[227]

Is this an overdrawn picture? Other reports suggest not. Although the Surgut–Urengoi railway line was named by the XXV Congress of the CPSU as being among 'the most important projects of the five-year period', '. . . the USSR Ministry of Transport and Communications has still not issued an official document sanctioning the construction of the line. The only document issued is a telegram from the minister, B. P. Beshchev, giving permission for preparatory work to proceed . . . In the same telegram the sum of expenditures for 1976 was finally fixed – altogether just 15 million rubles . . .'[228] Since then work on the line has gathered momentum, but has been plagued by a continuous imbalance between track-laying and bridge-building. The latter is, of course, unusually important in North Siberian conditions, and there is one 600 kilometre section of the Surgut–Urengoi line that requires no less than 300 bridges. Pressure on the bridge-builders is so great that in many cases they are building temporary bridges, so that the track-layers can get on. But in the long run this creates more than double work, because it takes twice as long to open up a 'window' in the track and complete a bridge than it would to lay the bridge properly in the first place.[229] It is clear that there are two principal problems lying behind this difficulty. The first is unreliable supply.[230] The other is pressure from the fuel ministries, which want everything to be temporary, and laid as quickly as possible. Only the Transport Ministry, we are told, wants to do the job properly.[231]

It seems, however, that what is involved here is not simply low priority, being the 'poor relation', with consequent supply difficulties and departmentalism. 'A difficult situation has emerged in the Ob' region with respect to the construction of hard-surface roads. The road-builders fulfil their plans. *The trouble is that these plans bear absolutely no relationship to the scale of oil extraction.*'[232] (Emphasis added – D.A.D.) Academician Aganbegyan reports that the decision taken ten years ago by the transport ministries not to refurbish and put back into operation the old Salekhard–Nadym–Urengoi road has cost the USSR at least a milliard rubles.[233] Thus acute problems of internal consistency in current plans conspire with specific instances of neglect of long-term planning to produce a scenario which is only further complicated by the more everyday problems of the Soviet economic system.

A strikingly similar picture emerges when we look at reports on progress in the other main transport sub-sector – pipelines.

This year [1976] the Pavlodar oil-processing factory will go into production . . . The raw materials for it will come via the Omsk–Pavlodar oil pipeline . . . There was a busy start to the current year . . . But suddenly everything came to a standstill.

The first hitch occurred when a telegram arrived over the signature of the chief engineer of Glavvostoktruboprovodstroi [*glavk* in charge of pipeline construction], V. Stepanov, informing the pipe-layers that yet another general contractor – the Chelyabinsk Uralneftegazstroi trust [specialist oil and gas construction organisation], based in Pavlodar – had been detailed to the job. Just when work was in full swing, it was necessary to revamp the organisational structure . . . The gremlins born of the organisational switch have still not been ironed out. When the work was divided up between the trusts by the *glavk*, Uralneftegazstroi . . . ended up a million rubles short. Now the trust is threatening not to do the corresponding volume of building work in value terms, and the *glavk* is showing no haste in examining the problem.

In March a new issue arose. By decision of the Ministry for Construction of Enterprises in the Oil and Gas Industries, men and equipment were to be transferred to Tyumen' *oblast'*. There, it was said, conditions were favourable for work. Later on, all efforts would again be turned onto the Omsk–Pavlodar pipeline, and lost time made up.

The fact that the complex has been planned for operationalisation without the inclusion of a number of important and necessary projects also gives cause for concern. The support base at Omsk . . . is not part of the complex *per se*. Over a period of two years an insignificant volume of work has been done on this project.'[234]

More recently the emphasis has shifted to gas pipelines, mostly in the Far North, and here difficult construction conditions combine with highly demanding targets to produce an apparently almost impossible situation. On the one hand, 'timber causeways [*lezhneviki*], six or seven logs deep, disappear without trace beneath the caterpillars of heavy pipe-laying cranes. Of the total length of the [Ukhta–Rybinsk section of the *Siyaniya Severa*] pipeline, only 15 kilometres could be delivered by helicopters, while 780 kilometres had to be dragged by caterpillar tractors, in twos and threes. Any other form of transport simply sank in the bogs.'[235] In these conditions pipelines tend to 'float', and have to be 'lashed down' with special anchors, or simply set solid in concrete.[236] On the other hand, we are now told that lead-times in pipeline construction will have to be reduced by 3–4 times against *norms*, if planned gas supplies are to be kept up.[237] As with the railways, coordination between different specialised functions is poor, and welders tend to go much faster than trench-diggers and fillers-in.[238] Supply problems are once again cited in explanation of this, and contemporary sources emphasise shortage, or absence, of high technology suitable for Far North conditions. Neither special lorries for carrying the giant pipes nor special diggers for digging the trenches have yet been invented,[239] and there is a particular shortage of high-quality insulating tapes.[240]

A key element in pipeline complexes is that of reservoir capacity. A *Pravda* report from 1975 noted that plans for the construction of reservoirs had not been fulfilled, and that consequently waste materials, like water, were being unnecessarily piped, while some oil wells had had to be shut off.[241] More recent reports once again highlight problems of an organisational nature. Local initiatives to bring into utilisation more advanced techniques and materials in reservoir construction meet with no support from the USSR Ministry for Installation and Special Construction. In particular, the latest technology for building large-scale reservoirs has not been applied.[242] There is no specialised organisation for the construction of reservoirs, though there is a special unit within Glavtyumen'neftegazstroi (specialised construction organisation subordinate to Minneftegazstroi). 'But this is hardly enough. The point is that the actual vessels are fitted by our subcontractor – the Tyumen'neftegazmontazh trust. It is subordinate to Glavgazspetsstroi [*glavk* of Minmontazhspetsstroi responsible for construction of special gas installations] which is located in Moscow. Various kinds of departmentalist hitches are continually arising in the interstices of the technological chain, and it sometimes takes a long time to clear them up.'[243]

Another major implementational issue has been that of utilisation of the two major by-products of oil and gas production – accessory gas and gas condensate. The bulk of the former is still being flared off,[244] not least because the problems of pipeline construction discussed above have affected this sub-sector, if anything, somewhat more emphatically than elsewhere. On the Nizhnevartovsk–Tomsk–Kuzbass pipeline, for example, the seriousness of supply problems suggests some lack of priority, but another major factor in the poor performance of the builders on this project may have been organisational fragmentation. No less than four construction trusts were involved – Nefteprovodmontazh, Tomskgazstroi, Vostokprovodmekhanizatsiya and Uralneftegazstroi.[245] At the ministerial level at least the Gas Ministry and Minn**eftegazstroi, and probably also Minmontazhspetsstroi, must have been involved.

The other major problem in relation to accessory gas has been processing capacity. The construction of the first Nizhnevartovsk gas-processing factory was finished in 1975, two years late,[246] and the second in late 1976 or early 1977. A third was to be completed by November 1977.[247] By 1980 four factories were in operation. Even so, 30 per cent of Samotlor gas is still being wasted.[248] Factories are also being built at Surgut and Pravdinskoe, and the flaring off of accessory gas (or, indeed, gas already partly processed) was to cease finally with the completion of the Tobol'sk petrochemical plant in 1979. We noted earlier the kind of overall planning problems that have afflicted this project, but it is fair to say that the 1979 completion date would in any case have almost certainly been missed. Over the period 1975–77 inclusive the Power Ministry fulfilled just 22 per cent of planned volume of work on the project.[249] Almost predictably, we discover that the plant is being built jointly by a number of ministries – the Ministry for the Oil-refining and Petrochemicals Industry, the Ministry for Industrial Construction, the Ministry for Power, and the Ministry for Transport Construction.[250] A similar picture emerges with respect to the Surgut factory, which appears to have been due for operationalisation in 1980.[251] As of mid-1980 100 million rubles' worth of equipment had been lying around doing nothing for two years. The main problem is quite simply the fact that the project is being handled by the Power Ministry, and it, or at least its subordinate organisation, Zapsibenergostroi (specialist energy project construction organisation) sees the factory as just 'not our kind of project'.[252]

Continuing on the same theme, it appears that up to 1975 there was no specialist design or construction organisation for accessory-gas-processing factories or pipelines. Each project was designed and constructed by a different organisation, and building organisations considered them a bad deal in success-indicator terms. In that year a specialised organisation, Sibneftegazrabotka, was formed, but it is not clear that this has made any substantial difference in relation to the degree of organisational integration in the sub-sector.[253]

The question of the utilisation of gas condensate is acquiring particular importance with the bringing into production of the Urengoi field (operating at one-third eventual capacity in 1980),[254] which is particularly rich in condensate.

It cannot be said that the people in Gosplan do not understand what a miserable share condensate has in the fuel balance of a country which has hundreds of millions of tons of this type of fuel. Not long ago there was a representative meeting, at which the problem of condensate was once again discussed. And once again the question was left open. Why? Complicated? Technically difficult? No one would argue the contrary. But no one is even making any effort to produce accurate estimates of 'costs', and of the relationship between the different kinds of fuel in the general energy balance, or to set institutes and ministers the appropriate assignments, so that they can get on with the practical solution of the problems of condensate.[255]

It seems that there are at present no plans to build a pipeline to bring condensate from Urengoi.[256]

The last major implementational problem that has been evident in West Siberia is one not confined to the oil and gas sectors. Since, however, these sectors play a dominating rôle in the regional economy, particularly in the more northerly parts, we need have no fear in applying facts of industrial life as a whole to the sectors we are particularly interested in. Labour is in very short supply throughout the region – Aganbegyan estimates that hundreds of thousands more workers will be needed in the future.[257] The labour shortage is closely related to a high rate of *tekuchest'* (excessive turnover of personnel) – in the Ob' region 70 people leave for every 100 who arrive.[258] This in turn is intimately connected with problems of infrastructure – especially of housing and amenities. In particular cases, such as that of the Tobol'sk petrochemical combine, reports on progress in this field have been highly favourable.[259] In other cases, and particularly further north, the picture has often been drawn in very dark colours. Taking the case of Nadym, where the plan for residential construction for the period 1971–75 was fulfilled to the extent of only a third, the Ministry for Construction of Enterprises in the Oil and Gas Industries is once again under suspicion, having 'mothballed' the Nadym housing materials and components factory, which should have originally gone into production in 1973, but was subsequently rescheduled for 1978.[260] Gas Ministry administrators have been no less under suspicion in this connection, inasmuch as they presumed that once the Medvezh'e field was operating at full capacity (i.e. as from 1977), the only people left in Nadym would be the gas-installation operators. In fact, Nadym has now become the construction base for the development of the Urengoi field, with a much larger permanent population than originally envisaged.[261] This has been a quite widespread phenomenon throughout the region – in 1979, for example, Raduzhnoe had a population of 40,000, as against 'planned' 15,000.[262] The general problem of lack of strategic planning is clearly in evidence here – elaboration of a general plan of development for Nadym did not begin until 1979[263] – and there are echoes of the fundamental disagreements between Gas Ministry and local gas-men discussed earlier.

Basic materials for house-building etc. are particularly heavy, and in the context of the transport problems discussed earlier it is difficult to see how the infrastructural problem can be solved without the development of a strong local building materials industry. But the attitude of Minneftegazstroi to the Nadym housing materials and components factory is clearly fairly typical of departmental attitudes to supply for residential construction. Timber components are still brought into Surgut, which is in the middle of a forest,[264] and building panels are still largely 'imported' into the regions as a whole.[265] Only in Tomsk *oblast'* has something been done to create an integrated local building materials industry. Clearly the fact that no less than 26 departments are involved in housing construction in Western Siberia must make coordination of supply very difficult.[266]

An adequate level of infrastructural investment would obviously cost a great deal in resources. When Medvezh'e went on full stream in

1977 costs were initially well below plan, for the simple reason that only 50 per cent of planned investments had actually been made. As builders caught up with the other 50 per cent – mainly infrastructural – cost and productivity indicators worsened fairly dramatically.[267] The 1976–80 plan envisaged construction of a million m^3 of housing in Tyumen'. It has been suggested, however, that the *oblast'* needs that amount every year.[268] The alternative 'tour of duty' (*vakhtovyi metod*) approach to manning problems was officially approved at the XXV Congress of the CPSU, but it has been admitted that this is nothing more than an expensive and rather ineffectual *pis aller*,[269] at least as it has been applied. The fact that lack of infrastructure affects base towns as much as 'frontier' posts in Western Siberia means that workers sometimes have to be flown – for two-week work stints – from Kuibyshev, Bashkiria and even Moldavia.[270] Clearly a manpower deficit of hundreds of thousands cannot be made up in this way. The strategic significance of the tour of duty system is surely in terms of *how* you allocate, rather than *whether* you allocate, large volumes of resources to infrastructural investment.

In the light of all this, it hardly needs saying that it is crucially important to economise on labour inputs to the maximum extent in Western Siberia. In fact, this has not been done systematically. As early as 1968, Federenko noted with disapproval that a number of labour-intensive engineering lines had been introduced in Novosibirsk and Omsk.[271] It was estimated in 1972 that fragmentation in auxiliary production and services in Tyumen' *oblast'* increased total labour requirements by 20 per cent.[272] The reasons for this are not hard to discover. 'In the Ob' region everyone still has "their own" . . . It is crucial that in West Siberia the different departments should not sprout "own" quarries, timber or chemical plants, or mini-factories.'[273] In 1967 there were no less than 37 supply (*snabzhenchesko-sbytovyi*) organisations in Novosibirsk – all subordinate to different departments – and one source estimated that cross-departmental rationalisation of the situation would have freed 163 managerial personnel.[274] There is no need to go into any more detail here – the reader can refer back to case study 4. The key point in the present context is the cost of departmentalism in a situation where the manpower balance is very strained. In principle at least, a proportion of the labour deficit in the oil and gas industries could be made up from within the region.

Analysis

There is little to add by way of conclusion to the earlier discussion of the general issue of the efficiency of the decision to go for rapid development of West Siberian power resources. One point that has emerged again and again from the discussion of implementation problems, however, is that we are dealing with a pioneer project, with an important dimension of technical progress.[275] Accounts of difficulties on Far North projects are testaments to the strength of the human spirit, as well as to the problems of the Soviet economic system. These elements may not affect m-t-p-h efficiency considerations very much, but if there were any doubts about whether the development of the complex does conform to the yardstick, they might point to the long-term planning horizon as the factor that should be turned to for an explanation, though one finds few references to the long term in the source material. We shall come back to this question in the concluding chapter. The putative constraint with respect to Soviet self-sufficiency in energy could be taken to represent the introduction of the strategic factor into the issue. Alternatively, it could simply be seen as a necessary condition for the maintenance of steady economic growth in the context of the political instability of the major oil-producing areas of the world.

The issue of implementation is more complex. A number of the aspects of implementational problems described are 'old hat'. Small-scale, excessively labour-intensive auxiliary establishments relate primarily to Factor C2, as they did in case study 4, while the insensitivity of executive organisations to infrastructural investment, and to the utilisation of by-products, is clearly largely a function of the operation of Factor C3. Departmentalism has had plenty of scope to manifest itself in all its forms, partly because of the weakness of central direction and lack of perspective planning, partly for reasons reminiscent of case study 1. The 'big three' ministries involved – the Ministry for the Gas Industry, the Ministry for the Oil Industry and the Ministry for Construction of Enterprises in the Oil and Gas Industries – have only been interested in fuel and fuel installations, while other organisations pulled in, rather haphazardly and without a clear division of labour, to handle parallel projects, have not had a big enough 'stake' to make energetic involvement worthwhile. But we have to go carefully on the question of infrastructure. It is difficult to see how the neglect of transport – conventional and pipeline – could fail to have fairly immediate internalised effects on the big three and their sub-units. Annual output performance must surely be affected. It emerged from the detailed discussion of the transport problem that plans have sometimes been very badly coordinated, while organisational shifts with little apparent rationale in any terms have also occurred. It seems, then, that a full explanation of these phenomena, and perhaps also of the neglect of accessory gas and condensate, must, as with case 3, include reference to some degree of *bad planning*, or policy error. There is, as we have seen, strong evidence in the West Siberian case of shortcomings in the work of the central planning authorities. Ministerial planning too seems to have left a good deal to be desired, perhaps due partly to the lack of a clearly defined overall framework. It is extraordinary, for instance, that the Oil Ministry actually squashed an organisational initiative emanating from local drilling units which could only have increased the rate of drilling, and hence ultimately of extraction.[276]

7

Investment planning and investment strategy

THE CASE STUDIES: A GENERAL SUMMING UP

Chapter 1 ended with a preliminary admission of the limitations of the essentially static, taxonomical approach which pervades this work. Chapter 6 began with the stated aim of bringing more realism into the treatment, by indicating how different factors may interact. It may have been almost embarrassingly successful in this respect, in that it has shown how in reality different factors can be almost inextricably intertwined. Has the whole 'yardstick' approach, then, proven too simple and too rigid to analyse an immensely complex situation? Certainly a more mathematically-based model would be at once more sophisticated and more flexible. But such a model is beyond the scope of the available information. More important, the really difficult problems centre round issues like externalities, priority and technology, which are by their nature unamenable to quantification. The yardstick approach may not have given us a measuring rod, but it has provided a compass which can help us to find our way through the labyrinth of the Soviet investment sphere. It has helped to narrow down and focus the discussion of efficiency, to highlight the potential complexity of policy, and to provide a basis for explaining difficult cases, like that of Nurek.

Beyond this, certain general points on specific factors have emerged from the case material. The infrequency with which long-term development factors are cited in published materials, even with reference to projects on the scale of West Siberian energy, surely reflects a key paradox in the Soviet system – a system which combines millenialist economic eschatology with an operational emphasis on the short run which pervades organisations from the enterprise level

175

up to that of Gosplan. But this cannot, of course, be the end of the discussion of the long-term, even if it is the end of the discussion of the long-term planning horizon. In relation to the Nurek complex, for example, one cannot help feeling that Tadzhik economic historians writing in the year 2000 may look back on the HES itself, and on the related projects, as the real turning-point in Tadzhik economic development. The fact that there could have been other turning-points, other roads, perhaps much shorter, will by then have been well and truly consigned to the 'dustbin of history'. The same sort of reasoning can be applied to the Bratsk and West Siberian cases. Giant projects 'get things going', whether the motivation is long-term planning horizon, state doctrine or investment good fetishism. To clarify the way in which they do so we have to return to the difficult question of externalities.

The Soviet system is, like most economic systems, comprehensively bad on production externalities, though some aspects of West Siberian development confirm that a higher degree of consciousness of environmental factors is emerging. Historically speaking, the system has surely been extremely good on linkage, though, as we shall argue later on, at least one of our case studies indicates that this is empirically as well as *a priori* an increasingly controversial proposition. What is controversial on any time scale is how effective the Soviet system has been in cashing in on external economies of scale and secondary agglomeration effects. Here the case studies can be of great assistance. The Bratsk case, in particular, helps to highlight and contrast the different elements. It gains, predictably, very low marks on production externalities, and not much better on linkage – excess capacity can provoke forward linkage, but in a command economy the latter must, by definition, be a much weaker force than backward linkage, since producers do not have to sell their goods. This proposition is clearly confirmed by the extent to which Bratsk excess capacity was *not* swiftly taken up. On secondary agglomeration effects, however, Bratsk does much better. However slow the authorities were in providing customers for Bratsk power, the scale of Bratsk permitted customer enterprises to be built on a scale which must have realised significant internal economies of scale. By the same token, as customer enterprises have been completed, as some kind of integrated industrial complex has begun to emerge in Eastern Siberia, so external economies of scale have begun to be reaped, admittedly to a less than maximal extent because of the failure to build up a stable local work force, an element largely related to infrastructural problems, and ultimately to C group factors. In a perverse, and surely very expensive way, the Bratsk complex has ended by even coming up trumps on linkage. The fact that by the time the timber complex and aluminium factory were completed Bratsk energy was already being fully utilised means that a powerful backward linkage effect was set in motion with respect to the Ust'-Ilim HES. Finally, the technology spin-off, which would normally appear as a kind of secondary agglomeration effect, with the experience gained on project A making it possible to lower costs on project B, was partially internalised in the Bratsk case, as Table 6.1 illustrates. It would be interesting to examine the extent to which the Ust'-Ilim HES benefitted from further technology spin-offs. The degree of capital cost escalation on that project cited in Table 3.1 suggests that the spin-off may not have been large.

There are considerable similarities, at least as long as we ignore basic cost indicators, between the Bratsk and Nurek cases. The latter has been characterised by insensitivity to production externalities, albeit not to a dramatic extent, and scores badly on linkage for exactly the same reasons as Bratsk. On the other hand, although the Regar and Yavan plants will not be very low-cost, they will be less high-cost than if limited electricity supplies had constrained the achievement of technically optimal capacity. Perhaps more important, they may themselves create a big enough market for auxiliary services and general equipment to permit local light and medium industry to break out of the vicious circle of smallness, departmental fragmentation and high costs so clearly documented in case study 4. The irrigation spin-off, however little it may change the basic cost-benefit profile of the project as it has developed since 1961, does mean that as of now Nurek provides a link between established specialised agriculture and the new heavy industry which may yet prove crucial to Tadzhik development – as long as the production externality situation does not get out of hand. Finally, one may speculate, though with even less basis than in the Bratsk/Ust'-Ilim case, that the experience of Nurek may help to lower costs on the 3.6 million kW Rogun HES, now under construction 70 km further up the Vakhsh.

The West Siberian case is more difficult to interpret. As usual, production externalities (in this case benefits rather than costs) are largely ignored. But the sheer scale of the undertaking, a scale which, it may be remembered, inclined even the Soviet state to feel that it might need some help from abroad,[1] has ensured that external economies of scale and secondary agglomeration effects have been exploited to a significant extent, though, in consequence of the coordinational problems described in detail in Chapter 6, by no means to a maximal extent. In particular, the neglect of transport has meant the loss of the opportunity to bring the long-term planning horizon back into the medium term (see discussion in Chapter 1, pp. 5–6). But it is when we turn to the linkage effect that the special features of the West Siberian case emerge.

It is a pity that none of our case studies give a good instance of backward linkage on a large scale – in this respect the sample is bad, basically because hydro-electric projects, which, once built, by their nature make few demands on the rest of the economy, have such disproportionate representation. But if we think, for example, of the way in which the development of Urals metallurgy spurred on the development of West Siberian coal, in the context of the Urals–Kuzbass combine, and subsequently that of Karaganda coal, we can perceive how very important backward linkage may be. Equally interestingly, when we think of the development of Kuzbass metallurgy, and more recently of Karaganda metallurgy (see discussion of case study 2), we can see how, in a situation where sectors widely disparate in technology have the closest input-output ties, forward linkage may be powerful even in a command economy, and appropriate government policies may go a considerable way towards actually *integrating* the two directions of linkage. In a word, Urals–Kuzbass in all its ramifications was very much a *leading* project, within the context of the overriding priority given in the 1930s and 1940s to the development of the heavy industrial complex. The key feature of West Siberian energy development is that, for all its gigantic scale and pioneering character, it is essentially a *following* development. The Soviet Union is, given the constraints discussed earlier, *short* of fuel, like the rest of the world. Indeed had the world fuel price revolution occurred a few years earlier, which it easily could have, plans for the development of Tyumen' would have looked very much like the classical response to a change in the relationship between supply and demand! Thus the aim was not to set the economy on a new growth and development path so much as to provide the energy base for maintaining an existing one. As noted in Table 6.4, however, production plans in Tyumen' have often remained underfulfilled. It is for this reason that I am reluctant to ascribe positive linkage effects to the various elements of discoordination which have been present in the West Siberian case. No doubt in twenty years time the West Siberian economy will be well and truly on its feet, largely owing to contemporary developments, but anything which reduces the potential flow of energy to Soviet industry, agriculture, etc. must have a direct and seriously deleterious effect on overall economic growth. This must surely swamp any positive effects that do exist. It seems not unreasonable to suggest that in this respect the Tyumen' case can be taken to represent a general tendency affecting the whole Soviet economy, as that economy becomes more sophisticated, and is increasingly faced with 'conventional' scarcity problems.

As with the big dams, the question of technological spin-off is an awkward one in relation to Western Siberia. That difficult problems of Far North technology are being solved every day in Tyumen' is beyond dispute. That the Soviet pioneers will have to move ever east and north in their search for new energy sources is fairly certain. But it has to be said that to some extent the heroic inventiveness of the pioneers is only brought into play because of problems of equipment and general supply which ought to be solved at Moscow level. In other words, we cannot assume that every piece of on-the-spot ingenuity represents a real 'bonus' on top of what would be included within a normal 'X-efficiency' definition. Finally, we must reckon with the possibility that each new Siberian energy complex will present many quite new and possibly unique problems of technology. After all, the greatest riches of Eastern Siberia are in the form of coal.

On the difficult question of investment good fetishism and the Nurek case, the reader may well feel dissatisfied with the essentially negative nature of the evidence, and in particular the shortage of highly suggestive circumstantial evidence. Given the basic methodological problem posed by investment good fetishism, as discussed in Chapter 1, it may not be out of place here to adduce a body of circumstantial evidence on another 'grand' project, the Concorde supersonic airliner, which, to my eyes at least, could almost, *mutatis mutandis*, cover the Nurek project.

. . . 'Concorde began as a dream among the boffins of Farnborough . . . The project gathered momentum and adherents as . . . enthusiasm spread to key civil servants. Dissent within Farnborough itself . . . was suppressed . . . The 1959 report of the technical studies . . . was presented with such enthusiasm that the difficulties were minimised.' A lobby was formed which '. . . faked the first, ludicrously low, cost estimates to get them past the politicians [and] excluded the Treasury from the scrutiny of the early research and development costs'.

In 1962 the Mills Committee appointed to assess the project went away from its meeting 'believing that all the technical problems of building . . . were already solved'. When realistic estimates for the project were required by the Treasury, it faced the typical kind of information problem in such situations:

'The Treasury, of course, had no aviation expertise of its own. It could only cross-examine the experts from the Ministry. The guts of the costings were done largely by the enthusiasts at Farnborough and their ex-colleagues now promoting the project in the Ministry.'

Step by step, the project was pushed through until recently it attained its well-deserved *technical* glory.[2]

Turning to implementational questions, the strength of C group factors is one of the things that emerges very strongly from the case material, not just in the Tadzhik engineering case, which could be said to be to some extent a 'set-up job', but equally in those of Bratsk and West Siberia. The modes of operation of intermediate bodies in particular have been shown to have most far-reaching effects, in terms not only of coordinational problems, but also of whole patterns of location. Soviet industrial ministries, *glavki, ob"edineniya*, etc. seem to go through the world ignoring external costs, insensitive to the exploitation of external benefits, bent only on their own aggrandisement and the material welfare of the men who run them. In other words, they seem to bear a remarkable similarity to many western business organisations. But it is very dangerous to press this analogy too far. The economic milieux of East and West remain totally different, and indeed one of the main distortive tendencies evinced by Soviet intermediate bodies, namely that towards organisational autarky, exists on a much smaller scale, if at all, in the West,[3] while any tendency to overbid for resources is constrained in the West by interest rates which may, admittedly, often be below equilibrium level. The key characteristic of Factors C1 and C2 is that they reflect what is basically a *defensive* syndrome. In the context of the perennial weaknesses of the Soviet supply system and success-indicator régime, no individual or organisation can survive without indulging in these practices. That they seriously distort investment patterns is indupitable. But these distortions are *ultimately* a function of the economic system as a whole, rather than of intermediate bodies, viewed as autonomous institutions. Less obviously than in the case of design organisations and building enterprises, intermediate bodies are anything but autonomous. But they are key *foci* of generalised tendencies and problems.

Both Chapters 3 and 4 ended with caveats on the degree of weight that Factors D and E should reasonably be expected to bear. The case studies confirm the picture of design and construction organisations, particularly the latter, being continually in the middle of the trouble, but often in a fairly helpless way. This generalisation should not, however, be pushed too far. One might argue, for instance, about the precise degree to which design organisations have been responsible for the problems of the Karaganda coal mines, but that they have played a major rôle is undeniable, even if there has been pressure from above. The really interesting general conclusion that emerges from all the material on design and construction organisations is that, once one gets beyond the basic, success-indicator/incentive-system-induced problems, everything tends to boil down ultimately to an *inadequate flow of resources into these sectors*. Is this just another form of tautness? Surely not. The tautness emanating from other dimensions of the economy often makes itself felt in design and construction, but when the push is on there is no question of resource mobilisation on a grand scale, as required by the classical priority principle. On the contrary, mobilisation in construction is often carried out on a shoe-string of vodka. As we shall see in the Appendix, not even projects with a big hard-currency element are immune from 'resource deprivation'. The obvious implication is that *high priority is not attached to the implementation of investment plans*. To such an extent does this proposition conflict with accepted ideas about the Soviet system (see discussion of the priority principle on pp. 13–14), that we must pause to try to dissect it as much as possible.

PRIORITY AND THE DESIGN AND CONSTRUCTION SECTORS

First of all, it would be dangerous to under-emphasise the importance of historico-sociological factors, particularly in relationship to the question of human resources. Evidence of a strong tendency for construction labour to come from the least socialised groups among Soviet society, and for lack of amenities on and around building sites to desocialise them even more, was cited in Chapter 4. Reference to Chapter 6, particularly to the section on Bratsk, will confirm just how poor living conditions may be even on top priority projects which are going well. If the generality of this point needs further underlining, note that workers on the BAM (Baikal–Amur) railway-line in Eastern Siberia were living in tents in 1974.[4] There is no comparable direct evidence on design workers, and one would be very surprised if they were not, on the whole, fairly sober citizens. But the material on 'petty tutelage', while no doubt partly simply reflecting a generalised aspect of Soviet reality, creates some *a priori* case that the quality of design manpower may not be of the highest. One possible historic explanation of this would be based on a consideration of the special conditions prevailing in the 1930s. General shortage of trained manpower, combined with the overwhelming emphasis on production *per se* which characterised the early stages of the industrialisation drive, may have produced a situation whereby only the most dispensable elements in the non-manual work force were considered worth 'wasting' on design. These elements might well have been the lower end of the old 'bourgeois specialist' spectrum, and this would provide a concrete political reason for a high initial level of petty tutelage. Thereafter, low esteem and little scope for creative work could have produced a vicious circle powerful enough to survive into the post-war period. However, this is all speculation – it is unfortunate that there appears to be, for design workers, none of the kind of journalistic sociology which puts flesh onto so many Soviet types, including that of the building worker.

But the design and construction sectors have been starved not just of human resources. Paint brushes have presented problems as often as has photo-copying equipment, and it is the *material* supply situation which is surely the key indicator as far as relative priorities are concerned. The Soviet system still places primary emphasis on production at the success-indicator level if not, perhaps, so much at the policy level, so that it is possible to generalise, and maybe 'dehistoricise' the speculative hypothesis just advanced in relation to design workers. Design organisations still do not contribute to aggregate or sectoral output indices, whatever their success-indicators, be they on *khozraschet* or no.

This argument cannot possibly, however, be extended to construction, which produces gross output, irrespective of final use, as effectively as any other sector. (For what it is worth, construction made a consistently greater, albeit only marginally so, contribution to gross social product – i.e. total transactions – than to net material product up to around 1971. Since then the relationship between the two series has been reversed, though the differences are still marginal.)

Why, then, has construction tended to be *de facto* non-priority? It is surely clear from the material presented in earlier chapters that the most important single reason – and it is an *ex ante* reason – why construction organisations have been starved of resources is, paradoxically enough, that executive bodies have felt their services to be so crucial that the purveyance of the same could not be left to the vagaries of the Soviet economic system at large. Departmentalism in its most general form has provided scope for fragmentation, while Factor C2, the tendency to organisational autarky, has virtually required it. As noted earlier, even ministries are far from all-powerful, and they have to pursue their autarkical ends by any means available to them. However successful they are in net overbidding for resources, however adroit in switching below-limit investment funds into auxiliary developments, however shameless in using 'reconstruction' as a cover-up for new construction, they are presented with ultimate resource constraints – after all Soviet planning is, even now, fairly taut – and rather strict constraints in terms of the locational pattern of existing enterprises. The general implications of this latter point in terms of transport patterns were discussed in Chapter 2, but in the specific case of construction – or indeed in that of construction materials – technological factors limit the scope for highly transport-intensive location patterns, just as they limit the scope for informal transformation of production profiles. You cannot turn a canning factory into a quarry in the way you can turn a machine-tool plant into a cable factory! Thus ministry X will not in this case switch around the production profiles and customer/supply patterns of peripheral enterprises, in the manner exemplified in case study 4, but will rather try to pick up, or even create, on the in-house basis, small construction organisations in areas where large-scale main-activity investment is going on. But the organisational-locational constraint – which affects other ministries as well as X – means that such organisations may be peculiarly ill-equipped. It is not difficult to see how this tendency may affect pioneer areas with particular severity, especially in cases like Western Siberia, where development has been very rapid, and has been largely the province of three major, specialised ministries.

Can any of the above reasoning be applied to design organisations? Because they do not produce output as such, their physical location is not very important, and is presumably not considered very important by central and intermediate planners alike. There would appear, then, to be no *a priori* reason why each ministry should not build up a fairly rationalised network of *proektnye organizatsii*. This has emphatically not been the case, however, and a number of cases where particular projects have been covered by a multitude of design organisations have been cited. Such unsystematic fragmentation may have, in part, a historical explanation. There never was a Ministry of Design, as there have always been ministries, or *glavki*, of construction, so that unsystematic fragmentation may have emerged, fully armed from the head of Zeus, in the *beginning*, i.e. around 1930. Design may have *remained* fragmented because no one thought it was important enough to try to rationalise – in Chapter 2 we cited attempts, or at least aspirations, to rationalise construction, if only at a departmental level: no corresponding material touching on the design sector has come to hand. Regional governmental bodies seem to have retained a much bigger stake in design than they have in most sectors relating to the material sphere, which could clearly be a factor in cases of overlapping competences. But this may not be correctly presented as an independent factor. In general, where they have felt their key interests to be at stake, the ministries have been very successful in 'imperialistic' ventures against other authorities. They may simply not have been sufficiently interested in design organisations, or in certain categories of design organisations.

We are, then, suggesting, or rather repeating the suggestion, that neglect of the design sector may have been a fairly straightforward case of genuine non-priority – odd at first sight, but not so much when one considers the intensity of the gross-output orientation of the Soviet system, particularly in the past. It is construction itself that is more interesting, with *de facto* non-priority, particularly in terms of supply, emerging as a result of complex tendencies on the part of executive bodies reflecting the very importance attached to construction organisations.

EFFICIENCY AND EFFECTIVENESS IN SOVIET INVESTMENT

Having established, then, that implementation of investment plans has indeed tended to be *ex post* non-priority, and given the well documented tendency for 'efficiency' in its most general sense to be at a much higher level in priority sectors than in non-priority sectors in the Soviet Union,[5] we clearly come up against the question of the overall 'efficiency' of investment. To be more specific, it is relevant to ask what sort of returns accrue to investment in the Soviet Union in terms of national income, ignoring completely the whole issue of whether maximisation of the national income is the only policy aim, taking the existing price system as given, etc. This concept of efficiency is essentially dynamic and macro-economic, and is clearly very far removed from that which has been employed throughout this work, so to avoid any possibility of confusion I intend to use the Soviet term 'effectiveness' (*effektivnost'*) to cover it. Now there are all sorts of problems in trying to measure effectiveness. Though sanctioned by UN usage,[6] the incremental capital-output ratio is an indicator that must be used with the greatest care. Quite apart from the question of lags – a key issue in the Soviet context, given the tendency to excessive gestation periods – there is the fundamental problem of the extent to which growth should be imputed to investment.[7] It is for this reason that I have contented myself with an approach of studied crudity. Investment ratios for respectively the Soviet Union and a group of high-growth western countries are presented in Tables 7.1 and 7.2.

Table 7.1. *The Soviet investment ratio*

	Gross fixed investment as percentage of NMP	Total operationalisations as percentage of NMP	Net fixed investment as percentage of NMP
1965	28.9	26.5	14.4
1966	28.7	26.1	14.3
1967	28.6	26.3	14.1
1968	28.5	25.0	13.9
1969	28.1	25.8	15.3
1970	28.7	27.2	17.7
1971	29.2	27.4	17.6
1972	30.1	27.3	17.6
1973	28.8	27.5	17.8
1974	29.3	27.4	17.5
1975	30.6	28.6	16.9

Note: The basic figures for the first two columns are in constant prices of 1969, and for the last column in current prices. Net investment is defined exclusive of change in unfinished construction
Source: Various editions of *Narodnoe Khozyaistvo SSR*

Table 7.2. Gross fixed capital formation as percentage of GDP in high-growth western countries (based on data in constant prices)

	1965	1966	1967	1968	1969	1970	1971	1972	1973	1974	1975
West Germany	26.7	26.2	24.1	24.2	25.1	26.4	26.8	26.6	25.5	23.3	23.0
Austria	27.2	28.1	27.6	27.5	26.1	27.2	29.0	30.8	30.0	29.0	28.0
Canada	23.0	23.8	22.9	21.8	21.7	21.2	21.6	21.6	22.3	22.9	23.3
Finland	27.5	27.6	26.0	24.5	24.8	25.8	26.1	26.0	25.7	25.7	25.2
Japan	28.4	28.8	30.2	32.5	34.3	35.1	35.7	36.2	37.2	34.0	32.1
Belgium	22.8	23.7	23.4	22.1	21.9	22.4	21.1	20.8	21.0	21.5	21.3
Italy	20.0	19.7	20.5	21.4	21.8	21.3	20.3	19.7	20.1	20.1	20.3
France						24.2	24.5	24.9	25.0	24.8	23.2
Norway						26.8	30.5	27.9	30.9	31.9	32.2
Netherlands					25.0	25.7	25.4	23.6	23.9	22.1	21.4
Australia	28.1	26.8	27.3	27.0	26.6	26.6	26.1	24.6	24.6	23.9	23.7

Note: All the countries included in the table exhibited annual rates of growth of GDP of 4.0–5.5% over the period 1965–75, with the exception of Japan, where the growth rate was around 8.5%, and of West Germany, where the rate for the decade as a whole was some 3.2%. This last figure, however, is distorted by one or two very bad years – the figure for the period 1965–73 is 4.4%, and that for 1967–73 5.4%. Figures for France and Norway for 1965–69, and for the Netherlands for 1965–67, are not given because of comparability problems relating to changes in price bases in official statistics

Source: UN and OECD statistics

Conclusions can be drawn from these about the extent to which high growth rates have been *accompanied* by high investment ratios, without any involvement in vexed questions of precise causality. But before drawing any conclusions, it is necessary to discuss the series presented, and the manifold methodological problems which limit their usefulness.

It is in principle quite indefensible to calculate *gross* investment (GI) as a proportion of *net* material product (NMP), whether Soviet depreciation allowances are at an adequate level or not.[8] But there is no official Soviet series for gross material product (GMP), and it is for this reason that in official publications, notably UN publications, the GI/NMP ratio is presented as 'the Soviet investment ratio'. The GI/GMP ratio would clearly be lower than the one presented in the first column of Table 7.1. The GI/GNP ratio would be even lower, since 'material product' excludes the so-called 'unproductive' or 'non-material' sphere.

But these elements have to be netted out against the effect of the Soviet practice of underpricing capital goods. In earlier years this factor would surely have swamped the others. For the more recent period, however, it is by no means clear that this is the case. Following on the general price reform of 1967, the proportion of investment made on the basis of own funds is now above the industrial average for most engineering sub-sectors (see Table 2.1), and this must reflect relatively high price levels for engineering products. A CIA research team has estimated that the rate of 'pure' inflation in Soviet machinery prices was about 2 per cent per annum 1955–78.[9] Construction output may still tend to be undervalued, but the price distortion factor is clearly no longer of dominant importance. (Note that the gross investment ratios presented in Table 7.1 are based on data in 1969 prices.)

There has been some controversy recently about the extent to which price-index peculiarities may distort the calculation of Soviet investment ratios.[10] In principle the gross investment figures are in constant prices, while those for NMP are in current (annual data for national income in constant prices is not systematically published). A detailed consideration of the vexed question of the general degree of concealed inflation present in the Soviet economy would take us too far afield, but the implication would appear to be that the gross investment ratios, as calculated, must represent some element of understatement in relation to putative ratios calculated on a wholly consistent price-index base. In fact, however, the constant prices of the gross investment series are, more precisely, 'constant estimate prices', under which rubric many machinery elements go in at current prices, though the great bulk of buildings elements are indeed valued at constant prices.[11] Given the inflationary trend in Soviet machinery prices, this must mean some inflationary bias in the gross investment series. On the basis of the CIA investigation quoted above, however, and given the roughly 40/60 proportion that has been normal between equipment and construction components in investment, that bias amounts to less than 1 per cent per annum. On balance the indications are that price-index inconsistencies distort the gross investment ratio downwards, but only to a minor extent. Cost hikes which are officially recognised by the authorities prior to completion are included in the constant estimate price data. Some cost escalations occurring at the actual construction stage may never be so recognised. The macro-economic implications of this are not straightforward, but they could strengthen the tendency for the price-index factor to distort the investment ratio downwards.

Taking all these factors into account, then, and as long as we stick to the recent period, there seems to be no reason to believe that the 'official' series for the Soviet investment ratio systematically understates the ratio as it would be on the basis of conventional western methodology. If anything, indeed, it may tend to overstate it. The best-known western recalculation puts Soviet gross fixed investment at 26.0 per cent of gross national product in 1965 and 28.4 per cent in 1974.[12] But the Soviet and western series are still not directly comparable, and the margin of error may be as great as a number of percentage points in either direction. What we can surely do with impunity is to compare investment ratios in terms of 'high', 'medium' or 'low'. If this seems somewhat too approximate, it should be remembered that problems of price and quality comparability can also make the margin of error on annual growth rates of national income rather large. The median growth rate for the countries included in Table 7.2 is around 4.5 per cent for the period covered, as compared with a corresponding Soviet figure, in terms of NMP, of 6.7 per cent. I would be inclined to suggest that, taking the quality factor into account, 4.5 per cent in a western market economy is well worth 6.5 per cent in a Soviet-type economy. In so doing, however, I am making it more difficult to demonstrate my argument. The smaller the allowance for quality differences, the stronger become the conclusions that follow, since Soviet investment ratios would have to be downwards adjusted to take account of higher growth rates. Price distortions could influence growth rates in either direction, but it seems reasonable to argue that, at least in the post-price-reform period, such distortions could not have been of major importance by themselves.

The clear conclusion that emerges from Tables 7.1 and 7.2 is that in the majority of this group of fast-growing western economies investment ratios appear to have been on about the same dimension as in the Soviet case, i.e. 'high' rather than 'medium' or 'low'. In the Japanese case the investment ratio appears, at least for some years, to have been significantly higher than the Soviet. But then the Japanese growth rate was consistently and significantly above that of any of the other countries, including the Soviet Union, throughout the period. France is certainly a borderline case, and the situation has been rather unstable in the case of the Netherlands, though it should be noted that the trend for the investment ratio for this country to drop in the 1970s has been paralleled by a dropping off in the growth rate. The comparatively low rates exhibited by West Germany and Australia 1974–75 correspond to around zero growth rates, and should probably be ignored. But there are countries which do not 'fit', and they are, indeed, as interesting as those that do. The fact that Canada gets away with spending significantly less than average on investment may be related to technological and geographical factors – in short, to 'North-Americanness' – but this will hardly do as an explanation for the Belgian case. And what about Italy – hardly the most efficient of the western economies? Even in these three cases, however, we are clearly presented with 'medium' rather than 'low' investment ratios. The conclusion that can legitimately be drawn from the statistics in Tables 7.1 and 7.2 is, then, a very general one, though it is quite 'strong' enough for present purposes; it has been the rule for fast-growing western economies to exhibit 'high' investment rates just as has been the case in the Soviet Union. Despite strong elements of implementational inefficiency, despite uncertain resource flows into the implementational process, despite the presence of policy elements not conducive to medium-term growth maximisation, there is little basis for arguing, at this very general level, that investment in the Soviet Union has been markedly ineffective in the context of high rates of growth by comparison with high-growth situations in western economies.

But how should this evidence be interpreted? Is, perhaps, the point simply that the investment process in the West is just as ineffectively implemented as in the Soviet Union? This is not a study of investment in the West, and there is, indeed, a lack of literature concentrating on implementational aspects of fixed capital formation in market economies. Certainly cost escalation and storming are not unknown in construction in western countries, particularly where government contracts are involved. But the problems of Soviet design and construction, and the distortive penchants of intermediate planning bodies, have been shown to be very clearly related to unique elements in the Soviet economic system, and the implementational process must be significantly less X-efficient in the USSR than, under normal conditions, in the West – the comparative figures on lead-times quoted on p. 36 surely confirm this. Specifically Soviet problems of X-efficiency have, furthermore, contributed to specifically Soviet problems of allocative efficiency. In 1977 only 39.2 per cent of Soviet investment in manufacturing, US definition, went into equipment, with 60.8 per cent going into buildings. For the United States the corresponding figures were 60.2 per cent and 39.4 per cent.[13] The predominant orientation of design and construction organisations to forms of gross output has clearly been a major factor here. Have there, perhaps, been other elements in the Soviet economic situation, possibly quite extraneous to the investment sphere as such, which give the Soviet system a plus on allocative efficiency to be netted out against these minuses? This brings us back to the whole issue of growth strategy, linkage, externalities, etc. To consider this issue in its most general form would clearly be beyond the scope of this work. If we are to throw further light on it while staying within the province of investment, we must proceed to a consideration of the structural pattern of investment.

Once again, the statistical problems are immense. Quite apart from price factors, there are differences in definitions of sectors between East and West which do, in some cases, make meaningful comparison on the basis of official data impossible.[14] In addition, it is often very difficult to find detailed figures on investment by sub-sectors of manufacturing for western countries. In comparing the figures presented in Tables 7.3 and 7.4, then, we can draw legitimate conclusions on the basis of only the most clearly delineated tendencies. Fortunately, there are a number of these. The most telling contrast emerges from a comparison of the figures for Soviet industry and

Table 7.3. *Percentage distribution by sector of gross investment in the Soviet Union (based on data in constant prices)*

	1950	1960	1965	1970	1975
Agriculture	15.0	14.1	16.7	17.2	20.4
Transport	12.2	9.4	9.7	9.5	11.2
Housing	18.3	22.5	16.9	16.4	14.2
Construction	2.6	2.8	2.6	3.7	3.8
Industry	38.2	35.0	37.1	36.0	35.6
of which:					
Electricity	3.4	4.0	4.5	4.1	3.3
Fuel	11.7	6.4	7.4	6.4	6.6
Ferrous metallurgy	4.2	3.3	3.3	2.6	2.6
Engineering	5.8	4.9	5.7	7.6	8.7
Other	13.7	16.2	17.0	17.2	14.8
Total	100.0	100.0	100.0	100.0	100.0

Sources: Various editions of *Narodnoe Khozyaistvo SSSR*

'industry' (for definition see note to Table 7.4) in western countries. There are only two out of sixteen 'observations' in the relevant row of Table 7.4 which do not show a significantly lower proportion of investment than for any of the years given for the Soviet Union. Noteworthy also is the particularly high figure for the Soviet Union in 1950 – a year in which 60 per cent of the Soviet population was still living in the countryside! It is surely reasonable to propose that the scope for exploitation of external economies of scale and secondary agglomeration effects is greater in industry than in any other major economic sector. The same may be true with respect to linkage – certainly the input-ouput ramifications of industrial production tend to be much more complex than those of trade and distribution or, say, an agriculture of the more traditional type. Housing, a sector where externality and linkage effects must be very weak, and where indeed there may be no *immediate* effects on productivity at all, has tended to receive proportionately less investment than in fast-growing western economies, though the difference appears, perhaps, less striking than we would expect. For earlier years, indeed, it is not clear that the generalisation can be sustained, and the figure for the Soviet Union for 1960 is really rather extraordinary. It is most interesting that the 'neglected' Soviet construction sector appears to have taken a larger share of investment resources than in the majority of fast-growing western economies, and to an increasing extent in recent years. We

Table 7.4. *Percentage distribution by sector of gross investment in selected western countries (total for each country = 100)*

	West Germany 1970	West Germany 1974	Canada 1970	Canada 1974	Finland 1970	Finland 1974	Japan 1971	Japan 1974	Belgium 1970	Belgium 1974	Italy 1970	Italy 1973	Norway 1970	Norway 1974	Netherlands 1970	Netherlands 1974	Australia 1970
Agriculture	3.1	2.7	5.1	6.7	8.1	6.8	4.8	5.1	2.6	2.7	6.5	6.3	7.0	6.3	4.0	5.2	4.8
Transport	8.4	8.8	16.2	15.2	17.6	15.7	5.4	3.9	9.5	11.2	8.7	10.9	20.5	13.7	8.9	9.9	9.4
Housing	18.9	20.4	19.4	23.2	22.4	24.3	20.7	22.8	25.0	25.8	28.7	25.6	19.6	16.5	20.5	22.7	18.6
Construction	2.9	1.8	1.5	1.5	2.3	2.2	2.6	2.3	3.0	2.2	1.3	1.1	2.0	1.8	2.1		1.5
Electricity, gas & water	4.6	6.4	9.7	8.8	4.8	8.0	4.1	3.9	5.5	4.9	6.2	5.0	8.1	6.1			8.3
Mining & quarrying	0.4	0.5	7.4	6.0	0.5	0.5	0.7	0.6	0.8	0.6 }	} 23.4	} 25.3	2.4	15.0	} 30.4	} 31.9	9.2
Manufacturing	25.0	17.7	17.1	14.5	24.0	22.5	21.3	20.1	25.6	24.6			15.2	15.1			13.7
of which: Metallurgy	2.7	1.6			2.2				5.2	5.2	2.9		3.1		2.2		
Engineering	5.9	4.1			4.4				4.3	4.9	6.1		3.5		8.9		
'Industry'	30.0	24.6	34.2	29.3	29.3	31.0	26.1	24.6	31.9	30.1	29.6	30.3	25.7	36.2	30.4	31.9	31.2
Energy & fuel									6.0	6.3	8.2				8.5		

Note: The list of selected countries is identical to that used in Table 7.2, minus Austria and France, for which countries adequate statistics are not available. The basic data are in constant prices for all countries except Australia, Canada and Japan, where they are in current prices. The 'Industry' row represents a summation of the *Electricity, gas & water, Mining & quarrying,* and *Manufacturing* rows. It is roughly comparable in coverage to the Soviet *Industry* category. The *Energy & fuel* category, available only for EEC countries for some years, is an 'extra', which cuts across the standard UN national accounts methodology. It is given here because it is roughly comparable to the Soviet categories of *Electricity* and *Fuel*, taken together.

Sources: UN and OECD statistics; *Eurostat Yearbook 2–1975*, Statistical Office of the European Community; *Beiträge zur Strukturforschung*, Heft 41, 1976, Deutsches Institut für Wirtschaftsforschung

will return to the question of the efficiency of input utilisation in construction later. At this point it is necessary only to say that all the qualitative evidence denies that this is a reflection of any kind of strategic priority. The high Soviet percentages for agriculture can be taken to reflect, for the earlier years, the still very large share of that sector in total output, rather than a high *rate* of investment. There cannot be the slightest question of agriculture having had any kind of priority in 1950! The particularly high figure for 1975, which corresponds fully to the medium-term trend, requires a somewhat different explanation, but this is another point to which we shall return later.

The figures for key industrial sectors in the selected western countries are incomplete except for some years in just three countries. It is, nevertheless, possible to pin-point certain key contrasts, or non-contrasts. In the case of metallurgy the situation is complicated by the fact that no figures at all have ever been published on Soviet non-ferrous metallurgy, so that it was not possible to present a *metallurgy* row in Table 7.3 for comparison with that in Table 7.4. Even so, the proportion of total Soviet investment going to what was, after all, one of the key priorities in terms of *output* during the industrialisation drive, does appear to have been remarkably small over the last quarter-century. No doubt it was much higher in the 1930s, and certainly a backward extrapolation would give a fairly high figure. But metallurgy has clearly not been an investment priority in the post-war period.

With *engineering* direct comparisons can be made with some impunity. The situation seems to be, in fact, that Soviet engineering has not claimed an especially high proportion of investment resources. Certainly it has recently taken a higher proportion than any other industrial sector, but then it accounts for at least 30 per cent of total industrial output. Once again investment trends seem not to have corresponded closely to output priorities. But the engineering share in investment has been increasing steadily, and stood at a very high level in 1975, albeit no higher than that of engineering in the Netherlands in 1970.

It is, however, when we turn to energy and raw material extraction that a strong contrast really begins to emerge between the high-growth western countries and the Soviet Union. There is no Soviet equivalent of the *Mining and quarrying* category, but, for all high-growth western countries for which figures are available except Australia,

Canada and Norway, rates of investment in this sector have been at an almost negligibly low level. In the Soviet Union *Electricity* and *Fuel*, taken together, have normally accounted for at least 10 per cent of total investment, and for some years the figure is significantly higher. For the selected western countries for which the figure is available, 8.5 per cent is the highest proportion recorded for *Energy and fuel*. A very rough adjustment of *Electricity, gas and water* figures, on the basis of the relationship of those figures to the *Energy and fuel* figures in cases where we have both series, suggests that only Australia, Canada, and possibly latterly Finland, of the countries for which *Energy and fuel* figures are not available, might be in the same bracket as the Soviet Union in this connection. Now the contrasts among the high-growth western countries tell us as clearly as the contrasts between the western countries taken together and the Soviet Union that natural resource endowment has been an important factor here. But at this stage we are concerned with *ex post* rather than *ex ante* analysis, and heavy investment in energy, fuel and raw material production is clearly a key feature of the structure of Soviet investment, whatever the reason for it.

An exhaustive discussion of how fruitful particular industrial branches might be in terms of internal and external economies of scale etc. would involve methodological and informational problems going beyond the scope of the present work. It is, indeed, not absolutely clear that one can meaningfully discuss external economies of scale in terms of individual branches, even at a high level of aggregation. The energy, fuel and raw materials extraction branches offer considerable scope for the exploitation of internal economies of scale, particularly in the Soviet context, as some of our case material has shown. But beyond this rather trite point there is not a great deal that can be said briefly, and with impunity. Much more productive at the level of branch analysis is a discussion of *linkage*. Here there are hard figures to work with, and a small body of literature to illuminate analysis.

In a classic article published in 1958 Chenery and Watanabe calculated, on the basis of input-output tables covering the US, Italian and Japanese economies, coefficients of the ratio of purchased inputs to the value of total production for a given sector (u_j), and the ratio of intermediate to total demand for a given sector (w_i).[15] Following Hirschman and Wilber,[16] we will interpret the former as a coefficient of potential backward linkage, and the latter as a coefficient of potential forward linkage. The sum of the two will give us, on this interpretation, a coefficient of total potential linkage. In the light of the problematic status of forward linkage in a command economy, we will work in terms of total linkage and backward linkage coefficients.

The most striking thing that emerges from the calculations is that ferrous metallurgy comes 'top of the league' on total linkage, out of a field of 24 industrial branches (plus five non-industrial sectors). On backward linkage iron and steel is slightly less impressive, as we would expect, but still manages to come fourth equal. There is, then, no difficulty in pin-pointing ferrous metallurgy as a major engine of economic development in the Soviet case, given its historical high priority in output terms, and if potential linkage can be allowed to be actual in the given context, at least as far as backward linkage is concerned. The problem is the extent to which investment has been a key variable in the development of the branch. Our figures suggest that it has not, but, as already noted, the availability of corresponding figures from the 1930s might change the picture.

Engineering does not show up strongly in terms of either forward or backward linkage in the Chenery and Watanabe calculations, except for transport equipment, the only sub-branch separately listed, which just makes it into 'Division I' (coefficient of more than 60) on backward linkage. Wilber rightly points out that had finished equipment not been construed as final rather than intermediate demand, much higher forward linkage coefficients would have emerged for engineering. Nevertheless, whatever the total linkage coefficient might have been, the backward linkage coefficient is not impressive. In any case, as noted earlier, investment has not been a major factor in the predominant position of engineering within Soviet industry. This key branch, then, helps us little in trying to pin-point elements which may have contributed to the Soviet 'residual', and not at all on the question of how much investment patterns may have contributed to these elements.

Given the evidence adduced in the foregoing paragraphs, it is clearly the energy, fuel and raw material extraction branches that are of greatest interest from the investment point of view. Sure enough, oil products, coal products, metal mining, oil and gas and coal mining all find themselves in 'Division I' on total linkage (combined coefficient of more than 110), with the first two branches occupying respectively fourth and sixth positions. On backward linkage alone, however, they fare less well. As we might expect, oil and coal products more or less hold their positions (sixth and seventh respectively), but the other three branches drop out. Thus the proposition that energy/fuel/raw materials has been a crucial nexus of 'residual creation' in the Soviet case can only be strongly defended on the basis of placing more weight than one might wish on the operationality of forward linkage in a command economy situation. As noted earlier, in connection with the Urals–Kuzbass combine, an argument can be made out that forward linkage might be powerful in the Soviet context in cases where backward linkage effects were in any case powerful. Even this proposition, however, does not seem wholly applicable to energy/fuel/raw materials, where backward linkage coefficients have been for some branches very low indeed. We must, then, leave the question of the interpretation of the effects of the high rate of investment in these primary branches in the Soviet Union in a state of somewhat tantalising irresolution.

In trying to tie in patterns of investment to possible sources of 'residual', we have come to firm conclusions only at the level of industry as a whole. At the branch level industries manifesting strong linkage characteristics have not shown up strongly in terms of shares of total investment, while industries accounting for unusually large shares of investment have not been shown unequivocally to be outstanding in linkage terms. On the other hand, there can be no doubt of the correlation between traditional Soviet production priorities and high linkage coefficients. The point is simply that output trends have not always been closely related to investment trends.

PROSPECTS FOR THE FUTURE

The aim of this work has been essentially to classify and analyse the phenomena of the past, but a little crystal-ball gazing is surely not out of place by way of conclusion, as long as it is not mistaken for systematic prediction. How effective is Soviet investment likely to be in the next decade or so? Clearly policy elements not conducive to medium-term growth maximisation will continue to be important, and indeed the long-term planning horizon may become much more important with the burgeoning development of Siberia and the Far East. The upward trend in the incremental capital-output ratio (ICOR) visible throughout the 1970s (6.1 for 1976–80 as compared to 5.2 for 1971–75 and 3.5 for 1966–70)[17] reflects, *inter alia*, that development. It also reflects a contrast which makes direct East–West comparison of the kind attempted in Tables 7.1 and 7.2 increasingly difficult in the post-oil-crisis world. In the Soviet Union growth rates have dropped, while investment ratios have stayed at about the same level. In most western countries growth rates *and* investment ratios have fallen. There is no evidence that the trends in ICORs reflect any significant intensification of the X-efficiency problems of Soviet investment activity. What they have done, however, is to focus the attention of the Soviet authorities on these problems, as an area where the economy might be able to make up ground lost for other reasons.

The fact is, however, that elements of inefficiency in the implementation of investment projects are unlikely to be excised unless changes of a striking degree of radicalism occur in the planning system. We noted in Chapter 3 that effective reform in the design sector would almost certainly be dependent on a degree of decentralisation within the sector going far beyond anything currently being contemplated. The great difficulties that have been experienced in evolving a new set of indicators for construction organisations suggest a similar, if less emphatic, conclusion. But we saw in Chapter 4 that the really dominant problem in construction is in any case the environment rather than the internal characteristics of the sector, for all the undoubted importance of the success-indicator syndrome. Returning to our remarks made earlier in this chapter *à propos* of the ministries, it is clear that a similar situation prevails with respect to non-specialised executive bodies. The continued development of the *ob"edinenie* may do something to limit and rationalise the kinds of tendencies discussed in Chapter 2, but administrative reshuffles, even on a grand scale, cannot be expected to change the economic milieu fundamentally, as was made amply clear in the case of the *sovnarkhoz* reform. To put the point at its very simplest, as long as there is supply uncertainty in the Soviet Union, the activity patterns of ministries, *glavki*, *ob"edineniya* and building organisations will be systematically distorted in the ways described. The overall conclusion, then, is that elements of inefficiency in the implementation of investment projects could only be eliminated, or reduced in strength to a significant degree, in the context of further *general* reform of the whole planning and management system.

Such a general reform is unlikely to happen in the foreseeable future. Meanwhile the Soviet authorities are bent on pushing vast volumes of investment resources not only into raw-material extraction projects in Siberia, but also into an agriculture which, for fundamental geographical reasons, will surely never, even on the long-term planning horizon, yield high returns (strategic factor again?). So far, then, the future does seem a little bleak for Soviet investment effectiveness. But there are other elements in the situation which must be considered, if only to be discounted.

Firstly, can increasing investment flows into construction be expected materially to alter the situation, even given that they do not solve the general problem of supply? In fact, the level of gross output per unit of fixed assets fell at an annual rate of 3.0 per cent in the period 1966–70, and at a rate of 4.7 per cent in the following five-year period.[18] Clearly, then, and even if the explanation for these figures is partly to be found in very long lags, no great stress ought to be laid on this factor, the more so given the very high coefficient of absolute effectiveness set for construction for 1981–85.

Secondly, given that the energy, fuel and raw materials sectors are likely to bulk even larger in the future than they have in the past, and brushing aside for the moment our doubts about how linkage-orientated these sectors really are, can we expect that positive linkage effects will continue to provide some degree of 'residual'? The big problem here is whether linkage effects can reasonably be expected to be a positive factor in a mature economy. As noted earlier, my own feeling is that they cannot, so that I would largely discount this factor.

There is one point, perhaps a rather academic one, relating to scale and capital intensity, which is rather well exemplified by the Nurek HES. As we saw in Chapter 6, it has been suggested that the long-run tendency may be for the marginal costs of non-hydro energy sources in Central Asia to rise steeply. If this does in fact happen, then Tadzhik hydro potential may look in a few decades time like a very good deal, and not just for Tadzhikistan, especially if transmission technology has in the meantime improved. Once Nurek is completed, there will be no possibility of increasing costs as far as that *tranche* of energy production is concerned. Now this point should certainly not be overstressed. Additional dams built in Tadzhikistan might well have less favourable running cost characteristics (no cost estimates for the Rogun dam have come to hand), and in any case HESs, virtually everlasting and with minimal running costs, are rather unique, and do not play more than a supporting rôle even in the Soviet energy balance. Were this situation to change radically in the future, the point would obviously become much more important.

Most of our case studies have been based on projects to a greater or less extent 'pioneering' in nature, and consideration of possible dynamic spin-offs has brought out the tantalisingly contradictory nature of such projects. Almost by definition, they foster major technological advances, almost by definition they tend to be so unique that these technological advances may find only limited further application. Permafrost technology is, surely, to a considerable extent indivisible, as may be anti-seismic technology. There is probably a good deal that the *world* can learn from, for example, West Siberian experience. But in terms of likely future *national-economic* policies of the Soviet government, we can only wonder whether the storming of each successive energy fortress will ever become even partially a routine matter.

Finally, let us return to the problem raised at the end of Chapter 1 in relation to the central organs involved in investment planning, namely Gosplan and Gosstroi. A picture of these organisations has emerged, often in a negative way, but ultimately rather strongly, in the intervening chapters. Gosstroi appears frequently in an essentially legislative rôle, promulgating building regulations, revising systems of norms, etc. It appears from time to time in a rather ineffectual *kontrol'* rôle. On the few occasions when we have seen it cast in a planning rôle, e.g. in the case of the Tobol'sk petrochemical plant, the picture is very unfavourable indeed. No doubt much good planning by Gosstroi goes unreported and unsung, but there is a suggestion of some basic problem with the way the organisation works. The frequency of reports of Gosstroi getting behind with its legislative work hints strongly that it is overburdened with this sort of thing, and perusal of any issue of *Ekonomika Stroitel'stva* presents graphic evidence of just how fussy much of this work is. But whatever the ultimate reasons, Gosstroi has probably been guilty in a number of the cases of apparently 'unforced' planning error, of *sheer bad planning* that we have come across. The sins of Gosplan may have been more of omission than of commission. It is well known that neglect on the part of Gosplan of long-term matters is often conditioned by the excessive workload imposed by an excessively centralised level of current planning. Lack of implementational teeth may sometimes have induced frustrated Gosplan planners simply to give up. Having said all that, the lack of an effective Gosplan presence in Western Siberia has been rather flabbergasting, and may, as we suggested earlier, have been the ultimate reason for all sorts of planning mistakes committed by ministries, Gosstroi, etc. Surely the quality of Soviet investment planning at the central level could be improved considerably, even outside the context of general changes in the economic system. But this conclusion should not be taken to represent more than a marginal modification of our general conclusion that it is the issue of general economic reform that is the key to the future in the investment sphere.

Appendix

THE IMPORT OF EQUIPMENT FROM HARD-CURRENCY COUNTRIES

'The basic principle of the plan for the import of machinery and equipment is that equipment, machines, instruments and vessels should be purchased on foreign markets only in cases where it is economically more advantageous to buy them abroad than to produce them at home, or when domestic production cannot be organised quickly enough, or in sufficient quantity or quality.'[1] Thus the official Soviet planning manual, and the statement is broad enough to leave a good deal of decision-making scope to the planners responsible. We begin by identifying who those planners are, before going on to assess how far their decisions are disciplined by unified appraisal criteria of the kind discussed in a general context in Chapter 5. We then look at how the actual installation of foreign equipment is organised, ending with some general remarks on how imported equipment fits into the Soviet planning system as a whole.

The loci of decision-making on the purchase of foreign equipment

The planning manual states simply that 'requests to purchase foreign equipment etc. are presented by USSR ministries and departments, and by councils of ministers of union republics, to Gosplan USSR and the Ministry for Foreign Trade, together with the necessary estimates and feasibility studies'.[2] More precisely, an *indent for import* (*zayavka na import*) has to be filled in. On this form the USSR ministry or equivalent is denominated the client (*zakazchik*), and the detailed correspondence is handled by its equipment supply administration (*upravlenie po snabzheniyu oborudovaniem*). A lower-level planning body –

main administration or industrial association – is normally denominated the payer (*platel' shchik*). The enterprise or plant only appears on the form as the addressee of the consignment. Details have to be entered on the technical characteristics of the piece of equipment, including its power consumption and other electrical details, and the implications in terms of spare parts. The main administration/industrial association level has to verify that the piece of equipment 'conforms to the demands of contemporary technology'. The planning manual states that the relevant machine-building ministries have to confirm this, and also verify that similar equipment cannot be provided by domestic industry.[3]

The *zayavka na import* is formally addressed to the appropriate all-union association of the Ministry for Foreign Trade. There are a number of these associations specialising in the import of particular types of equipment. Mashinoimport, for example, imports rolling stock, electrical equipment, equipment for the oil and gas industries, and transporting equipment. Avtopromimport imports sets of equipment for car factories. There is, however, no evidence to suggest that the all-union foreign trade association is an important nexus of decision-taking on what equipment is to be imported. Rather its rôle appears to be restricted to the technical problems of organising consignment.

It is clear that it is the ministry and the relevant main administration/industrial association that are normally the main movers in any initiative to import equipment. The relative importance of Gosplan and the Ministry for Foreign Trade in vetting proposals is not altogether clear. The planning manual does make provision for 'decisions of Party and government' on the purchase of equipment for specific sectors.[4]

Appraisal criteria

Accounting prices of imported machinery are calculated by multiplying the hard-currency price by one of a set of special coefficients. These, however, bear only an approximate relationship to ratios of domestic and foreign prices for comparable pieces of equipment, and are not adjusted in cases where, for example, something has been purchased at a bargain price. They cannot, therefore, be used to assess the 'effectiveness of import'. Feasibility studies of particular imports are, in fact, done on the basis of widely differing methodologies by branch organisations, subordinate in most cases to industrial ministries. An article published in 1975 'by way of formulating the question' puts forward proposals for an integrated set of criteria.[5] These must clearly have had some degree of official blessing, but their precise status is still not clear. The formal expressions of the criteria are as follows:

1 For the assessment of the import of equipment analogous to equipment already produced in the Soviet Union:

By comparison of the price of the piece of imported equipment with the difference between the cost of producing the equipment at home and the cost to the Soviet frontier of the exports required to pay for the imported equipment. This to be based on a careful study of analogous pieces of machinery in each individual case.[6]

2 For the assessment of the import of equipment with no analogue produced in the Soviet Union:

On the basis of the formula

$$R = \frac{\Pi 6.7}{PX + W},$$

where R is the effectiveness of import, Π is annual profit from the output of the equipment, P is the price of the piece of imported equipment plus any associated licences or know-how, X is a 'coefficient of effectiveness of export equivalent', and W is the working capital expenditure associated with the imported equipment.[7] The coefficient 6.7 represents the pay-off period in years corresponding to a 'normal' coefficient of effectiveness for the national economy as a whole of 0.15. The cost of purchase of licences etc. is said to be usually 2–5 per cent of the cost of equipment, and it is recommended that in cases where the former cost is not precisely known, price planners should apply a standard coefficient of 5 per cent to the cost of the equipment.[8] X is defined as the normative difference between the hard-currency earnings of exports and the cost of producing the exported goods – essentially the average rate of profit on exports, presumably by sector.[9] Basically, then, the stream of profits from the piece of imported equipment over the normative pay-off period is compared to the cost of purchase adjusted by a coefficient which expresses the opportunity cost of using that particular tranche of exports to finance that particular foreign purchase. It is recommended that world prices be used in all parts of the calculation, even for domestically produced raw materials.

3 For the assessment of the import of equipment with no analogue produced in the Soviet Union, taking account of (a) the number of years by which the economy gets the equipment quicker than if domestic production had been set up; (b) any delay in installing the equipment:

On the basis of the formula

$$R = \frac{\Pi 6.7 + \Pi T_a}{[PX + W]1.08^{T_b}},$$

where T_a is the number of years gained through using imported equipment, and T_b the number of years lost through any delay in installation. The coefficient 1.08 represents the standard 'norm for differently timed expenditures' (see p. 107 above).[10]

4 A precise formulation is also given for the appraisal of deals involving foreign licences and *domestic* investment:

$$R = \frac{[C_1 - C_2]N6.7}{LX_L + D1.08^{T_b}},$$

where C is the current cost of production (including depreciation – see p. 104 above), and the subscripts $_1$ and $_2$ denote, respectively, production without, and production with, the utilisation of the licence. N is the annual rate of output, L is the price of the licence in foreign-exchange rubles, X_L is the 'coefficient of effectiveness of export equivalent for the hard-currency zone of purchase of licences and patents', and D represents the value of related investments in domestic rubles.[11]

There are a number of obscurities in relation to these formulae. In particular, it is not at all clear precisely how domestic prices are converted into hard-currency prices for items other than machinery. Given that we are also unsure about the precise status of the formulae, they may be best interpreted as simply representing a desire on the part of the Soviet authorities to bring some systematisation into this particular area of foreign trade criteria. There are obvious parallels with the situation relating to general investment criteria, as discussed in Chapter 5.

The installation of foreign equipment
This is primarily the responsibility of the Ministry of Installation and Special Construction. Minmontazhspetsstroi was until recently

organised into 21 Union-wide main administrations.[12] It now seems to be organised into a similar number of all-union 'industrial' associations.[13] Formed in 1966 as successor to a State Production Committee that had been created in 1963, the Ministry's remit is in the fields of specialised electrical, heating and ventilation, and automatic systems installation work.[14] In 1978 in the Tatar autonomous republic 58 per cent of the work of the Ministry related to the installation of technological equipment', 17.2 per cent to 'hydro-technical and special works', and 6.8 per cent to energy construction. The only other construction ministries doing a significant amount of work under any of these three headings were the Energy Ministry and the Ministry for the Construction of Enterprises in the Oil and Gas Industries. But note that 26.3 per cent of the construction work done by non-construction ministries related to the 'installation of technological equipment' category.[15]

At a more general level, it is clear that Minmontazhspetsstroi is organised on the basis of Union-wide *technological*, rather than sectoral specialisation, with a certain amount of regionalisation at the lowest decision-taking instance. Trust No. 7, for example, specialises in the construction of oil-processing plants. When it was instructed to do the installation work on a big plant in the Baltic region it immediately created a Baltic Installation Administration (*montazhnoe upravlenie*). But it also decided to pull in 10–12 of its installation administrations from other regions. These included the Moscow Installation Administration, which specialises in the construction of reservoirs and pipelines, and the First Saratov Installation Administration, which specialises in work with reagents.[16] No doubt installation administrations tend to have their seat in areas which will give them plenty of local work, but it is quite clear that they can be commandeered for any project anywhere in the Soviet Union. An article on the Soyuzteplostroi trust, which specialises in building furnaces, confirms this general picture, but also confirms that proposals have been made for the integration of installation and special construction trusts into big regional production-construction associations (see pp. 74–5 above).[17] Whether this would mean more regionalisation within the structure of Minmontazhspetsstroi, or indeed the abolition of the Ministry altogether, is not clear. But the proposed new arrangement is attacked because it could never guarantee the 'unified technological policy on every kind of specialised work'[18] which is the key principle of Minmontazhspetsstroi work.

Imported equipment and the Soviet planning system as a whole

All of this makes it sound as if the Soviet authorities attach great importance to imported equipment, as a vehicle for technology transfer, and are prepared to devote a good deal of special attention to its organisation. But while this is undoubtedly true in some general sense, we find strong evidence at the level of the particular to suggest that goals relating to imported equipment are not necessarily implemented more efficiently than other plans in the Soviet economy, and that the apparent fully committed priority to the sub-sector may in practice be less than clear-cut.

We noted on p. 90 that the problem of excessively early consignment of equipment can involve imported as well as domestically produced plant. A recent *cause célèbre* revealed a much more dramatic case of wastage of imported machinery, with 36 million rubles' worth of equipment for the oil industry left to rust.[19] Much more than just discoordination in plans was involved here. In 1976 the Oil Ministry was set the task of raising rates of recovery from oil fields (*nefteotdacha plastov*) from their prevalent levels of under 50 per cent. Special funds were set aside for implementing the programme, including finance for the import of equipment. Initially the project was entrusted to a number of administrations within the Ministry, but they could not cope with the new work. Accordingly a special administration for increasing recovery rates was formed. In practice, however, even this approach failed to get off the ground. The new administration was never properly staffed, and it is now admitted that its creation did more harm than good to the organisation of the project. At this stage the responsible deputy minister, E. Khalimov, started to cover up the true state of affairs by fiddling the plan fulfilment reports. Key imported supplies, of which equipment formed only part, were left lying by the roadside, in disused quarries, or even ended up as ballast in the foundations of railway lines.

There was clearly a good deal of sheer incompetence involved here – Khalimov was 'moonlighting' on teaching and editing jobs throughout the period involved, and could not possibly have been paying due attention to his work with the Ministry. But there are also powerful echoes of some of the strategic problems that have affected West Siberian oil and gas development, with ministries, it seems, always reckoning that it is easier to fulfil output targets by opening up new fields than by increasing efficiency on old. This clearly represents a microcosm of the whole extensive/intensive development issue, and suggests a strategic dimension to the question of the efficiency of utilisation of imported machinery. It is not just that plans are often discoordinated, not just that planners are sometimes incompetent or irresponsible. The Soviet planning system is still rather insensitive to costs, and is still strongly inclined to try to get things done through campaigns and priorities. We have quoted a number of examples of investment projects suddenly being deprived of all or part of their basic labour force. Hanson and Hill confirm that this happens quite frequently on projects involving a lot of imported equipment.[20] We discussed on pp. 93–4 the problem of quality in the construction labour force. Though programmed as the crack, high-technology wing of the Soviet construction industry, the Ministry of Installation and Special Construction often has difficulty in finding workers to match this specification – not surprisingly, perhaps, given that it faces the same problems of poor infrastructure and living conditions for its workers as other construction ministries.

None of this is really to suggest that the Soviet authorities care less than they pretend about imported equipment. As we have just noted, they are obviously sufficiently worried about the work of Minmontazhspetsstroi to contemplate a major reorganisation. As we saw on p. 82, the new bonus arrangements for on-time completion provide for a special increment of 25 per cent on top of the basic bonus in cases where large amounts of imported equipment are involved. The problem is that this kind of priority tends to cut across, or even contradict, the more traditional priority on fulfilling short- and medium-term output targets for key industrial products. At the level of intermediate planning body or lower, it is clearly still these latter priorities that ultimately prevail, and that means that in times of stress projects involving imported equipment may be treated as badly, or indeed as well, as any other project.

Glossary

'AKT PRIEMKI' operationalisation certificate.

'BLAT' personal connections as a basis for 'oiling the wheels'.

'BRAK' substandard production, 'rejects'.

CC CPSU Central Committee of the Communist Party of the Soviet Union.

CPSU Communist Party of the Soviet Union.

CRE coefficient of relative effectiveness.

'EDINYI ZAKAZCHIK' 'single client' – term used when local authority takes on the rôle of general contractor for all 'in-house' basis residential construction in its area.

'EKSPERTIZA' design-monitoring organisation.

'GLAVK' (PLURAL 'GLAVKI') 'main administration' – main sub-division of ministry.

'GORISPOLKOM' city government.

'GORKOM' city committee of the CPSU.

GOSBANK State Bank.

GOSPLAN State Planning Commission.

GOSSTROI State Committee for Construction.

GOSUDARSTVENNAYA PRIEMOCHNAYA KOMISSIYA (GPK) State Operationalisation Commission.

'GOTOVAYA STROITEL'NAYA PRODUKTSIYA' finished construction output.

GRES local thermal power-station.

HES hydro-electric station.

ICOR incremental capital-output ratio.

'INDUSTRIYA' term for industry normally used only in a general, historical sense; construction is the only sector ever described as an *industriya*.

'KHOZRASCHET' (ADJ. 'KHOZRASCHETNYI') 'business accounting'.

'KHOZYAISTVENNYI SPOSOB' 'in-house' basis.

'KOMBINAT' (PLURAL 'KOMBINATY') combine, conglomerate.

'KONSTRUKTORSKOE BYURO' (PLURAL 'KONSTRUKTORSKIE BYURO') 'constructor bureau' – specialist organisation designing machines.

'KONTROL'' checking, monitoring.

'KRAI' province.

L-T-P-H long-term planning horizon.

M-T-P-H medium-term planning horizon.

MATERIAL SPHERE the 'productive' (in the Marxian sense) sectors of the economy.

'MESTNICHESTVO' localism.

'METIZ' (PLURAL 'METIZY') general metal goods.

MINMONTAZHSPETSSTROI Ministry of Installation and Special Construction.

MINNEFTEGAZSTROI Ministry for the Construction of Enterprises in the Oil and Gas Industries.

MINPROMSTROI Ministry of Industrial Construction.

MINSTROI Ministry of Construction.

MINTYAZHSTROI Ministry for Heavy Industrial Construction.

'NEPRERYVKA' continuous planning.

NMP (NET MATERIAL PRODUCT) Marxian-based definition of National Income which excludes so-called 'unproductive' services.

NNO (NORMED NET OUTPUT ('NORMATIVNAYA CHISTAYA PRODUKTSIYA')) form of value-added-based planning indicator.

'NORMATIVNAYA USLOVNO-CHISTAYA PRODUKTSIYA' normed conventional-net output – a variant of NNO.

'NORMATIVY ZADELOV' norms for volumes of unfinished construction.

NOT ('NAUCHNAYA ORGANIZATSIYA TRUDA') a form of Taylorist time study.

NSR ('NORMATIVNAYA STOIMOST' RABOT') normed value of work, a form of value-added-based planning indicator.

'OB″EDINENIE' (PLURAL 'OB″EDINENIYA') 'association' – general term which may describe anything from a conglomerate of enterprises up to a sub-ministerial intermediate planning authority.

'OB″EM REALIZUEMOI PRODUKTSII' total marketed output.

'OBKOM' provincial committee of the CPSU.

'OBLAST″' (PLURAL 'OBLASTI') province.

'OSVOENIE' 'assimilation' – bringing up to full-capacity operation.

'OTDEL KAPITAL′NOGO STROITEL′STVA' (OKS) capital investment department.

'PODRYAD' (ADJ. 'PODRYADNI') contract.

'PODRYADNYI SPOSOB' contractual basis.

'POSTANOVLENIE' decision, decree.

'PREDPRIYATIE' enterprise.

'PRODOLZHITEL′NOST′ STROITEL′STVA' 'duration of construction', total investment cycle.

'PRODUKTSIYA' output.

'PROEKT' (PLURAL 'PROEKTY') design.

'PROEKT PROIZVODSTVA STROITEL'NO-MONTAZHNYKH RABOT' design for the implementation of construction work.

'PROEKTNAYA ORGANIZATSIYA' (PLURAL 'PROEKTNYE ORGANI-ZATSII') (PO) design organisation.

'PROEKTNOE ZADANIE' design assignment.

'PROIZVODSTVO' production.

'PROIZVODSTVO PRODUKTSII V NATURAL'NOM VYRAZHENII' production in physical terms.

'PROMYSHLENNOST'' industry, industrial branch.

'PUSKONALADOCHNYE RABOTY' on-streaming operations.

'PUSKOVYI OB"EKT' (PLURAL 'PUSKOVYE OB"EKTY') project due to be finished in the current plan period.

'RABOCHII PROEKT' working design.

'RAION' district.

'RASPYLENIE', 'RASPYLENIE SREDSTV' excessively broad investment front.

'RASSHIRENIE' expansion.

'REALIZATSIYA' sales.

'REKONSTRUKTSIYA' reconstruction.

'RESHENIE' decision, decree.

'RUKOVODITELI' top management.

'SEBESTOIMOST'' cost.

'SHABASHNIK' 'lump' worker, moonlighter.

'SHTURMOVSHCHINA' storming.

'SMETNOE DELO' estimating, quantity surveying.

'SMETY' estimates.

'SNABZHENIE PO ZAKAZAM' supply by order.

SNT ('SMETNO-NORMATIVNAYA TRUDOEMKOST'') estimated normed labour-intensity.

'SOTSIALISTICHESKOE SOREVNOVANIE' socialist competition.

'SOVNARKHOZ' (PLURAL 'SOVNARKHOZY') regional economic council. In 1957 Khrushchev largely replaced the ministerial system with a system of *sovnarkhozy*, in an attempt to combat departmentalism. The *sovnarkhozy* were abolished in 1965.

STROIBANK Construction Bank.

'STROITEL'NO-MONTAZHNOE UPRAVLENIE' (PLURAL 'STROI-TEL'NO-MONTAZHNYE UPRAVLENIYA') construction and installation administration – subdivision of construction trust.

'TEKHNICHESKII PROEKT' technical design.

'TEKHNICHESKOE ZADANIE' (PLURAL 'TEKHNICHESKIE ZADANIYA') technical assignment.

'TEKHNIKO-EKONOMICHESKIE OBOSNOVANIYA' (TEOs) feasibility studies.

'TEKHNO-RABOCHII PROEKT' technico-working design.
'TEKUCHEST'' excessive turnover of personnel.
'TITUL'NYI SPISOK' (PLURAL 'TITUL'NYE SPISKI') 'title list'.
'TOVARNAYA PRODUKTSIYA' marketable output.
'TREST' (PLURAL 'TRESTY') trust.
'UCHASTOK' section.
'UNIVERMAG' department store.
'UPRAVLENIE KAPITAL'NOGO STROITEL'STVA' (UKS) capital investment department.
'USLOVNO-CHISTAYA PRODUKTSIYA' conventional-net output, a form of value-added-based planning indicator.
'VAKHTOVYI METOD' tour of duty method.
'VAL', 'VALOVAYA PRODUKTSIYA' gross output.
'VALOVOI OB″EM RABOT' gross volume of work.
'VEDOMSTVENNOST'' departmentalism.
'VNUTRIPOSTROECHNYI TITUL'NYI SPISOK' intra-project title list.
'VREMYA STROITEL'NOGO PROIZVODSTVA' building time.
'VVOD V DEISTVIE' operationalisation, commissioning.
'ZADANIE NA PROEKTIROVANIE' assignment for design work.
'ZADEL' planned volume of unfinished construction.
'ZAYAVKA NA IMPORT' indent for import.
'ZVENO' (PLURAL 'ZVEN'YA') link.

Notes

1. A conceptual framework for the study of investment activity in the Soviet Union

1 D. W. Pearce, *Cost-Benefit Analysis*, London, Macmillan, 1971, p. 26.
2 See D. A. Dyker, 'Industrial location in the Tadzhik republic', in *Soviet Studies*, vol. xxi, no. 4, April 1970.
3 *The Collected Essays, Journalism and Letters of George Orwell*, Harmondsworth, Penguin, 1970, vol. ii, p. 29.
4 See Dyker, 'Industrial location'. The original context was purely locational, but there are no obstacles to generalisation of the concepts.
5 See A. N. Ustinov, *Statistika Kapital' nogo Stroitel' stva*, Moscow, Statistika, 1980, p. 63.
6 G. M. Heal, *The Theory of Economic Planning*, Amsterdam–Oxford, North Holland Publishing House, 1973, p. 30.
7 See A. N. D. McAuley, 'Rationality and central planning', in *Soviet Studies*, vol. xviii, no. 3, January 1967.
8 It is worth noting that Heal concludes a discussion of collective choice problems with the statement that 'in practice, then, the objective function has to be seen as representing the collective preferences of a relatively small number of planners chosen to make social choices' (Heal, *The Theory*, p. 59). It may, then, be not only in a Soviet context that classical welfare concepts are difficult to apply.
9 T. C. Koopmans, *Three Essays on the State of Economic Science*, New York, McGraw-Hill, 1957, p. 84.
10 *Ibidem*.
11 See T. C. Koopmans, 'Analysis of production as an efficient combination of activities', in T. C. Koopmans (ed.), *Activity Analysis of Production and Allocation*, New York, John Wiley, London, Chapman and Hall, 1951, p. 37.
12 H. Leibenstein, 'Allocative efficiency vs. "X-efficiency"', in *American Economic Review*, vol. lvi, no. 3, June 1966, pp. 394–5.
13 *Ibidem*, p. 413.
14 T. Scitovsky, 'Two concepts of external economies', in A. N. Agarwala and S. P. Singh (eds.), *The Economics of Underdevelopment*, Bombay, Oxford University Press, 1958.
15 S. K. Holland, *Capital versus the Regions*, London, Macmillan, 1976, p. 198.
16 *Ibidem*, p. 51.

17 The term is taken from A. Weber, *The Theory of the Location of Industries*, trans. C. J. Friedrich, Chicago and London, University of Chicago Press, 1929, chapter 5. Note, however, that Weber includes under the agglomeration factor *internal* economies of scale, as long as they are of a locational nature.

18 For a general discussion of the question of externalities see E. J. Mishan, 'The postwar literature on externalities: an interpretative essay', in *Journal of Economic Literature*, vol. 9, no. 1, March 1971, especially p. 6.

19 See 'Problemy razrabotki novoi metodiki sostavleniya narodno-khozyaistvennykh planov', in *Planovoe Khozyaistvo*, No. 7, 1977, p. 115.

20 For a discussion of taut planning see H. S. Levine, 'Pressure and planning in the Soviet economy', in M. Bornstein and D. R. Fusfeld (eds.), *The Soviet Economy. A Book of Readings*, Homewood, Illinois, Irwin, 3rd edition, 1970.

21 A. Nove, *The Soviet Economy*, London, Allen and Unwin, 3rd edition, 1968, p. 329.

22 See A. O. Hirschman, *The Strategy of Economic Development*, New Haven, Yale University Press, 1958; C. K. Wilber, *The Soviet Model and Under-developed Countries*, Chapel Hill, University of North Carolina Press, 1969.

23 Keren argues that, while tautness may increase effort, uncertainty reduces it. It is not clear to the present author that tautness is meaningful except in the context of certain types and degrees of uncertainty. But Keren's point that tautness in the targets set for enterprise A may discourage effort in enterprise B, a customer of enterprise A, because it increases the degree of supply uncertainty facing it, seems a valid one. The conclusion is, of course, that 'the longer the chain of supply relationship, the more weighty is this element in favouring lower but surer targets'. See M. Keren, 'On the tautness of plans', in *Review of Economic Studies*, vol. xxxix (4), no. 120, October 1972, p. 482.

24 See H. Hunter, 'Priorities and shortfalls in pre-war Soviet planning', in J. Degras and A. Nove (eds.), *Soviet Planning. Essays in Honour of Naum Jasny*, Oxford, Blackwell, 1964.

25 See the latest decree on planning published in *Ekonomicheskaya Gazeta*, No. 32, 1979, special supplement.

26 For a full discussion of all these points see D. A. Dyker, 'Decentralisation and the command principle – some lessons from Soviet experience', in *Journal of Comparative Economics*, vol. 5, no. 2, June 1981.

27 The classic discussion of this problem is A. Nove, 'The problem of "success indicators" in Soviet industry', in *Economica*, vol. xxv, no. 97, February 1958.

28 'Pork-barrel' is defined as covering 'legislation which benefits local areas. Traditionally [in the USA], rivers and harbours were the basic area for pork-barrel activity; in recent years the term has been used for a much wider scope of activities.' See G. Tullock, *The Vote Motive*, Hobart Paperback no. 9, Institute of Economic Affairs, London, 1976, p. xv.

29 For an excellent discussion of *blat*, see J. Berliner, *Factory and Manager in the USSR*, Cambridge, Mass., Harvard University Press, 1957.

30 As was done in Dyker, 'Industrial location'.

2. The economic system as a whole: non-specialised, subordinate executive bodies

1 'Ob uluchshenii planirovaniya i usilenii vozdeistviya khozyaistvennogo mekhanizma na povyshenie effektivnosti proizvodstva i kachestva raboty', in *Ekonomicheskaya Gazeta*, No. 32, 1979, special supplement.

2 Statement by V. Ivanov, in *Ekonomicheskaya Gazeta*, No. 21, 1979, p. 9.

3 A. Boldyrev, 'Planirovanie v otrasli – na novuyu stupen'', in *Ekonomicheskaya Gazeta*, No. 48, 1979, p. 7.

4 The idea of tying investment votes to planned increment in production was mooted at the XXV Congress of the CPSU, and is embodied in the new planning decree. See V. Kulikov, 'Glavnyi orientir – vvod ob"ektov', in *Ekonomicheskaya Gazeta*, No. 6, 1977, p. 9, and 'V TsK KPSS i Sovete Ministrov SSSR', in *Pravda*, 29/7/79, pp. 1–2.

5 A. Stepun and V. Kozlov, 'Novoe v planirovanii kapital'nykh vlozhenii', in *Planovoe Khozyaistvo*, No. 10, 1966, p. 83.

6 A. Khikmatov, *Rezervy Povysheniya Effektivnosti Kapital'nykh Vlozhenii*, Tashkent, Uzbekistan, 1969, p. 73.

7 N. S. Shumov, *Finansirovanie i Kreditovanie Promyshlennosti*, Moscow, Finansy, 1973, p. 114; source quoted under note 1.

8 Stepun and Kozlov, 'Novoe v planirovanii', p. 83.

9 N. Martsenitsen and P. Temnov, 'Chto pokazala ekspertiza proektov', in *Ekonomika Stroitel'stva*, No. 7, 1965, p. 41.

10 V. Krasovskii, 'Ekonomicheskaya reforma i problemy kapital'nykh vlozhenii', in *Voprosy Ekonomiki*, No. 10, 1968, p. 41.

11 Stepun and Kozlov, 'Novoe v planirovanii', p. 78.

12 S. Ziyadullaev, 'Vazhnoe uslovie planovogo rukovodstva', in *Ekonomicheskaya Gazeta*, No. 23, 1968, p. 11.

13 I. D. Sher, *Finansirovanie i Kreditovanie Kapital'nykh Vlozhenii*, Moscow, Finansy, 1972, p. 26.

14 See second source quoted under note 4, and 'Deistvennost' plana', in *Ekonomicheskaya Gazeta*, No. 38, 1979, p. 5.

15 'Stroit' kompleksno', in *Pravda*, 31/8/77, p. 1.

16 N. Zenchenko, 'Povyshat' deistvennost' territorial'nogo planirovaniya', in *Planovoe Khozyaistvo*, No. 6, 1977, p. 63.

17 I. Tsitsin, 'Upravlenie stroitel'stvom v gorodskom raione', in *Ekonomicheskaya Gazeta*, No. 36, 1976, p. 9.

18 See M. Moro, 'V plane li stroika', in *Pravda*, 20/8/79, p. 2; V. Kulikov, 'Tselevym naznacheniem', in *Ekonomicheskaya Gazeta* No. 39, 1976, p. 9.

19 See details of new decree on this matter in 'Polozhenie o sluzhbe edinogo zakazchika', in *Ekonomicheskaya Gazeta*, No. 12, 1980, p. 6.

20 S. Vtorushin, 'Stali ulitsy tupiki', in *Pravda*, 19/10/79, p. 3.

21 N. Baibakov, 'Plan i proizvodstvo v novykh usloviyakh', in *Pravda*, 1/10/68, p. 2.

22 N. Baibakov, 'O gosudarstvennom plane razvitiya narodnogo khozyaistva SSSR na 1973 god', in *Pravda*, 19/12/72, p. 3.

23 'Vypolnenie plana stroitel'stva – vazhneishaya narodno-khozyaistven-naya zadacha', in *Planovoe Khozyaistvo*, No. 5, 1972, p. 3.

24 S. Kas'yanov, 'O povyshenii effektivnosti kapital'nykh vlozhenii', in *Planovoe Khozyaistvo*, No. 11, 1976, p. 76.

25 P. Poletaev, 'Kapital'nye vlozheniya v sel'skom khozyaistve', in *Voprosy Ekonomiki*, No. 7, 1971, p. 54.

26 V. Gribov, 'Sovershenstvovanie planirovaniya i finansirovaniya kapital'nykh vlozhenii', in *Planovoe Khozyaistvo*, No. 7, 1976, p. 88.

27 V. Isaev, 'Puti povysheniya effektivnosti kapital'nykh vlozhenii', in *Voprosy Ekonomiki*, No. 8, 1973, p. 32.

28 V. Solomin, 'Kachestvo planirovaniya i organizatsiya kapital'nogo stroitel'stva', in *Voprosy Ekonomiki*, No. 1, 1977, p. 62.

29 V. V. Dementsev, 'Finansovyi mekhanizm ob"edinenii', in *Ekonomiches-kaya Gazeta*, No. 25, 1975, p. 8.

30 Gribov, 'Sovershenstvovanie planirovaniya', p. 88.

31 V. V. Muzhitskikh, 'Novoe v finansirovanii kapital'nykh vlozhenii', in *Den'gi i Kredit*, No. 4, 1977, pp. 75–6.

32 M. Pessel', 'Kredit kak faktor intensifikatsii kapital'nogo stroitel'stva', in *Planovoe Khozyaistvo*, No. 1, 1977, p. 56.

33 For a discussion of these defects see Nove, *The Soviet Economy*, 3rd edition, pp. 178–9.

34 See M. Chistyakov, '1968 god. Plan predpriyatiya', in *Ekonomicheskaya Gazeta*, No. 40, 1967, p. 11.

35 See A. Illarionov, 'Ot zven'ev k mekhanizirovannym otryadam', in *Ekonomika Sel'skogo Khozyaistva*, No. 10, 1974; 'Sovershenstvovanie planirovaniya', in *Ekonomicheskaya Gazeta*, No. 22, 1975, p. 16; Sher, *Finansirovanie i Kreditovanie*, p. 211; L. Frankel', 'S uchetom vyyavlennykh rezervov', in *Ekonomicheskaya Gazeta*, No. 46, 1975, p. 7.

36 See 'Sovershenstvovanie khozyaistvennogo mekhanizma', in *Ekonomicheskaya Gazeta*, No. 33, 1979, pp. 3–4.

37 See S. Rogin, 'Ispytany', in *Pravda*, 9/10/79, p. 2.

38 See 'Planovye pokazateli i kriterii otsenki', in *Ekonomicheskaya Gazeta*, No. 35, 1979, p. 5.

39 A. Nove, 'Soviet Union 1967', Institute of Soviet and East European Studies, University of Glasgow, p. 11 (unpublished manuscript).

40 Chistyakov, '1968 god.', p. 11.

41 N. Drogichinskii and V. Starodubrovskii, 'Otrasl' na khozraschete', in *Ekonomicheskaya Gazeta*, No. 18, 1970, p. 7.

42 A. K. Zhakupov, 'Otrasl' na khozraschete', in *Ekonomicheskaya Gazeta*, No. 36, 1976, p. 8.

43 A. E. Andreev, 'V usloviyakh khozrascheta', in *Ekonomicheskaya Gazeta*, No. 46, 1976, p. 8.

44 See interview with V. N. Doenin, 'S uchetom otraslevykh osobennostei', in *Ekonomicheskaya Gazeta*, No. 16, 1976, p. 5, and interview with K. I. Galanshin, 'Tsel' – kontsentratsiya proizvodstva', in *Ekonomicheskaya Gazeta*, No. 19, 1976, p. 6.

45 'Proizvodstvennye ob"edineniya', in *Pravda*, 3/7/79, p. 1.

46 V. D. Shtundyuk, 'Voprosy formirovaniya i ispol'zovaniya fondov i

rezervov promyshlennykh ob"edinenii', in *Finansy SSSR*, No. 2, 1976.
47 See, for example, V. Danilov and G. Yastrebtsov, 'Ot slov – k delu', in *Pravda*, 27/5/75, p. 2; V. Podskrebkin, 'Eksperiment v deistvie', in *Ekonomicheskaya Gazeta*, No. 48, 1975, p. 9.
48 I. Kuznetsov, 'Khozyaistvennyi raschet: novye perspektivy', in *Pravda*, 14/9/79, pp. 2–3.
49 V. P. Krasovskii, *Problemy Ekonomiki Kapital'nykh Vlozhenii*, Moscow, Ekonomika, 1967, p. 49; I. V. Maevskii and V. I. Maevskii, *Nekotorye Voprosy Izmereniya Ekonomicheskoi Effektivnosti*, Moscow, Nauka, 1970, p. 95.
50 V. A. Gnatov and Yu. V. Uvarov, 'Nekotorye voprosy stimulirovaniya sokrashcheniya investitsionnogo protsessa', in *Finansy SSSR*, No. 7, 1977, p. 48; P. Hanson and M. R. Hill, 'Soviet assimilation of western technology; a survey of UK exporters' experience', in US Congress JEC, *Soviet Economy in a Time of Change*, Washington, US GPO, 1979, vol. 2, p. 594.
51 N. Kachalov, 'Sredstva vlozheny, chto sdelano?', in *Ekonomicheskaya Gazeta*, No. 46, 1979, p. 17.
52 N. Geidarov, 'Dolgo – znachit dorogo', in *Ekonomicheskaya Gazeta*, No. 26, 1975, p. 9; I. Pogosov, 'V polnuyu situ!', in *Pravda*, 19/10/74, p. 2.
53 V. Matvienko, 'Kogda smeta – ne predel', in *Ekonomicheskaya Gazeta*, No. 28, 1977, p. 9.
54 See G. I. Frumkin, 'O proverke smet', in *Den'gi i Kredit*, No. 12, 1976; O. Kolotov, 'Puskonaladochnye raboty: nazrevshie voprosy', in *Ekonomicheskaya Gazeta*, No. 9, 1978, p. 9.
55 T. Khachaturov, 'Kapital'nye vlozheniya: kurs na effektivnost'', in *Pravda*, 29/8/79, p. 2.
56 A. Mitrofanov, 'O kontsentratsii kapital'nykh vlozhenii', in *Planovoe Khozyaistvo*, No. 3, 1970, p. 35.
57 Isaev, 'Puti povysheniya', p. 32. See also V. Isaev, 'Nekotorye voprosy khozyaistvennoi reformy i stroitel'stva', in *Voprosy Ekonomiki*, No. 5, 1970; 'Sovershenstvovanie planirovaniya kapital'nykh vlozhenii – vazhneishaya narodnokhozyaistvennaya zadacha', in *Planovoe Khozyaistvo*, No. 2, 1971.
58 Isaev, 'Puti povysheniya', p. 47.
59 V. Shilov, 'Ne dopyskat' "razdvoeniya plana"', in *Pravda*, 17/7/76, p. 2.
60 Isaev, 'Puti povysheniya', p. 47.
61 See V. Il'in, 'Uskorenie stroitel'stva – vazhnaya narodnokhozyaistvennaya zadacha', in *Voprosy Ekonomiki*, No. 1, 1976, p. 7.
62 V. S. Bard and A. P. Zubkov, 'Finansovye i kreditnye metody vozdeistviya na nezavershennoe stroitel'stvo', in *Finansy SSSR*, No. 4, 1977, p. 49.
63 I. Dmitriev, 'Glavnoe – vvod v deistvie', in *Pravda*, 7/9/77, p. 2.
64 Krasovskii, *Problemy Ekonomiki Kapital'nykh Vlozhenii*, p. 18.
65 V. Solomin, 'Nereshennye voprosy planirovaniya i organizatsii kapital'nogo stroitel'stva', in *Planovoe Khozyaistvo*, No. 10, 1968, p. 40.
66 A. Nove, 'The industrial planning system: reforms in prospect', in *Soviet Studies*, vol. xiv, no. 1, July 1962.

67 V. Dymshits, 'O nasushchnykh zadachakh kapital'nogo stroitel'stva', in *Ekonomicheskaya Gazeta*, 18/12/61, p. 6.

68 See, for example, O. Hoeffding, 'The sovnarkhoz reform', in F. Holzman (ed.), *Readings in the Soviet Economy*, Chicago, Rand McNally, 1962.

69 Yu. Sakharov and N. Petrov, 'Leningradskii eksperiment', Part 1, in *Pravda*, 11/5/69, p. 2.

70 *Ibidem*, Part 3, in *Pravda*, 14/5/69, p. 2.

71 E. Manevich, 'Problemy vosproizvodstva rabochei sily i puti uluchsheniya ispol'zovaniya trudovykh resursov v SSSR', in *Voprosy Ekonomiki*, No. 10, 1969, p. 37.

72 F. Kokhonov, 'Iskusstvo ekonomiki', in *Pravda*, 21/1/76, p. 3.

73 S. Meikshan, 'Dva aspekta odnoi problemy', in *Sotsialisticheskaya Industriya*, 29/10/70, p. 2.

74 V. D. Shashin, 'Sovershenstvovanie organizatsii proizvodstva, truda i upravleniya v neftedobyvayushchei promyshlennosti', in *Neftyanoe Khozyaistvo*, No. 1, 1970, pp. 3–6.

75 M. Poltoranin and V. Sevest'yanov, 'Na beregakh Irtysha', in *Pravda*, 3/7/77, p. 2.

76 I. Sergienkov, 'Kak griby posle dozhdya', in *Pravda*, 8/5/76, p. 2.

77 M. Medvedev, 'Planirovanie i programnoe upravlenie otrasl'yu', in *Planovoe Khozyaistvo*, No. 10, 1976, p. 88.

78 I. V. Chirgadze, 'Mashinostroenie Tadzhikistana i Osnovnye Napravleniya ego Razvitiya', unpublished dissertation for the degree of Candidate of Economic Sciences, Dushanbe, 1965, p. 133; D. A. Alyshbaev, *Perspektivy Razvitiya i Razmeshcheniya Vazhneishikh Otraslei Promyshlennosti Kirgizii*, Frunze, no date, p. 49.

79 Martsenitsen and Temnov, 'Chto pokazala', p. 41.

80 V. Shavlyuk, 'Pochemu dorozhaet stroika', in *Pravda*, 27/6/79, p. 2.

81 See Dyker, 'Industrial location', p. 499.

82 P. Merkin, 'Voprosy ekonomicheskogo obosnovaniya plana kapital'nykh vlozhenii', in *Planovoe Khozyaistvo*, No. 2, 1965, p. 29.

83 See Khikmatov, *Rezervy Povysheniya*, pp. 137–8.

84 A. Ferberg, 'O kapital'nykh vlozheniyakh na rekonstruktsiyu deistvuyushchikh predpriyatii', in *Voprosy Ekonomiki*, No. 1, 1966, p. 118; for a more recent statement of the same point see R. R. Novik, 'Fondootdacha i rost effektivnosti', in *Ekonomicheskaya Gazeta*, No. 24, 1975, p. 13.

85 N. I. Kal'mus *et al.*, 'Ekonomicheskoe stimulirovanie pri rekonstruktsii', in *Ekonomika Stroitel'stva*, No. 2, 1980, p. 19.

86 S. Kas'yanov, 'Kursom tekhnicheskogo perevooruzheniya', in *Ekonomicheskaya Gazeta*, No. 26, 1976, p. 9.

87 I. Plakhotin, 'Nado vnesti yasnost'', in *Ekonomicheskaya Gazeta*, No. 3, 1980, p. 9.

88 N. Budunova, 'Metodicheskie voprosy opredeleniya ekonomicheskoi effektivnosti rekonstruktsii promyshlennykh prepriyatii', in *Planovoe Khozyaistvo*, No. 2, 1977, p. 17.

89 Martsenitsen and Temnov, 'Chto pokazala', pp. 39–40.

90 *Ibidem*, p. 46.

91 Il'in, 'Uskorenie stroitel'stva', p. 8.
92 *Economic Survey of Europe in 1976*, Part II, New York, United Nations, 1977, p. 98.
93 L. Ginzburg, 'Povysit' effektivnost' kapital'nykh vlozhenii v rekonstruktsiyu predpriyatii', in *Planovoe Khozyaistvo*, No. 6, 1965, p. 14.
94 *Ibidem*, p. 13.
95 See Ferberg, 'O kapital'nykh vlozheniyakh', p. 119.
96 L. I. Bugaets and Z. A. Parshina, 'O snizhenii sebestoimosti produktsii na rekonstruiruemykh i novykh predpriyatiyakh', in *Finansy SSSR*, No. 3, 1978, p. 21.
97 See A. Gnidenko and E. Makarov, 'Rekonstruktsiya: opyt i problemy', in *Ekonomicheskaya Gazeta*, No. 22, 1975, p. 8; I. Vorotyntsev, 'Otvetstvennost'za rekonstrukstsiyu', in *Ekonomicheskaya Gazeta*, No. 3, 1976, p. 12; M. I. Charkov, 'Effektivnost' kapitalovlozhenii pri rekonstruktsii predpriyatii', in *Finansy SSSR*, No. 10, 1976, p. 57.
98 'Khozyaistvennyi mekhanizm v stroitel'stve', in *Ekonomicheskaya Gazeta*, No. 39, 1979, p. 5; 'Otraslevye popravochnye koeffitsienty', in *Ekonomicheskaya Gazeta*, No. 25, 1980, p. 6.
99 N. Semizorov and N. Abramov, 'Effekt rekonstruktsii', in *Pravda*, 5/8/74, p. 2.
100 E. Orzhekhovskii, in *Ekonomicheskaya Gazeta*, No. 30, 1975, p. 9.
101 G. Klimenko, 'Rekonstruktsiya: opyt i problemy', in *Ekonomicheskaya Gazeta*, No. 36, 1975, p. 14.
102 Il'in, 'Uskorenie stroitel'stva', p. 8.
103 See, for example, N. Federenko, 'Ob ekonomicheskoi otsenke prirodnykh resursov', in *Voprosy Ekonomiki*, No. 3, 1968; V. Pavlenko, 'O edinykh metodikakh', in *Ekonomicheskaya Gazeta*, No. 46, 1970, p. 7; A. E. Probst, *Voprosy Razmeshcheniya Sotsialisticheskoi Promyshlennosti*, Moscow, Nauka, 1971, p. 158.
104 See source quoted under note 1.
105 N. Baguzov, 'Effektivnost' kapital'nykh vlozhenii i proektirovanie', in *Ekonomika Stroitel'stva*, No. 2, 1966, p. 23.
106 K. Abrosimova, 'Raionnye planirovki i razmeshchenie promyshlennosti', in *Narodnoe Khozyaistvo Uzbekistana*, No. 12, 1960, pp. 13–14.
107 'Obmen mneniyami. Problemy razmeshcheniya promyshlennosti v Uzbekistane', in *Kommunist Uzbekistana*, No. 5, 1963.
108 B. Mironov, 'Abalakovskii spor', in *Pravda*, 23/1/80, p. 2.
109 M. Dobrorodnykh, 'Kaspii dolzhen ostavat'sya chistym', in *Ekonomicheskaya Gazeta*, No. 36, 1977, p. 14.
110 M. Mkrtchyan, 'Metodologicheskie voprosy razmeshcheniya proizvoditel'nykh sil', in *Planovoe Khozyaistvo*, No. 12, 1969, p. 43.
111 Sh. N. Zakirov, *Voprosy Razvitiya i Razmeshcheniya Promyshlennosti Uzbekistana*, Tashkent, Nauka UzSSR, 1965, p. 67.
112 See K. Baidal, 'Za kirpichnoi stenoi', in *Pravda*, 9/4/80, p. 2.
113 I. S. Zen'kov and M. A. Rusakov, *Ekonomika Stroitel'stva*, Moscow, Vysshaya Shkola, 1967, pp. 116–17.
114 Sher, *Finansirovanie i Kreditovanie*, p. 31.
115 Charkov, 'Effektivnost' kapitalovlozhenii', p. 56.

116 V. F. Babak, 'Vliyanie dolgosrochnogo kredita na effektivnost' kapitalovlozhenii', in *Finansy SSSR*, No. 6, 1977, p. 45.

3. Specialised, subordinate non-executive bodies – design organisations

1 I. Galkin (ed.), *Organizatsiya Planirovanie i Upravlenie Stroitel'nym Proizvodstvom*, Moscow, Vysshaya Shkola, 1978, p. 8.
2 Yu. Bocharov and V. Lyubovnyi, 'Kompleksnoe razvitie krupnykh gorodov', in *Planovoe Khozyaistvo*, No. 12, 1976, p. 84.
3 P. Podshivalenko (ed.), *Ekonomika Stroitel'stva*, Moscow, Izdatel'stvo Politicheskoi Literatury, 1965, p. 165; see also R. Hutchings, *Soviet Science, Technology, Design*, London, Oxford University Press, 1976, pp. 155–61.
4 'Stroikam – vysokuyu effektivnost'', in *Pravda*, 13/8/79, p. 1.
5 F. Nazarov, 'Sovershenstvovat' proektno-smetnoe delo', in *Planovoe Khozyaistvo*, No. 7, 1966, p. 69.
6 A. A. Borovoi, 'Novyi etap sovershenstvovaniya proektno-smetnogo dela', in *Ekonomika Stroitel'stva*, No. 6, 1981, p. 3.
7 *Narodnoe Khozyaistvo v 1974 g.*, Moscow, Statistika, 1975, p. 541.
8 Borovoi, 'Novyi etap', p. 3.
9 G. Shiryaev, 'Uluchshenie proektno-smetnogo dela – vazhnaya narodno-khozyaistvennaya zadacha', in *Planovoe Khozyaistvo*, No. 1, 1977, p. 29.
10 See Borovoi, 'Novyi etap', p. 6.
11 M. R. Jackson, 'Information and incentives in planning Soviet investment projects', in *Soviet Studies*, vol. xviii, no. 1, July 1971, p. 7.
12 Podshivalenko, *Ekonomika Stroitel'stva*, p. 135.
13 *Ibidem*, p. 137.
14 'Ob uluchshenii proektno-smetnogo dela', in *Ekonomicheskaya Gazeta*, No. 26, 1969, pp. 12–13.
15 V. A. Shavrin, *Gosudarstvennyi Byudzhet SSSR*, Moscow, Gosfinizdat, 4th edition, 1953, p. 87.
16 A. M. Aleksandrov, *Gosudarstvennyi Byudzhet SSSR*, Moscow, Gosfinizdat, 1961, p. 255.
17 Khikmatov, *Rezervy Povysheniya*, pp. 66–7.
18 'Po sledam neopublikovannykh pisem', in *Ekonomicheskaya Gazeta*, No. 2, 1980, p. 56.
19 L. Gatovskii, 'Ekonomicheskaya nauka i nekotorye problemy tekhnicheskogo progressa', in *Voprosy Ekonomiki*, No. 12, 1969, p. 14.
20 A. N. Grammatikov, *Ekonomicheskaya Reforma v Oblasti Planirovaniya, Finansirovaniya i Kreditovaniya Kapital'nykh Vlozhenii*, Moscow, Nedra, 1968, p. 58; E. Pliskovskii and I. Zaretskii, 'Puti uluchsheniya proektno-smetnogo dela', in *Ekonomicheskaya Gazeta*, No. 24, 1970, p. 9.
21 F. Nazarov, 'Khozyaistvennyi raschet proektnykh organizatsii', in *Planovoe Khozyaistvo*, No. 5, 1968, p. 61; O. Sitnikov, 'Tekhnicheskii progress i khozyaistvennaya reforma', in *Planovoe Khozyaistvo*, No. 9, 1969, p. 32.

22 Sher, *Finansirovanie i Kreditovanie*, p. 229.
23 P. Podshivalenko, 'Sovershenstvovat' ekonomicheskie metody rukovodstva stroitel'stvom', in *Ekonomika Stroitel'stva*, No. 2, 1972, p. 7.
24 'Proekt i stroika', in *Pravda*, 30/9/75, p. 1.
25 See N. Galiaskarov, 'Ne otstavat' ot trebovanii zhizni', in *Ekonomika Stroitel'stva*, No. 4, 1966, p. 46.
26 M. Zotov, 'Kredit dlya stroiki', in *Pravda*, 13/1/76, p. 3.
27 'Ob uluchshenii' (see note 1 to Chapter 2).
28 'V TsK KPSS i Sovete Ministrov SSSR', in *Pravda*, 29/7/79, pp. 1–2.
29 'Plata za proizvodstvennye fondy', in *Ekonomicheskaya Gazeta*, No. 20, 1980, special supplement.
30 'Premirovanie za vvod ob"ektov', in *Ekonomicheskaya Gazeta*, No. 42, 1979, pp. 9–10; 'Khozyaistvennyi mekhanizm v stroitel'stve', in *Ekonomicheskaya Gazeta*, No. 39, 1979, p. 5.
31 'Khozyaistvennyi mekhanizm' (see preceding note).
32 *Ibidem.*
33 Sher, *Finansirovanie i Kreditovanie*, p. 229.
34 Podshivalenko, *Ekonomika Stroitel'stva*, p. 167; Zen'kov and Rusakov, *Ekonomika Stroitel'stva*, p. 109.
35 G. Shiryaev, 'O sovershenstvovanii proektno-smetnogo dela', in *Planovoe Khozyaistvo*, No. 8, 1969, p. 58; Sitnikov, 'Tekhnicheskii progress', p. 32.
36 Podshivalenko, *Ekonomika Stroitel'stva*, p. 140.
37 M. Bershinin, 'Povysit' uroven' gradostroitel'stva', in *Ekonomicheskaya Gazeta*, No. 39, 1975, p. 9.
38 N. Kirillov, 'Kazhdoi stroike – ekonomichnyi proekt', in *Ekonomicheskaya Gazeta*, No. 47, 1975, p. 9.
39 I. Perepechin and L. Apraksina, 'Kakov proekt – takov ob"ekt', in *Ekonomicheskaya Gazeta*, No. 6, 1980, p. 7.
40 Ferberg, 'O kapital'nykh vlozheniyakh', p. 41.
41 Galiaskarov, 'Ne otstavat'', pp. 44–5.
42 V. Malyugin and M. Turianskii, 'Progress smetnogo normirovaniya', in *Ekonomika Stroitel'stva*, No. 12, 1967.
43 V. Shtanskii, 'Tekhnicheskii progress i ekonomika proektirovaniya', in *Voprosy Ekonomiki*, No. 9, 1976, p. 50.
44 G. A. Kosatykh, 'UPSS dolzhny stat' normativnoi bazoi razrabotki tekhnicheskikh proektov', in *Ekonomika Stroitel'stva*, No. 3, 1980, p. 72.
45 *Ibidem.*
46 Khikmatov, *Rezervy Povysheniya*, pp. 87–8.
47 *Ibidem*, p. 66.
48 In *Pravda*, 23/5/74, p. 1.
49 'Tekhnicheskii progress v stroitel'stve', in *Ekonomicheskaya Gazeta*, No. 49, 1978.
50 V. Radchenko, 'Pochemu "tyazhely" oblegchennye konstruktsii', in *Ekonomicheskaya Gazeta*, No. 20, 1980, p. 9.
51 Galiaskarov, 'Ne otstavat'', p. 46.
52 Ya. Rubins, 'Kak sberech' metall?', in *Ekonomicheskaya Gazeta*, No. 52, 1978, p. 9.
53 P. Podshivalenko, *Novoe v Finansirovanii Stroitel'stva*, Moscow, Finansy,

1968, pp. 54–5.

54 Podshivalenko, 'Sovershenstvovat' ekonomicheskie metody', p. 7.

55 See E. Kozlov and M. Makhlin, 'Chto sokratit "nezavershenku"?', in *Ekonomicheskaya Gazeta*, No. 34, 1975, p. 9; I. Kulya and I. Trushkin, 'Raschetam – stroinuyu sistemu', in *Ekonomicheskaya Gazeta*, No. 13, 1976, p. 9.

56 E. L. Pliskovskii, 'Opyt kreditovaniya proektnykh organizatsii', in *Den'gi i Kredit*, No. 6, 1976.

57 V. Gladyshev, 'Po zakonchennym ob"ektam', in *Ekonomicheskaya Gazeta*, No. 2, 1980, p. 9.

58 P. Podshivalenko, 'Usilenie roli finansovo-kreditnykh rychagov v povyshenii effektivnosti kapital'nykh vlozhenii', in *Voprosy Ekonomiki*, No. 4, 1980, p. 63.

59 See 'Uluchshat' upravlenie stroitel'stvom', in *Pravda*, 17/1/80, p. 1; M. Makhlin, 'Podtverzhdaet praktika', in *Ekonomicheskaya Gazeta*, No. 7, 1980, p. 9.

60 G. Kulagin, 'Statut prikladnogo instituta', in *Trud*, 5/4/73, p. 2.

61 'Proekty – v srok!', in *Pravda*, 18/7/79, p. 1.

62 M. Cherkasov, ' "Perekhodyashchii" ob"ekt', in *Pravda*, 11/11/68, p. 2.

63 See, for example, interview with L. Bibin, 'Vazhnyi etap', in *Ekonomicheskaya Gazeta*, No. 47, 1971, p. 9; V. I. Kuraruru, 'Ukreplenie dogovornoi i finansovo-raschetnoi distsipliny', in *Finansy SSSR*, No. 5, 1976, p. 54; S. I. Linskii and V. U. Dubkov, 'Kreditovanie nezavershennogo proizvodstva stroitel'no-montazhnykh rabot', in *Ekonomika Stroitel'stva*, No. 4, 1980, pp. 47–8.

64 Shiryaev, 'O sovershenstvovanii', p. 57.

65 Khikmatov, *Rezervy Povysheniya*, pp. 77–8.

66 Pogosov, 'V polnuyu situ!'

67 A. Lyashko, 'Kachestvo i distsiplina plana', in *Pravda*, 25/6/75.

68 See V. Parfenov, 'Slovo sozdatelei novykh zavodov', in *Pravda*, 18/1/76, p. 3; Shtanskii, 'Tekhnicheskii progress', p. 51.

69 Ya. Orlov and V. Shimanskii, *Reforma i Torgovlya*, Moscow, Politizdat, 1970.

70 Kirillov, 'Kazhdoi stroike'.

71 See K. Glukhovskoi, 'Ekspertizu proektov provodyat stroiteli', in *Ekonomicheskaya Gazeta*, No. 19, 1977, p. 9; V. Kamenev, 'Rezervy snizheniya smetnoi stoimosti', in *Ekonomicheskaya Gazeta*, No. 13, 1978, p. 9; V. K. Bobkov, 'Glavnaya tsel' – povyshenie effektivnosti stroitel'nogo proizvodstva', in *Ekonomika Stroitel'stva*, No. 5, 1980, p. 66.

72 Shiryaev, 'O sovershenstvovanii', pp. 56–7.

73 Shiryaev, 'Uluchshenie', p. 30.

74 Shiryaev, 'O sovershenstvovanii', pp. 56–7.

75 Krasovskii, *Problemy Ekonomiki Kapital'nykh Vlozhenii*, p. 47.

76 *Ibidem.*

77 A. Kostousov, 'Videt' konechnyi rezul'tat', in *Pravda*, 22/9/76, p. 2.

78 V. Eremenko, 'Kak otsenivat' vklad konstruktora', in *Pravda*, 25/1/76, p. 3.

79 K. G. Federenko and G. V. Yandovskii, 'Kapitalovlozheniya i kontrol'

Stroibanka', in *Finansy SSSR*, No. 2, 1976, p. 36.
80 Shtanskii, 'Tekhnicheskii progress', p. 54.
81 Nazarov, 'Sovershenstvovat' proektno-smetnoe delo', pp. 69–70.
82 P. Rakhatov and P. Antonov, 'Kontsentratsiya sredstv – zakon', in *Ekonomicheskaya Gazeta*, No. 14, 1979, p. 10.
83 'Proekty – v srok!', in *Pravda*, 18/7/79, p. 1.
84 See V. Vitkovskii, 'Sovershenstvovanie upravleniya kapital'nym stroitel'stvom', in *Voprosy Ekonomiki*, No. 6, 1977, p. 28; K. A. Tsai, 'Strozhe kontrol' za kachestvom proektov i smet', in *Finansy SSSR*, No. 2, 1978, p. 36.
85 See V. Ustinov and V. Volkov, 'Komu snimat' mikrofil'my?', in *Pravda*, 3/1/75, p. 2; M. G. Chentemirov, 'Povyshat' kachestvo stroitel'stva', in *Ekonomika Stroitel'stva*, No. 5, 1980, p. 7.
86 Krasovskii, *Problemy Ekonomiki Kapital'nykh Vlozhenii*, p. 45.
87 Zen'kov and Rusakov, *Ekonomika Stroitel'stva*, p. 203.
88 Khikmatov, *Rezervy Povysheniya*, pp. 68–9.
89 I. Markelov, 'Algoritmy upravleniya, dva vzglyada na ASU', in *Nash Sovremennik*, No. 10, 1974.
90 Gladyshev, 'Po zakonchennym ob"ektam'.
91 A. Vozyakov, 'Povyshat' effektivnost' kapital'nogo stroitel'stva', in *Finansy SSSR*, No. 8, 1967, p. 5; V. Isaev, 'Osnovnoi pokazatel' – vvod v deistvie', in *Ekonomika Stroitel'stva*, No. 8, 1969, p. 12.
92 Shtanskii, 'Tekhnicheskii progress', p. 47.
93 P. Podshivalenko, 'Effektivnost' kapital'nykh vlozhenii i finansovyi kontrol' v stroitel'stve', in *Planovoe Khozyaistvo*, No. 10, 1966, p. 3.
94 See, for example, Isaev, 'Sovershenstvovanie planirovaniya', p. 38.
95 Il'in, 'Uskorenie stroitel'stva', p. 9.
96 L. G. Kapshii, 'Ob organizatsii finansovogo kontrolya za stoimost'yu oborudovaniya v stroitel'stve', in *Finansy SSSR*, No. 7, 1976, p. 50.
97 Shtanskii, 'Tekhnicheskii progress', p. 47.
98 V. Krasovskii, 'Ekonomicheskie problemy fondootdachi', in *Voprosy Ekonomiki*, No. 1, 1980, p. 110.
99 Perepechin and Apraksina, 'Kakov proekt'.
100 N. Vovchenko, 'Bystree osvaivat' proizvodstvennye moshchnosti', in *Ekonomika Stroitel'stva*, No. 10, 1965, p. 25.
101 See, for example, R. Merkin, 'Effektivnost' kapital'nykh vlozhenii i ekonomika novykh predpriyatii', in *Voprosy Ekonomiki*, No. 12, 1968, pp. 48–50.
102 See Perepechin and Apraksina, 'Kakov proekt'.
103 One source estimates that design organisations are responsible for 8–10 per cent of defects in construction work leading to excessive maintenance costs. See A. Tregubov, 'Kachestvo – zabota obshchaya', in *Ekonomicheskaya Gazeta*, No. 42, 1975, p. 9.
104 Yu. Shatalin and A. Volkov, 'Planirovanie kapital'nogo stroitel'stva i optimizatsiya general'nykh skhem razmeshcheniya proizvodstva', in *Planovoe Khozyaistvo*, No. 3, 1977, p. 90.
105 Shiryaev, 'Uluchshenie', p. 29.
106 *Ibidem*.

107 K. Krupitsa, V. Ozhiganov and E. Peryshkin, 'Na prostorakh krainego severa', in *Ekonomika Stroitel'stva*, No. 6, 1965, p. 35.
108 'Uporyadochit' tekhniko-ekonomicheskie obosnovanie stroitel'stva', in *Ekonomika Stroitel'stva*, No. 11, 1965, p. 11.
109 See report in *Ekonomicheskaya Gazeta*, No. 23, 1974, p. 9.
110 Shtanskii, 'Tekhnicheskii progress', p. 49.
111 See *ibidem*, p. 52.
112 See Kostousov, 'Videt' konechnyi rezul'tat'.
113 Federenko and Yandovskii, 'Kapitalovlozheniya i kontrol'', p. 37.
114 Khikmatov, *Rezervy Povysheniya*, p. 86.
115 See Borovoi, 'Novyi etap', pp. 5–7.
116 Podshivalenko, *Ekonomika Stroitel'stva*, p. 162.
117 Tsai, 'Strozhe kontrol'', p. 35.
118 'Obnovlenie fondov', in *Pravda*, 20/5/80, p. 2.
119 See N. G. Kazhlaev, *Povyshenie Effektivnosti Kapital'nykh Vlozhenii*, Moscow, Ekonomizdat, 1963, p. 50; Khikmatov, *Rezervy Povysheniya*, p. 81.
120 P. Shitenkov, 'K chemu provodyat proschety ekspertizy', in *Ekonomika Stroitel'stva*, No. 1, 1967, p. 49.
121 Zen'kov and Rusakov, *Ekonomika Stroitel'stva*, p. 256.
122 P. Podshivalenko and I. D. Sher, *Finansirovanie i Kreditovanie Kapital'nykh Vlozhenii*, Moscow, Finansy, 2nd edition, 1965, p. 61.
123 Charkov, 'Effektivnost' kapitalovlozhenii', p. 56.
124 See 'V Tsentral'nom Komitete KPSS', in *Ekonomicheskaya Gazeta*, No. 36, 1975, p. 3.
125 'Stroit'bystro, ekonomichno, kachestvenno', in *Finansy SSSR*, No. 3, 1977, p. 42.
126 See G. A. Khmel'nitskii, 'Povyshat'effektivnost' kapitalovlozhenii', in *Finansy SSSR*, No. 10, 1976, p. 20.
127 See V. P. Matvienko, 'Povyshat' rezultativnost' kontrolya', in *Finansy SSSR*, No. 7, 1976.
128 See *ibidem*, p. 48.
129 V. Kudryadtsev, V. Sarychev and V. Didkovskii, 'Ekonomicheskie etalony i konkursnoe proektirovanie', in *Ekonomika Stroitel'stva*, No. 3, 1968, p. 51.

4. Specialised, subordinate executive bodies – the building industry

1 Galkin, *Organizatsiya Planirovanie*, p. 282.
2 L. I. Mazurin, 'Organizatsiya upravleniya v stroitel'stve', in *Finansy SSSR*, No. 8, 1976, p. 42.
3 *Narodnoe Khozyaistvo SSSR v 1978 godu*, Moscow, Statistika, 1979, pp. 355–6.
4 Podshivalenko, *Ekonomika Stroitel'stva*, p. 75.
5 G. P. Papliyan, 'Osnovnoe zveno upravleniya stroitel'nym proizvodstvom', in *Ekonomika Stroitel'stva*, No. 3, 1980, p. 26.
6 Galkin, *Organizatsiya Planirovanie*, pp. 288–9.
7 A. Yakovlev, 'Stroitel'nye ob"edineniya', in *Pravda*, 4/2/80, p. 2.

8 See 'Snizu doverkhu', in *Ekonomicheskaya Gazeta*, No. 32, 1976, p. 9.
9 Mazurin, 'Organizatsiya upravleniya', p. 43.
10 See Vitkovskii, 'Sovershenstvovanie upravleniya', pp. 29–30.
11 See I. A. Sukhachev, 'Brigadnyi podryad i sovershenstvovanie upravleniya stroitel'nym proizvodstvom', in *Ekonomika Stroitel'stva*, No. 1, 1980, p. 28.
12 'Stil' upravleniya', in *Izvestiya*, 13/3/68, p. 1; M. Odinets, 'Chto skryvaetsya za obshchimi slovami', in *Pravda*, 26/11/68, p. 2.
13 See article cited under note 8.
14 Yakovlev, 'Stroitel'nye ob"edineniya'.
15 N. N. Kachalov, 'O nekotorykh aspektakh sovershenstvovaniya organizatsii upravleniya stroitel'stvom', in *Ekonomika Stroitel'stva*, No. 5, 1980, p. 17.
16 See 'Polozheni o proizvodstvennom stroitel'no-montazhnom ob"edinenii', in *Ekonomicheskaya Gazeta*, No. 49, 1979, special supplement.
17 Papliyan, 'Osnovnoe zveno', pp. 26–7.
18 *Ibidem*, p. 27.
19 See Podshivalenko, *Ekonomika Stroitel'stva*, pp. 12–13.
20 *Narodnoe Khozyaistvo SSSR v 1978 godu*, p. 352.
21 Podshivalenko, *Ekonomika Stroitel'stva*, p. 72.
22 G. V. Benza, N. M. Zaslavskii, A. G. Sandler, and N. M. Tsalik, *Novaya Sistema Planirovaniya v Stroitel'stve*, Kiev, Budivel'nik, 1967, pp. 28–30.
23 V. Malyugin and B. Vainshtein, 'Ekonomicheskii eksperiment v stroitel'stve', in *Planovoe Khozyaistvo*, No. 2, 1965; 'Vvod v deistvie i rentabel'nost' – glavnoe', in *Ekonomika Stroitel'stva*, No. 3, 1965, p. 19.
24 Benza *et al.*, *Novaya Sistema*, pp. 13–14.
25 *Ibidem*, pp. 40–5; Martsenitsen and Temnov, 'Chto pokazala'.
26 G. Smirnov and E. Kudryavtsev, 'Glavmosstroi na puti k khozyaistvennoi reforme', in *Ekonomicheskaya Gazeta*, No. 42, 1968, p. 18.
27 See I. Matyushchenko and S. Luchinskii, 'Nekotorye vyvody iz analiza eksperimenta', in *Ekonomika Stroitel'stva*, No. 5, 1966.
28 *Ibidem*; P. Gorbushin, 'Sovershenstvovanie planirovaniya i ekonomicheskogo stimulirovaniya stroitel'nogo proizvodstva', in *Voprosy Ekonomiki*, No. 2, 1967, p. 5.
29 V. Zabelin and I. Veremkroit, 'Pregrada vedomstvennosti i mestnichestvu', in *Ekonomicheskaya Gazeta*, No. 27, 1975, p. 9.
30 See G. Zubatkin, 'Planirovanie stroitel'nogo proizvodstva', in *Planovoe Khozyaistvo*, No. 1, 1976, pp. 87–8.
31 I. Komarov, 'Effektivnost' nauchnogo poiska', in *Ekonomicheskaya Gazeta*, No. 32, 1975, p. 9.
32 Gorbushin, 'Sovershenstvovanie planirovaniya', p. 3.
33 Ya. Kvasha and V. Krasovskii, 'Kapital'noe stroitel'stvo i nakoplenie', in *Voprosy Ekonomiki*, No. 7, 1965, p. 9.
34 E. Zolotnikov and L. Remezov, 'Novoe v pravilakh priemki v ekspluatatsiyu ob"ektov proizvodstvennogo naznacheniya', in *Ekonomika Stroitel'stva*, No. 5, 1966, pp. 28–9.
35 See P. Podshivalenko, 'Finansirovanie i kreditovanie podryadnykh organizatsii', in *Ekonomicheskaya Gazeta*, No. 6, 1970, p. 9.

36 Sher, *Finansirovanie i Kreditovanie*, p. 62.
37 V. Il'in, 'Vmesto avansa – kredit', in *Ekonomicheskaya Gazeta*, No. 51, 1978, p. 9.
38 Podshivalenko, 'Usilenie roli', p. 66.
39 S. D. Movshovich, 'Za progressivnuyu formu raschetov', in *Finansy SSSR*, No. 1, 1977, p. 46; M. Kerezhin and M. Makhlin, 'Glavnaya zadacha – vvod ob"ektov', in *Ekonomicheskaya Gazeta*, No. 10, 1979, p. 7.
40 See V. Bukato, 'Kredit i effektivnost'', in *Ekonomicheskaya Gazeta*, No. 28, 1976, p. 9.
41 'Finansy i kredit v kapital'nom stroitel'stve', in *Ekonomicheskaya Gazeta*, No. 36, 1979, p. 5.
42 Il'in, 'Vmesto avansa – kredit'.
43 S. A. Monich and V. V. Muzhitskikh, 'Razvivat' finansovo-kreditnye otnosheniya v stroitel'stve', in *Finansy SSSR*, No. 11, 1976, p. 58.
44 Linskii and Dubkov, 'Kreditovanie nezavershennogo proizvodstva', p. 48.
45 V. Krasovskii, 'O dolgosrochnykh planakh i prognozakh kapital'nykh vlozhenii', in *Voprosy Ekonomiki*, No. 4, 1967, p. 56.
46 V. Parfenov, 'Pervoprokhodtsy', in *Pravda*, 30/12/68, p. 2.
47 V. Isaev, 'Obshchaya zadacha stroitelei, zakazchikov, proektirov-shchikov', in *Ekonomicheskaya Gazeta*, No. 2, 1972, p. 9.
48 I. Komzin and M. Podnos, 'Pochemu trest otstaet', in *Pravda*, 24/5/74, p. 2.
49 V. Zatvan, 'Stimuly uskoreniya', in *Pravda*, 19/1/75, p. 2.
50 A. Bogatyrev *et al.*, 'Dal'neishii shag po puti khozyaistvennoi reformy', in *Ekonomicheskaya Gazeta*, No. 23, 1975, p. 9.
51 M. G. Chentemirov, 'Vse ob"ekty vvodit' v srok', in *Ekonomicheskaya Gazeta*, No. 33, 1977, p. 9.
52 Zubatkin, 'Planirovanie stroitel'nogo proizvodstva', p. 88.
53 Il'in, 'Vmesto avansa – kredit'.
54 See *ibidem*; V. Petrov and M. Kazarin, ' "Avansov" gusto – na schete pusto', in *Ekonomicheskaya Gazeta*, No. 30, 1976, p. 9.
55 Yu. Rakhmanov, 'Reforma: shag za shagom', in *Ekonomicheskaya Gazeta*, No. 43, 1975, p. 9.
56 *Ibidem*.
57 Podskrebkin, 'Eksperiment v deistvie'.
58 P. Podshivalenko and V. D. Evstigneev, 'Puti sovershenstvovaniya stroitel'nogo proizvodstva', in *Ekonomika Stroitel'stva*, No. 5, 1980, p. 49.
59 Galkin, *Organizatsiya Planirovanie*, p. 483.
60 See V. Sevast'yanov, 'Ekonomicheskoe obozrenie', in *Pravda*, 25/5/76, p. 2.
61 N. Utkin, 'Ne tol'ko vshir'', in *Pravda*, 23/3/75, p. 2; N. Kozlov, 'Spetsializatsiya v brigade', in *Ekonomicheskaya Gazeta*, No. 30, 1976, p. 9.
62 Chentemirov, 'Povyshat' kachestvo stroitel'stva', p. 10.
63 Podshivalenko, 'Usilenie roli', p. 63.
64 See E. Channov, '. . . I otmenili podryad', in *Pravda*, 24/3/75, p. 2; G. Khaliletskii, 'Chto meshaet novoi forme khozrascheta', in *Ekonomiches-kaya Gazeta*, No. 44, 1975, p. 9; N. Burnasheva, 'Ot brigady k potoku',

and R. Pereskokov, 'Narushil – otvechai', in *Ekonomicheskaya Gazeta*, No. 1, 1976, p. 11; L. Ya. Terman, 'Chetkaya tekhnologicheskaya komplektatsiya – vazhnoe uslovie uspekha brigadnogo podryada', in *Ekonomika Stroitel'stva*, No. 3, 1980.

65 See Channov, '. . . I otmenili podryad'; A. Kucherenko, 'Kto narushaet dogover', in *Pravda*, 21/7/75, p. 2.

66 See interview with I. A. Lanshin in *Pravda*, 18/6/75, p. 2; Podshivalenko and Evstigneev. 'Puti sovershenstvovaniya', p. 50; Sukhachev, 'Brigadnyi podryad'.

67 G. Ivanov, 'Po-Zlobinskii!', in *Pravda*, 14/2/76, p. 2; interview with Lanshin quoted under previous note.

68 I. Dmitriev, 'Vazhneishii faktor povysheniya effektivnosti stroitel'nogo proizvodstva', in *Ekonomika Stroitel'stva*, No. 1, 1980, p. 4; 'V chest' znamenatel'nogo yubileya', in *Ekonomika Stroitel'stva*, No. 3, 1980, pp. 9–10.

69 For instance on the construction of the Ust'-Ulim HES. See letter from Yu. Sokolov, in *Pravda*, 20/2/76, p. 2.

70 M. Makhlin, 'Slet brigadirov khozraschetnykh brigad', in *Ekonomicheskaya Gazeta*, No. 8, 1976, p. 2.

71 See G. I. Smirnov, 'Sovershenstvovat' upravlenie ekonomicheskimi poiskami', in *Ekonomika Stroitel'stva*, No. 4, 1980.

72 I. Dmitriev, 'Vazhnye zadachi stroitel'stva', in *Trud*, 6/9/79, p. 2.

73 Podshivalenko and Evstigneev, 'Puti sovershenstvovaniya', p. 49.

74 See source quoted under note 41.

75 Podshivalenko, *Ekonomika Stroitel'stva*, pp. 283–93.

76 A. S. Vishnevskii, 'Vazhnyi faktor obespecheniya vypolneniya planov vvoda v deistvie ob"ektov', in *Ekonomika Stroitel'stva*, No. 2, 1980, pp. 17–18.

77 M. F. Semenova and L. I. Maslennikova, 'Uvelichit' material'nuyu zainteresovannost' rabochikh i sluzhashchikh stroitel'nykh organizatsii', in *Finansy SSSR*, No. 10, 1977, p. 33.

78 See 'Vyshe kachestvo stroitel'stva', in *Pravda*, 4/8/76, p. 1.

79 N. N. Zhilenkov and E. M. Giller, 'Stimulirovanie konechnykh rezul'tatov stroitel'nogo proizvodstva', in *Ekonomika Stroitel'stva*, No. 3, 1980, p. 23.

80 Semonova and Maslennikova, 'Uvelichit' material'nuyu zainteresovannost'', p. 34.

81 'Premirovanie za vvod ob"ektov', in *Ekonomicheskaya Gazeta*, No. 42, 1979, pp. 9–10; O. Sopov, 'O poryadke premirovaniya za vvod moshchnostei i ob"ektov', in in *Ekonomicheskaya Gazeta*, No. 11, 1980, p. 8.

82 V. Zolotarev, 'Podryad i premii', in *Pravda*, 15/1/79, p. 2.

83 'Otvety na voprosy chitatelei o primenenii brigadnogo podryada', in *Ekonomika Stroitel'stva*, No. 1, 1980, p. 33.

84 See V. Kolosov, 'Doska pocheta v zerkale sotsiologii', in *Literaturnaya Gazeta*, 22/9/71, p. 10.

85 See V. P. Kolosov, 'Pravil'no ispol'zovat' fond zarabotnoi platy', in *Finansy SSSR*, No. 10, 1976, p. 53; P. Podshivalenko, 'Puti usileniya kontrolya za raskhodovaniem fondov zarabotnoi platy v stroitel'stve', in

Finansy SSSR, No. 12, 1976, p. 21; L. Kurin, 'Za protsentom – pustotsvetom', in *Pravda*, 16/5/77, p. 2.

86 See V. G. Frolov, 'Sotsialisticheskomy sorevnovaniyu – shirokii razmakh', in *Ekonomika Stroitel'stva*, No. 2, 1980, p. 9.

87 Zolotarev, 'Podryad i premii'.

88 See M. N. Kreinina and N. V. Makarov, 'Effektivnee primenyat' akkordnuyu oplatu truda', in *Ekonomika Stroitel'stva*, No. 5, 1980, p. 55.

89 G. Kalmykov and V. Filipenko, 'Zolotoe Dno', in *Don*, No. 10, 1966.

90 *Pravda Vostoka*, 15/3/72, p. 2, abstracted in *ABSEES* vol. iii, no. 1, July 1979, p. 20.

91 T. Kozhevnika and L. Tairov, 'Na perelome', in *Pravda*, 27/4/76, p. 3.

92 *Tiesa*, 31/7/71, p. 2, abstracted in *ABSEES*, vol. ii, no. 1, July 1978, p. 105.

93 A. Nikolaev, 'Vvod, da ne tot', in *Ekonomicheskaya Gazeta*, No. 51, 1976, p. 9.

94 Zubatkin, 'Planirovanie stroitel'nogo proizvodstva', p. 88.

95 'Zarabotnaya plata – po gotovoi produktsii', in *Ekonomicheskaya Gazeta*, No. 27, 1968, p. 20.

96 See I. Komarov, 'Zarplata stroitelya', in *Ekonomicheskaya Gazeta*, No. 12, 1979, p. 9.

97 See A. S. Dronov, 'Vazhnyi ekonomicheskii rychag', in *Ekonomika Stroitel'stva*, No. 5, 1980, p. 58; *Ekonomika i Zhizn'*, No. 5, 1971, pp. 51–2, abstracted in *ABSEES* vol. ii, no. 2, October 1971, p. 84.

98 The letter of the law limits overtime to four hours in two days, and 120 hours in a year. The rate should be time-and-a-half for the first two hours and double time thereafter.

99 A. Solomakhin, 'Ukrali voskresen'e', in *Pravda*, 14/1/69, p. 2.

100 P. Pronyagin, 'Zven'ya stroiki', in *Pravda*, 8/10/79, p. 2.

101 Podshivalenko, 'Puti usileniya kontrolya', p. 22.

102 See, for instance, I. P. Khizhnyak, 'Ratsional'no ispol'zovat' sredstva na zarplatu', in *Finansy SSSR*, No. 4, 1977, p. 46.

103 Kolosov, 'Pravil'no ispol'zovat'', p. 53.

104 'Berech' materialy na stroikakh', in *Pravda*, 16/6/79, p. 1.

105 D. Stoyanova, 'Vazhen faktor za povishavane na efektivnostta', in *Ikonomicheskii Zhivot* (Sofia, Bulgaria), 8/6/77, p. 13.

106 V. Isaev, 'Povyshenie effektivnosti kapital'nogo stroitel'stva', in *Voprosy Ekonomiki*, No. 2, 1977, p. 10.

107 Yu. Butlitskii, 'Dorogam – prochnuyu odezhdu', in *Pravda*, 5/7/71, p. 2.

108 V. Krasovskii, 'Oborot kapital'nykh vlozhenii i rezervy kapital'nogo stroitel'stva', in *Voprosy Ekonomiki*, No. 8, 1973, p. 47.

109 See Yu. Tsygankov, 'Effektivnost' nepreryvnogo planirovaniya kapital'nogo stroitel'stva', in *Voprosy Ekonomiki*, No. 2, 1976; V. Arkhipenko, 'Uroki i opyt odnoi stroiki', in *Kommunist*, No. 2, 1976, p. 52.

110 Galkin, *Organizatsiya Planirovanie*, p. 484.

111 See interview with A. M. Tokarev, in *Ekonomicheskaya Gazeta*, No. 22, 1976, p. 9.

112 M. Kerezhin and M. Makhlin, 'Stroitel'nomu konveieru – chetkii ritm', in *Ekonomicheskaya Gazeta*, No. 47, 1976, p. 9.

113 See V. Rybal'skii, 'Elektronika – stroitel'stvu', in *Pravda*, 22/3/76, p. 2.

114 E. Gritsevskii and L. Golub, 'EVM i podgotovka proizvodstva', in *Ekonomicheskaya Gazeta*, No. 48, 1978, p. 9.

115 Benza *et al.*, *Novaya Sistema*, p. 73.

116 Vovchenko, 'Bystree osvaivat'', p. 25.

117 Il'in, 'Uskorenie stroitel'stva', p. 10.

118 L. Bibin, 'Plan i resursy', in *Pravda*, 17/9/79, p. 2.

119 L. Grishmanov, 'Na uroven'rastushchikh trebovanii stroitel'stva', in *Ekonomicheskaya Gazeta*, No. 46, 1968, pp. 17–18.

120 See, for example, *ibidem*; V. Popov and V. Rusakova, 'Kvartire nuzhen remont', in *Pravda*, 19/11/69, p. 3; G. Gel'fer, 'Gde konchaetsya asfal't . . .', in *Sovetskaya Rossiya*, 15/10/70, p. 2; Tregubov, 'Kachestvo – zabota obshchaya'.

121 A. Boldyrev, 'Planirovanie v otrasli – na novuyu stupen'', in *Ekonomicheskaya Gazeta*, No. 48, 1979, p. 7.

122 A. Murzin and F. Chursin, 'Nastuplenie na Obi', Part II, in *Pravda*, 13/7/74, p. 2.

123 *Narodnoe Khozyaistvo SSSR v 1979 godu*, Moscow, Statistika, 1980, p. 133.

124 See L. Chernyavskii, 'Navesti poryadok v material'no-tekhnicheskom snabzhenii', in *Ekonomika Stroitel'stva*, No. 10, 1965, pp. 17–18; 'Plan, stroika, ritm', in *Pravda*, 24/1/76, p. 3.

125 *Kommunist Uzbekistana*, No. 1, 1970, pp. 73–81, abstracted in *ABSEES* vol. i, no. 1, July 1970, p. 86.

126 Letter from A. Nalivaev, in *Pravda*, 7/1/69, p. 2.

127 'Mashiny na stroikakh', in *Pravda*, 17/7/75, p. 1.

128 See G. Pavlov, 'Videt' perspektivu', in *Pravda*, 14/6/76, p. 3; A. Bogachuk and Yu. Kishlev, 'Montazh na zavodskoi konveier', in *Pravda*, 8/1/75, p. 2.

129 A. Etmekdzhiyan, 'Vazhnyi rezerv povysheniya effektivnosti kapital'nykh vlozhenii', in *Planovoe Khozyaistvo*, No. 12, 1966, p. 3.

130 Pavlov, 'Videt' perspektivu'.

131 Hanson and Hill, 'Soviet assimilation', p. 597.

132 F. A. Dronov, *Effektivnost' Ispol'zovaniya Osnovnykh Fondov Promyshlennosti*, Minsk, Nauka i Tekhnika, 1966, p. 81.

133 See, for example, *Kazakhstanskaya Pravda*, 24/2/70, p. 2, abstracted in *ABSEES* vol. i, no, 1, July 1970, p. 98.

134 G. Buravkin, 'Upovaya na avral', in *Pravda*, 26/11/68, p. 2.

135 L. Chernyavskii, 'Stroikam – snabzhenie po zakazam', in *Ekonomicheskaya Gazeta*, No. 6, 1976, p. 10.

136 N. T. Arkhipets, 'Snabzhenie stroek cherez organy Gossnaba SSSR', in *Ekonomika Stroitel'stva*, No. 1, 1980, p. 35.

137 D. Yazykov, 'Komplekt dlya stroiki', in *Pravda*, 19/6/80, p. 2.

138 See text of decree in *Ekonomicheskaya Gazeta*, No. 4, 1980, pp. 7–8.

139 S. Palevskii, 'Dva glavka po sosedstvu', in *Ekonomicheskaya Gazeta*, No. 2, 1979, p. 9.

140 A. P. Lifatov, 'Uporyadochit' obespechenie stroek nerudnymi materialami', in *Ekonomika Stroitel'stva*, No. 4, 1980, p. 20.

141 Kazhlaev, *Povyshenie Effektivnosti*, p. 175.

142 See source cited under note 133.

143 See I. Razumkov, 'Zamerzli na "nule" ', in *Sotsial'noe Obespechenie*, No. 1, 1972.

144 A. Yakovlev, 'Kak razvit' eksperiment', in *Pravda*, 25/3/79, p. 2.

145 V. Bratchenko, 'Perevooruzhenie ugol'noi promyshlennosti', in *Ekonomicheskaya Gazeta*, No. 16, 1969, p. 5.

146 Kazhlaev, *Povyshenie Effektivnosti*, pp. 144–5.

147 *Ibidem*.

148 F. Koppel' and B. Brig, 'Bol'shoi gorod i ministerstva', in *Pravda*, 21/5/69, p. 2.

149 E. N. Gromov and L. M. Chernyak, 'Faktor povysheniya effektivnosti', in *Ekonomika Stroitel'stva*, No. 5, 1980, p. 29.

150 M. Postnikov, 'Planirovanie razvitiya gorodskogo khozyaistva', in *Planovoe Khozyaistvo*, No. 4, 1965, p. 22.

151 C. A. Krylov, *The Soviet Economy*, Lexington, Mass., Lexington Books, 1979, p. 234.

152 *Ibidem*.

153 'Zhilishchnoe stroitel'stvo', in *Ekonomicheskaya Gazeta*, No. 28, 1979, p. 2.

154 See leader in *Pravda*, 6/12/74, p. 1; A. Dauksa, 'Demesio centre – darbo nasumas', in *Tiesa*, 25/2/75.

155 See G. Makhlinovskii, 'Orlovskoi "nepreryvke" – dorogu na stroiki', in *Ekonomicheskaya Gazeta*, No. 19, 1975, p. 9; Yu. Tsygankov, 'Geografiya "nepreryvki" ', in *Pravda*, 28/9/75, p. 2; Ya. Glezer, 'Zasluzhivaet rasprostranenie', in *Ekonomicheskaya Gazeta*, No. 37, 1975, p. 9; N. Petrov and D. Shnyukas, 'Gde rvetsya "nepreryvka" ', in *Pravda*, 29/6/80, p. 2.

156 See A. Volkov, 'Zarabotnaya plata i trud stroitelei', in *Pravda*, 4/1/69, p. 2.

157 For an estimate of the Soviet rate of unemployment, see P. J. D. Wiles, 'A note on Soviet unemployment by US definitions', in *Soviet Studies*, vol. xviii, no. 4, April 1972.

158 See V. Zhurnist, 'Trudnyi prolog', in *Komsomol'skaya Pravda*, 18/11/67, p. 1.

159 For a literary treatment of this theme, see V. I. Belov, 'Vospitanie po doktoru Spoku', in *Sever*, No. 7, 1974.

160 S. D. Reznik, 'Trudovaya distsiplina', in *Ekonomika Stroitel'stva*, No. 3, 1980, p. 53.

161 I. Ganichev, 'Ruchnoi trud – na plechi mashin', in *Kazakhstanskaya Pravda*, 4/4/75, p. 2.

162 See L. Timofeev, 'Maslovy – na sele i v gorode', and V. Perevedentsev, 'Nado li trevozhit'sya?', in *Literaturnaya Gazeta*, 29/9/71, p. 10; Krylov, *The Soviet Economy*, p. 162.

163 'V Tsentral'nom Komitete KPSS i Sovete Ministrov SSSR', in *Pravda*, 13/2/79, p. 1; 'V Tsentral'nom komitete KPSS', in *Ekonomicheskaya Gazeta*, No. 24, 1980, p. 2.

164 Tsygankov, 'Effektivnost' nepreryvnogo planirovaniya', p. 15.

165 M. Makhlin, 'Chetkii ritm stroitel'nogo konveiera', in *Ekonomicheskaya Gazeta*, No. 33, 1979, p. 9.

166 Krasovskii, *Problemy Ekonomiki Kapital'nykh Vlozhenii*, p. 59.

167 See P. Afanas'ev, 'God nachalsya, a gde zhe plan?', in *Trud*, 18/1/64, p. 2.

230 *Notes*

168 See Kozhevnika and Tairov, 'Na perelome'; 'Vysshe kachestvo stroitel'stva', in *Pravda*, 13/5/75; G. Petrov, 'Rekonstruktsiya "na oshchup"'', in *Pravda*, 13/2/77, p. 2.
169 I. Shatunovskii, 'Zavod kotorogo net', in *Pravda*, 30/1/80, p. 3.
170 See 'V Gosstroe SSSR', in *Ekonomika Stroitel'stva*, No. 2, 1980, p. 64.
171 See E. Kazakov, 'Kompromissy vokrug nepodelok', in *Ekonomicheskaya Gazeta*, No. 22, 1976, p. 9; V. Shilov, 'Simvolicheskii klyuch', in *Pravda*, 31/1/79, p. 3.
172 N. Geidarov, 'Dolgo – znachit dorogo'.
173 Yu. Kuplyauskas, 'Chto za strokoi otcheta', in *Ekonomicheskaya Gazeta*, No. 10, 1980, p. 9.
174 See Kulya and Trushkin, 'Raschetam – stroinuyu sistemu'.
175 For a positive assessment see M. M. Geidarov, 'Kontrol' – na uroven' trebovanii', in *Den'gi i Kredit*, No. 3, 1977, p. 68.
176 See V. Taratuta, 'Po real'nym planam', in *Pravda*, 22/6/79, p. 2.
177 V. I. Gresik, 'Povysit' effektivnost' kapital'nogo stroitel'stva', in *Finansy SSSR*, No. 5, 1976, p. 58.
178 V. A. Gurov and E. D. Yartseva, 'Effektivnost' kontrolya', in *Finansy SSSR*, No. 4, 1977, pp. 44–5.
179 Tregubov, 'Kachestvo – zabota obshchaya'.

5. Official state doctrine

1 G. A. Kozlov (ed.), *Politicheskaya Ekonomiya. Sotsializm*, Moscow, Politizdat, 1975, p. 110.
2 J. S. Berliner, 'Marxism and the Soviet economy', in M. Bornstein and D. R. Fusfeld (eds.), *The Soviet Economy. A Book of Readings*, Homewood, Illinois, Irwin, 2nd edition, 1966, pp. 23–6.
3 G. A. Kozlov (ed.), *Politicheskaya Ekonomiya*, Part 2, Moscow, Mysl', 1968, pp. 57 and 71.
4 See Nove, *The Soviet Economy*, pp. 302–5.
5 See Berliner, 'Marxism', pp. 25–6.
6 See Nove, *The Soviet Economy*, pp. 307–13.
7 See National Bureau of Economic Research, 54th Annual Report, September 1974, *Issues for Research*, pp. 103–5.
8 See K. M. Bartol, 'Soviet computer centres: network or tangle?' in *Soviet Studies*, vol. xxiii, no. 4, April 1972. The computer networks of both Aeroflot and Morflot are based on imported systems. See J. A. Dillon, 'Aeroflot to use General Automation mini-computers in Soviet message switching network', in *Computers and People*, September 1975, p. 34.
9 For a discussion of the last price reform, see G. E. Schroeder, 'The 1966–67 Soviet industrial price reform: a study in complications', in *Soviet Studies*, vol. xx, no. 4, April 1969.
10 A. E. Probst, *Voprosy Razmeshcheniya Sotsialisticheskoi Promyshlennosti*, Moscow, Nauka, 1971, p. 158.
11 *Ibidem.*
12 See P. Korablev, 'Territorial'naya kontsentratsiya promyshlennogo proizvodstva', in *Voprosy Ekonomiki*, No. 2, 1978, pp. 124–5.

13 See A. Bergson, *The Economics of Soviet Planning*, New Haven, Yale University Press, 1964, p. 252.
14 See G. Grossman, 'Scarce capital and Soviet doctrine', in *Quarterly Journal of Economics*, vol. 67, no. 3, August 1953; on development of the CRE in general, see J.-M. Collette, *Politique des Investissements et Calcul Economique*, Paris, Editions Cujas, 1964.
15 *Tipovaya Metodika Opredeleniya Ekonomicheskoi Effektivnosti Kapital'nykh Vlozhenii i Novoi Tekhniki v Narodnom Khozyaistve SSSR*, Moscow, Gosplan SSSR; Akademiya Nauk SSSR, Institut Ekonomiki, 1960.
16 '*Tipovaya Metodika Opredeleniya Ekonomicheskoi Effektivnosti Kapital'nykh Vlozhenii*', in *Ekonomicheskaya Gazeta*, No. 39, 1969; '*Metodika Opredeleniya Ekonomicheskoi Effektivnosti Kapital'nykh Vlozhenii*', in *Ekonomicheskaya Gazeta*, Nos. 2 and 3, 1981.
17 Bergson, *The Economics*, p. 252.
18 A. Mitrofanov, 'Kompas ekonomicheskoi effektivnosti', in *Ekonomicheskaya Gazeta*, No. 39, 1969, p. 13. For a severe critique of the 1969 *Methodology* see M. Mkrtchyan, 'Ob opredelenii effektivnosti kapital'nykh vlozhenii pri razmeshchenii proizvodstva', in *Planovoe Khozyaistvo*, No. 7, 1970.
19 *Tipovaya Metodika*, 1960, pp. 10–11; *Tipovaya Metodika*, 1969, pp. 11–12; *Metodika*, p. 5.
20 *Tipovaya Metodika*, 1960, p. 12; *Tipovaya Metodika*, 1969, p. 12; *Metodika*, p. 5.
21 For a formal treatment of the Present Value criterion see M. M. Dryden, 'Capital budgeting: treatment of uncertainty and investment criteria', in *Scottish Journal of Political Economy*, vol. xi, no. 3, November 1964.
22 F. Durgin, 'The Soviet 1969 Standard Methodology for investment allocation versus "universally correct" methods', in *ACES Bulletin*, vol. xix, no. 2, Summer 1977, p. 43.
23 The whole of the foregoing relies heavily on Bergson, *The Economics*, pp. 257–9. See also P. J. D. Wiles, 'Soviet investment decision-making', in *The USSR in the 1980s*, Brussels, NATO-Directorate of Economic Affairs, 1978.
24 *Tipovaya Metodika*, 1960, p. 13.
25 *Tipovaya Metodika*, 1969, p. 12; *Metodika*, p. 6.
26 Bergson, *The Economics*, p. 255.
27 *Tipovaya Metodika*, 1960, p. 10.
28 See I. K. Narzikulov (ed.), *Problemy Razvitiya i Razmeshcheniya Proizvoditel'nykh Sil Tadzhikskoi SSR*, Dushanbe, Donish, 1967, p. 40.
29 L. Vaag, 'Effektivnost', zainteresovannost'', in *Ekonomicheskaya Gazeta*, 20/10/65, p. 9.
30 See Bergson, *The Economics*, p. 262.
31 See T. S. Khachaturov, 'Metodicheskie voprosy opredeleniya ekonomicheskoi effektivnosti kapital'nykh vlozhenii', in T. S. Khachaturov (ed.), *Metody i Praktika Opredeleniya Effektivnosti Kapital'nykh Vlozhenii i Novoi Tekhniki*, Issue 11, Moscow, Nauka, 1967, p. 12.
32 See Mitrofanov, 'Kompas'.
33 T. Khachaturov, 'Razvitie teorii effektivnosti kapital'nykh vlozhenii', in *Voprosy Ekonomiki*, No. 11, 1977, p. 77.
34 R. Bazov, 'Puti povysheniya effektivnosti rekonstruktsii predpriyatii', in

Planovoe Khozyaistvo, No. 1, 1977, pp. 40–1.

35 See V. A. Trapeznikov, '"Glagoli" upravleniya: znaet – mozhet – khochet – uspevaet', in *Literaturnaya Gazeta*, 12/5/70, p. 10; Vaag, 'Effektivnost'', p. 8.

36 L. V. Kantorovich and A. L. Vainshtein, 'Ob ischislenii normy effektivnosti na osnove odnoproduktovoi modeli razvitiya khozyaistva', in *Ekonomika i Matematicheskie Metody*, No. 5, 1967; A. L. Lur"e, 'O raschetakh normy effektivnosti i ob odnoproduktovoi modeli narodnogo khozyaistva', in *Ekonomika i Matematicheskie Metody*, No. 3, 1969; L. V. Kantorovich and A. L. Vainshtein, 'Eshche ob ischislenii normy effektivnosti na osnove odnoproduktovoi modeli razvitiya narodnogo khozyaistva', in *Ekonomika i Matematicheskie Metody*, No. 3, 1970.

37 See Durgin, 'The Soviet 1969 SM', p. 41; Wiles, 'Soviet', p. 93.

38 *Metodika*, pp. 2–5.

39 P. J. D. Wiles, *The Political Economy of Communism*, Oxford, Basil Blackwell, 1964, pp. 126–7.

40 See F. Diderikhs, 'O pravomernosti differentsiatsii normativa effektivnosti kapital'nykh vlozhenii', in *Voprosy Ekonomiki*, No. 4, 1967.

41 Durgin, 'The Soviet 1969 SM', pp. 43–4.

42 The 'repeal' of the laws became official with the publication of the documents for the 1971–75 five-year plan. See *Directives of the Five-Year Economic Development Plan of the USSR for 1971–75, A Report by Alexei Kosygin*, Moscow, Novosti Press Agency Publishing House, 1971, p. 22; for a theoretical underpinning of the new position see V. N. Cherkovets (ed.), *Dva Podrazdeleniya Obshchestvennogo Proizvodstva*, Moscow, Mysl', 1971.

43 See K. Marx, *Capital*, Moscow, Progress Publishing House, 1967, vol. II, chapters XX and XXI.

44 *Narodnoe Khozyaistvo v 1959 godu*, Moscow, Gosstatizdat, 1960, p. 149.

45 Wiles, *The Political Economy of Communism*, chapters 14–16.

46 A. Pashkov, *Ekonomicheskii Zakon Preimushchestvennogo Rosta Proizvodstva Sredstv Proizvodstva*, Moscow, Gosplanizdat, 1958, pp. 52, 55, 51.

47 A. Notkin, 'Uroven' razvitiya obshchestvennogo proizvodstva i ego proportsii', in *Voprosy Ekonomiki*, No. 1, 1967, pp. 15–16.

48 See statement on annual plan for 1975 published in *Pravda*, 21/12/74, p. 1, and 'Osnovnye Napravleniya Razvitiya Narodnogo Khozyaistva SSSR na 1976–1980 gody, Doklad Predsedatelya Soveta Ministrov SSSR tovarishcha A. N. Kosygina', in *Ekonomicheskaya Gazeta*, No. 10, 1976, p. 6.

49 *Tipovaya Metodika*, 1960, p. 18. The 1969 *Methodology* is not explicit on this point.

50 See, for example, V. G. Lebedev, *Narodnokhozyaistvennaya Effektivnost' Razvitiya Tekhniki*, Moscow, Mysl', 1971, chapter IV.

51 See Bergson, *The Economics*, pp. 248–9.

52 See F. G. Denton, 'A recent Soviet study of economic growth 1951–63', in *Soviet Studies*, vol. XIX, no. 4, April 1968; *Economic Survey of Europe in 1976*, New York, United Nations, 1977, Part I, p. 101 and Part II, p. 94. But note that the unlagged incremental capital-output ratios presented in the latter sources should be interpreted with caution.

53 See S. Kuznets, *Economic Growth of Nations*, Cambridge, Mass., Harvard

University Press, 1971, p. 74.
54 See I. W. Koropeckyj, 'The development of Soviet location theory before the Second World War', Part I, in *Soviet Studies*, vol. xix, no. 1, July 1967.
55 F. Engels, *Anti-Dühring*, Moscow, Foreign Languages Publishing House, 3rd edition, 1962, p. 401. Translation corrected for style by D.A.D.
56 *Ibidem*, pp. 406–7.
57 *Ibidem*, p. 408.
58 V. I. Lenin, *Izbrannye Proizvedeniya*, Moscow, Izdatel'stvo Politicheskoi Literatury, 1966, vol. II, p. 626.
59 See E. H. Carr, *The Bolshevik Revolution*, London, Macmillan, 1950, vol. 1, chapter 10.
60 Wiles, *The Political Economy of Communism*, pp. 150–2.
61 V. V. Kistanov, *Kompleksnoe Razvitie i Spetsializatsiya Ekonomicheskikh Raionov SSSR*, Moscow, Nauka, 1968, pp. 28–9.
62 A. E. Probst, *Razmeshchenie Sotsialisticheskoi Promyshlennosti, Teoreticheskie Ocherki*, Moscow, Ekonomizdat, 1962, p. 140.
63 N. I. Troshev, *Planirovanie Razmeshcheniya Promyshlennosti v SSSR*, Moscow, Gosplanizdat, 1960, p. 6.
64 *Ekonomika Sotsialisticheskoi Promyshlennosti*, Moscow, Izdatel'stvo Politicheskoi Literatury, 1966, p. 294.
65 Probst, *Voprosy Razmeshcheniya Sotsialisticheskoi Promyshlennosti*, chapter 1.
66 Sh. N. Zakirov, *Problemy Ratsional'nogo Razmeshcheniya Promyshlennosti Uzbekistana*, Tashkent, Nauka UzSSR, 1972, p. 13.
67 For a discussion of this concept, see R. E. Lonsdale, 'The Soviet concept of the territorial-production complex', in *Slavic Review*, vol. xxiv, no. 3, September 1965.

6. Some case studies

1 V. F. Mal'tsev (ed.), *Bratskaya GES. Sbornik Dokumentov i Materialov*, vols I and II, Irkutsk, Vostochno-Sibirskoe, Knizhnoe izdatel'stvo, 1964 and 1967.
2 *Sbornik*, vol. I, p. 43.
3 *Ibidem*, p. 47.
4 *Ibidem*, p. 49
5 *Ibidem*, pp. 51–2.
6 *Ibidem*, p. 51 and pp. 47–8.
7 *Ibidem*, p. 55.
8 *Ibidem*, p. 52.
9 *Ibidem*, pp. 55–6.
10 *Ibidem*, p. 58
11 *Ibidem*, pp. 59–60.
12 *Ibidem*, p. 67.
13 *Ibidem*, p. 69.
14 *Ibidem*, pp. 68–9.
15 *Ibidem*, pp. 72–6.
16 *Ibidem*, p. 126.
17 *Sbornik*, vol. II, p. 355.

18 V. Fridenberg, 'Voprosy kombinirovaniya proizvodstva', in *Voprosy Ekonomiki*, No. 9, 1957, p. 50.
19 *Sbornik*, vol. I, pp. 106–8.
20 *Ibidem*, p. 110.
21 *Ibidem*, p. 79.
2 *Ibidem*.
23 *Ibidem*, pp. 83–4.
24 *Ibidem*, pp. 109–10.
25 *Ibidem*, pp. 122–3.
26 *Ibidem*, pp. 106–7.
27 *Ibidem*, p. 138
28 *Ibidem*, pp. 147–51.
29 *Ibidem*, p. 141.
30 *Ibidem*, p. 143.
31 *Ibidem*, pp. 154–6.
32 *Ibidem*, p. 140.
33 *Ibidem*, pp. 163–5.
34 *Sbornik*, vol. II, pp. 370–2.
35 *Sbornik*, vol. I, p. 267.
36 *Ibidem*, p. 201.
37 *Ibidem*, pp. 201–2
38 *Ibidem*, p. 212.
39 *Ibidem*, p. 214.
40 *Ibidem*, pp. 232–3.
41 *Ibidem*, p. 253.
42 *Ibidem*, pp. 259–60.
43 *Ibidem*, p. 266.
44 *Ibidem*, p. 254.
45 *Ibidem*, p. 287.
46 *Ibidem*, p. 267.
47 *Ibidem*, p. 297.
48 *Ibidem*, p. 320.
49 *Ibidem*, p. 299.
50 *Ibidem*, pp. 301–3 and 320–1.
51 *Ibidem*, p. 316.
52 *Ibidem*, p. 324.
53 *Ibidem*, p. 329.
54 *Sbornik*, vol. II, p. 395.
55 *Ibidem*, p. 396.
56 *Ibidem*, p. 407.
57 *Sbornik*, vol. I, p. 412.
58 *Sbornik*, vol. II, pp. 408–9.
59 *Sbornik*, vol. I, p. 427.
60 *Sbornik*, vol. II, pp. 398–9.
61 *Ibidem*, pp. 46–9, 54 and 62–3.
62 *Sbornik*, vol. I, p. 419.
63 *Ibidem*, p. 439.
64 *Sbornik*, vol. II, pp. 441–8.

65 *Sbornik*, vol. I, p. 437.
66 *Sbornik*, vol. II, p. 51.
67 *Ibidem*, p. 62.
68 *Ibidem*, p. 74.
69 *Ibidem*, p. 85.
70 *Ibidem*, pp. 46–9.
71 *Ibidem*, p. 74.
72 *Ibidem*, p. 453.
73 *Ibidem*, p. 161.
74 *Ibidem*, p. 133.
75 *Ibidem*, p. 132.
76 E. Gorbunov and B. Orlov, 'O narodnokhozyaistvennoi effektivnosti razvitiya promyshlennosti v Sibiri', in *Voprosy Ekonomiki*, No. 8, 1966, pp. 55–6.
77 *Sbornik*, vol. II, pp. 459–60.
78 *Ibidem*, p. 464.
79 *Ibidem*, pp. 424–5.
80 *Ibidem*, pp. 424–6.
81 R. M. Merkin and A. I. Mitrofanov, *Snizhenie Udel'nykh Kapital'nykh Vlozhenii v Promyshlennosti*, Moscow, Gosudarstvennoe izdatel'stvo literatury po stroitel'stvu, arkhitekture i stroitel'nym materialam, 1963, p. 75.
82 V. Krasovskii, 'Ekonomicheskaya reforma i problemy kapital'nykh vlozhenii', p. 48.
83 V. A. Nemtsev, 'Puti optimizatsii administrativno-territorial'nogo deleniya SSSR', in *Sovetskoe Gosudarstvo i Pravo*, No. 6, 1972, p. 85.
84 Gorbunov and Orlov, 'O narodnokhozyaistvennoi effektivnosti', pp. 55–6.
85 P. Potemkin, G. Devyatov and V. Sorokin, 'Ekonomicheskie voprosy sozdaniya i osvoeniya novykh predpriyatii Sibiri', in *Voprosy Ekonomiki*, No. 5, 1965, p. 32.
86 A. Bochkin and A. Sukhodrev, 'Svet nad Eniseem', in *Pravda*, 5/11/68, p. 2.
87 *Sbornik*, vol. II, p. 469.
88 *Ibidem*, p. 206.
89 *Ibidem*, p. 481.
90 *Ibidem*, p. 206.
91 *Ibidem*, p. 530.
92 *Ibidem*, p. 525.
93 V. Krasovskii, 'Oborot kapital'nykh vlozhenii i rezervy kapital'nogo stroitel'stva', p. 44.
94 P. I. Lyashchenko, *Istoriya Narodnogo Khozyaistva SSSR*, vol. III, Moscow, Gosudarstvennoe izdatel'stvo politicheskoi literatury, 1956, p. 291.
95 *Narodnoe Khozyaistvo SSSR v 1965 g.*, Moscow, Statistika, 1966, p. 179. The figure is actually for the whole of the Kazakh SSR, but Karaganda is the only major producer of coking coal in that republic.
96 Yu. G. Saushkin *et al.* (eds.), *Ekonomicheskaya Geografiya Sovetskogo Soyuza*, Part I, Moscow, Izdatel'stvo Moskovskogo universiteta, 1967, p. 157.

97 For discussion of the numerous problems that have arisen in connection with this development see G. Petrov, 'Porogi ognennoi reki', in *Pravda*, 22/5/71, p. 2; N. Khromagin *et al.*, 'Proekty vdogonku', in *Pravda*, 20/3/74, p. 2.

98 G. E. Khrapkov, *Ekonomicheskaya Effektivnost' Kapital'nykh Vlozhenii v Razvitie Karagandinskogo Basseina*, Alma-Ata, Nauka, 1965, pp. 162–81.

99 *Kazakhstanskaya Pravda*, 20/3/71, p. 2, abstracted in *ABSEES*, vol. ii, no. 1, July 1971, p. 110; see also R. I. Kosmambetova and E. M. Federova, *Sovershenstvovanie Proizvodstvennoi Struktury Ugol'nykh Shakht*, Alma-Ata, Nauka Kazakhskoi SSR, 1976.

100 B. M. Sokolov, 'Ekonomicheskaya effektivnost' kapital'nykh vlozhenii i puti sokrashcheniya ob"emov nezavershennogo stroitel'stva', in T. S. Khachaturov (ed.), *Ekonomicheskaya Effektivnost' Kapital'nykh Vlozhenii i Novoi Tekhniki*, Moscow, Nauka, 1965, p. 256, citing *Peredovaya Pravda*, 13/8/58.

101 See D. Gridasov, 'Planam – kompleksnost', optimal'nost''', in *Ekonomicheskaya Gazeta*, 20/10/65, p. 13.

102 See, for example, N. A. Karaulov, 'Gidroenergeticheskie resursy severnogo i zapadnogo Tadzhikistana', in *Tadzhiksko-Pamirskaya Ekspeditsiya 1933 g.*, Leningrad, Akademiya Nauk SSSR.

103 I. T. Novikov, 'Osushchestvlenie leninskikh idei elektrifikatsii SSSR', in *Partiinaya Zhizn'*, No. 7, 1966, p. 21.

104 L. V. Talasov, 'Kaskad vakhshskikh GES i ego rol'v energetike Srednei Azii', in K. T. Porshin and F. S. Mazitova (eds.), *Nurekskaya GES i Zadachi Nauki*, Stalinabad, AN TadzhSSR, 1961.

105 Porshin and Mazitova, *Nurekskaya GES*, p. 5.

106 A. E. Probst and I. K. Narzikulov (eds.), *Narodnokhozyaistvennoe Znachenie Nurekskoi GES*, Dushanbe, Irfon, 1964, p. 77.

107 F. S. Mazitova, 'Osnovnye napravleniya razvitiya toplivno-energeticheskogo balansa Tadzhikistana', in Porshin and Mazitova, *Nurekskaya GES*, p. 22.

108 N. T. Lolaev, 'Transport i mezhraionnye ekonomicheskie svyazi Tadzhikistana', in *Voprosy Razvitiya Proizvoditel'nykh Sil Tadzhikistana, Uchenye Zapiski*, Dushanbe, Dushanbinskii gosudarstvennyi pedogogicheskii institut, 1964, vol. 43, p. 181.

109 Narzikulov, *Problemy Razvitiya*, p. 39.

110 U. Kh. Kletsel'man, *Kompleksnoe Razvitie Promyshlennosti Tadzhikskoi SSR*, Dushanbe, Donish, 1969, p. 133.

111 Oral communication from member of the Academy of Sciences of the Tadzhik SSR, 1968.

112 *Kommunist Tadzhikistana*, 26/1/74, p. 1, abstracted in *ABSEES*, vol. 5, no. 3, July 1974, p. 54.

113 'Podnimaetsya plotina', in *Pravda*, 25/8/74, p. 1.

114 D. Rasulov, 'Opirayas' na opyt', in *Pravda*, 6/1/76, pp. 2–3.

115 D. Chernysh, 'Rastet Nurek elektricheskii', in *Pravda*, 26/3/77, p. 2.

116 'Po kompleksnym programmam', in *Pravda*, 24/9/77, p. 1.

117 Reported in *Trud*, 15/9/79, p. 1.

118 A. D. Dadabaev, '"Rabochaya estafeta": stupeni rosta', in *Ekonomiches-*

kaya Gazeta, No. 18, 1980, p. 5.
119 *Ibidem.*
120 See *Kommunist Tadzhikistana*, 27/11/65, 10/12/65 and 23/1/66, quoted in V. Conolly, *Beyond the Urals*, London, Oxford University Press, 1967, p. 150.
121 *Kommunist Tadzhikistana*, 3/11/72, p. 2, abstracted in *ABSEES*, vol. 3, no. 3, January 1973, pp. 50–1.
122 See L. Makhkamov and D. Chernysh, 'Rabochaya estafeta', in *Pravda*, 7/12/74, p. 2; O. Latifi, 'Komu nesti estafetu', in *Pravda*, 13/5/76, p. 2.
123 Narzikulov, *Problemy Razvitiya*, p. 42.
124 S. V. Klopov and V. A. Ryl'skii, *Energopromyshlennyi Kompleks Yuzhnogo Tadzhikistana*, Moscow, Nauka, 1967, p. 19.
125 Probst and Narzikulov, *Narodnokhozyaistvennoe Znachenie*, p. 107.
126 *Ibidem*, p. 108.
127 M. M. Albegov, 'O lokalizatsii zadach razvitiya i razmeshcheniya proizvodstva', in A. A. Ivanchenko (ed.), *Ekonomicheskie Problemy Razmeshcheniya Proizvoditel'nykh Sil SSSR*, Moscow, Nauka, 1969, pp. 100–1.
128 *Ibidem.*
129 Klopov and Ryl'skii, *Energopromyshlennyi Kompleks*, pp. 22 and 94.
130 O. Latifi, '. . . i shlyut telegrammy', in *Pravda*, 17/10/74, p. 2.
131 *Direktivy XXIII S"ezda KPSS po Pyatiletnemu Planu Razvitiya Narodnogo Khozyaistva SSSR na 1966–70 gody*, Moscow, Politizdat, 1966, p. 69.
132 O. Latifi, 'Svet nad dolinoi', in *Pravda*, 28/7/80, p. 3.
133 Probst and Narzikulov, *Narodnokhozyaistvennoe Znachenie*, p. 159.
134 Narzikulov, *Problemy Razvitiya*, p. 55.
135 Baguzov, 'Effektivnost' kapital'nykh vlozhenii', p. 23.
136 *Kommunist Tadzhikistana*, 30/5/71, p. 2, abstracted in *ABSEES*, vol. 2, no. 2, October 1971, p. 86.
137 Rasulov, 'Opirayas' na opyt'.
138 *Ibidem.*
139 See V. Beketov and O. Latifi, 'Taktika i strategiya kompleksa', Part I, in *Pravda*, 14/11/76, p. 2.
140 A. O. Stepun, 'Zavershayushchii god pyatiletki', in *Ekonomika Stroitel'stva*, No. 1, 1980, p. 10.
141 Latifi, '. . . i shlyut telegrammy'.
142 O. Latifi, 'Metall Regara', in *Pravda*, 2/4/75, p. 2.
143 V. Sevast'yanov, 'Puskovye pered finishom', in *Pravda*, 10/10/74, p. 2.
144 'Budet pervyi metall', in *Kommunist Tadzhikistana*, 1/1/75, p. 2.
145 Latifi, 'Metall Regara'.
146 S. Makhkambaev, 'Problemy stroyashchegosya zavoda', in *Ekonomicheskaya Gazeta*, No. 4, 1976, p. 11.
147 'Rastet tadzhikskii alyuminievyi', in *Pravda*, 21/12/75, p. 1.
148 O. Latifi, 'Energiya Vakhsha', in *Pravda*, 4/8/79, p. 2.
149 *Ibidem.*
150 D. Chernysh, 'Gigant v stroyu!', in *Pravda*, 15/10/80, p. 1.
151 Makhkambaev, 'Problemy stroyashchegosya zavoda'.
152 V. Beketov and O. Latifi, 'Taktika i strategiya kompleksa', Part II, in *Pravda*, 15/11/76, p. 2.

153 Beketov and Latifi, 'Taktika i strategiya kompleksa', Part I.
154 Latifi, 'Energiya Vakhsha'.
155 Narzikulov, *Problemy Razvitiya*, p. 45.
156 Probst and Narzikulov, *Narodnokhozyaistvennoe Znachenie*, p. 28.
157 *Kommunist Tadzhikistana*, 19/10/72, p. 2, abstracted in *ABSEES*, vol. 3, no. 3, January 1973, p. 48.
158 Probst and Narzikulov, *Narodnokhozyaistvennoe Znachenie*, p. 67.
159 Beketov and Latifi, 'Taktika i strategiya kompleksa', Part II.
160 Beketov and Latifi, 'Taktika i strategiya kompleksa', Part I.
161 Latifi, 'Energiya Vakhsha'.
162 Chernysh, 'Rastet Nurek elektricheskii'.
163 'Ispolin na Vakhshe', in *Ekonomicheskaya Gazeta*, No. 27, 1980, p. 1.
164 Latifi, 'Svet nad dolinoi'.
165 P. Volin and V. Fainberg, 'Mertvyi ob"em', in *Literaturnaya Gazeta*, 24/12/80, p. 12.
166 Latifi, 'Energiya Vakhsha'; A. Nikolaev, 'Nazrevshie problemy gidroenergetiki', in *Ekonomicheskaya Gazeta*, No. 18, 1980, p. 9.
167 *Narodnoe Khozyaistvo SSSR v 1965 godu*, Moscow, Statistika, 1966, p. 538.
168 Reported in *Pravda*, 11/8/58.
169 See N. Stroganov, '"Tsena" kilovatta', in *Ekonomicheskaya Gazeta*, 4/7/64, p. 5.
170 See report of VII Plenum CC CP Tadzhikistan, in *Kommunist Tadzhikistana*, 14/4/61; V. Bulargin, 'Krepit' sotsialisticheskuyu zakonnost'', in *Kommunist Tadzhikistana*, 17/12/61, p. 2.
171 *Narodnoe Khozyaistvo SSSR v 1975 godu*, Moscow, Statistika, 1976, p. 513.
172 Latifi, '. . . i shlyut telegrammy'.
173 Latifi, 'Energiya Vakhsha'.
174 Kletsel'man, *Kompleksnoe Razvitie*, p. 38.
175 *Ibidem*, p. 40.
176 *Ibidem*.
177 *Ibidem*, p. 42.
178 See R. Rakhimov *et al.*, 'Voprosy spetsializatsii i dal'neishego razvitiya mashinostroitel'noi promyshlennosti Tadzhikistana', in *Voprosy Ekonomiki Narodnogo Khozyaistva Tadzhikistana*, Dushanbe, AN TadzhSSR, 1963, pp. 10–11.
179 Kletsel'man, *Kompleksnoe Razvitie*, p. 43.
180 See I. V. Chirgadze, 'Nekotorye voprosy razvitiya mashinostroeniya v Tadzhikistane', in *Izvestiya Akademii Nauk Tadzhikskoi SSR, Otdelenie Obshchestvennykh Nauk*, No. 2 (40), 1965, p. 57.
181 M. N. Nurnazarov, *Razvitie i Razmeshchenie Promyshlennosti Severnogo Tadzhikistana*, Dushanbe, Donish, 1974, p. 61.
182 Chirgadze, *Mashinostroenie Tadzhikistana*, p. 137.
183 T. E. Dyrin and V. P. Sherstnev, *Mashinostroitel'naya i Elektrotekhnicheskaya Promyshlennost' Tadzhikistana*, Stalinabad, Tadzhikgosizdat, 1961, pp. 8–9; Rakhimov *et al.*, 'Voprosy spetsializatsii', pp. 7–8; I. K. Narzikulov, Kh. S. Saidmuradov and G. Ya. Kurtser (eds.), *Ocherki Istorii Narodnogo Khozyaistva Tadzhikistana*, Dushanbe, Donish, 1967, pp. 213–14.

184 *Kommunist Tadzhikistana*, 2/4/74, p. 1, abstracted in *ABSEES*, vol. 5, no. 3, July 1974, p. 49.

185 Rakhimov *et al.*, 'Voprosy spetsializatsii', p. 18.

186 Chirgadze, *Mashinostroenie Tadzhikistana*, p. 133.

187 Rakhimov *et al.*, 'Voprosy spetsializatsii', p. 13.

188 Nurnazarov, *Razvitie i Razmeshchenie*, p. 100.

189 V. Pinskii and V. Sharaev, 'Kogda interesy raskhodyatsya', in *Ekonomicheskaya Gazeta*, No. 26, 1968, p. 20.

190 A. Shifrin and Yu. Khokhryakov, 'Vpred' bez rasresheniya', in *Ekonomicheskaya Gazeta*, No. 41, 1968, pp. 12–13.

191 *Ibidem*, p. 13.

192 Kletsel'man, *Kompleksnoe Razvitie*, p. 42.

193 See, for example, G. I. Granik, *Ekonomicheskie Problemy Razvitiya i Razmeshcheniya Proizvoditel'nykh Sil Evropeiskogo Severa SSSR*, Moscow, Nauka, 1971, p. 142.

194 'Zapadnaya Sibir' – glavnaya', in *Ekonomicheskaya Gazeta*, No. 16, 1977, pp. 12–13.

195 *Ibidem*, p. 13.

196 A. I. Il'ichev and R. M. Buryndin, *Zapadnaya Sibir'*, Novosibirsk, Zapadno-Sibirskoe knizhnoe izdatel'stvo, 1971, p. 143.

197 'Stroiki zapadnoi Sibiri', in *Pravda*, 27/5/80, p. 1.

198 S. Bogatko, 'Potentsial Sibiri', in *Pravda*, 11/2/80, p. 2.

199 'Prognozirovanie perspektiv gazonosti', in *Gazovaya Promyshlennost'*, No. 11, 1975.

200 F. K. Salmanov *et al.*, 'Syr'evaya baza gazovoi promyshlennosti Zapadnoi Sibiri', in *Gazovaya Promyshlennost'*, No. 2, 1975.

201 See I. F. Elliot, *The Soviet Energy Balance*, New York, Washington and London, Praeger, 1974, chapter 3.

202 S. Vtorushin and A. Murzin, 'Tyumenskii gaz', Part I, in *Pravda*, 26/2/77, p. 2.

203 K. G. Davarashvili and A. D. Timoshevskaya, 'Osobennosti kapital'nogo stroitel'stva v Sibiri', in *Ekonomika i Organizatsiya Promyshlennogo Proizvodstva*, No. 2, 1972, pp. 28–9 and 31.

204 A. Probst, 'Puti razvitiya toplivnogo khozyaistva SSSR', in *Voprosy Ekonomiki*, No. 6, 1971, p. 57.

205 Ya. Mazover, 'Razmeshchenie toplivodobyvayushchei promyshlennosti', in *Planovoe Khozyaistvo*, No. 11, 1977, p. 146.

206 A. Khaitun, 'Sotsial'no-ekonomicheskie problemy osvoeniya neftyanykh i gazovykh raionov strany', in *Planovoe Khozyaistvo*, No. 9, 1977, p. 94.

207 N. Nekrasov, 'Industrial'naya karta strany', in *Pravda*, 20/4/76, p. 2.

208 Khaitun, 'Sotsial'no-ekonomicheskie problemy', p. 94.

209 A. Aganbegyan, 'Territoriya i otrasli', in *Pravda*, 7/12/79, pp. 2–3.

210 For a general discussion of the Soviet energy balance see D. Zhimerin, 'Energetika: segodnya i zavtra', in *Pravda*, 17/12/76, p. 2.

211 Vtorushin and Murzin, 'Tyumenskii gaz', Part I.

212 *Ibidem*.

213 V. Lisin, 'Tugoi uzel tobol'skii' in *Pravda*, 20/8/80, p. 2; there may have

240

Notes

been international complications here. Western technology is involved at Tobol'sk, as at the Tomsk petro-chemical plant. The German chemical industry feared that in the uncertain market conditions of the 1970s compensation deals such as had been proposed for Tomsk, with the involvement of a German consortium, might produce embarrassingly high levels of Soviet infiltration into the German market. Political pressure to cut the size of the project was then successfully applied by the Germans on the Soviet authorities. See V. Sobeslavsky and P. Beazley, *The Transfer of Technology to Socialist Countries*, Farnborough, Gower, 1980, pp. 96–7.

214 Bogatko, 'Potentsial Sibiri'.
215 V. Orlov and R. Shniper, 'Territorial'nyi plan: perspektivy, problemy, funktsii', in *Ekonomicheskaya Gazeta*, No. 29, 1967, p. 11; V. K. Savel'ev, 'Osnovnye problemy razvitiya ural'skogo ekonomicheskogo raiona', in N. N. Nekrasov (ed.), *Razvitie i Razmeshchenie Proizvoditel'nykh Sil Ekonomicheskikh Raionov SSSR*, Moscow, Nauka, 1967, p. 110.
216 'Planirovanie – na uroven' zadach, postavlennykh XXIV s"ezdom KPSS', in *Ekonomika i Organizatsiya Promyshlennogo Proizvodstva*, No. 3, 1972, p. 7.
217 S. Vtorushin and V. Sevest'yanov, 'Tyumen': vtoroi etap', Part 3, in *Pravda*, 17/5/79, p. 2.
218 See A. Murzin, 'Vsled za Samotlorom', in *Pravda*, 11/6/75, p. 3; A. Murzin, 'Gazovyi kontinent', in *Pravda*, 12/6/75, p. 3; S. Vtorushin and A. Murzin, 'Tyumenskii gaz', Part II, in *Pravda*, 27/2/77, p. 2.
219 A. A. Trofimuk, 'Kompleksnaya programma "Sibir"'', in *Ekonomicheskaya Gazeta*, No. 30, 1979, p. 6.
220 Vtorushin and Murzin, 'Tyumenskii gaz', Part II.
221 'Strategiyu vybrat' segodnya', in *Ekonomika i Organizatsiya Promyshlennogo Proizvodstva*, No. 2, 1979, pp. 17–18.
222 Orlov and Shniper, 'Territorial'nyi'.
223 F. Salmanov, 'Tyumenskie gorizonty', in *Pravda*, 13/2/81, p. 3.
224 Yu. Permikin, 'Starye bedy novogo metoda', in *Pravda*, 1/9/75, p. 2.
225 A. Goretskii *et al.*, 'O gosudarstvennom ruble', in *Ekonomicheskaya Gazeta*, No. 46, 1975, p. 9.
226 S. Vtorushin and A. Murzin, 'Doroga k bogatstvam severa', in *Pravda*, 4/8/76, p. 2.
227 Vtorushin and Murzin, 'Tyumenskii gaz', Part II.
228 Vtorushin and Murzin, 'Doroga k bogatstvam severa'.
229 A. Medushchenko, 'Cherez trista rek', in *Pravda*, 3/1/79, p. 2.
230 See G. Yastrebtsov, 'Doroga na Urengoi', in *Pravda*, 15/9/80, p. 2.
231 S. Vtorushin, 'Severnoi magistral'yu', in *Pravda*, 22/5/79, p. 2.
232 R. Kuzovatskii, 'K bogatstvam Priob'ya', in *Pravda*, 20/1/76, p. 3. See also S. Vtorushin and A. Murzin, 'Na novom etape', in *Pravda*, 5/6/78, p. 2.
233 Aganbegyan, 'Territoriya i otrasli'.
234 'Nefteprovod Omsk – Pavlodar', in *Ekonomicheskaya Gazeta*, No. 14, 1976, p. 9.
235 Il'ichev and Buryndin, *Zapadnaya Sibir'*, p. 147.

236 'Urengoi–Vyngapur–Chelyabinsk', in *Ekonomicheskaya Gazeta*, No. 9, 1978, p. 2.
237 B. Shcherbina, 'Po toplivnym arteriyam', in *Pravda*, 26/4/79, p. 2.
238 E. Gromov, 'V usloviyakh sibirskoi zimy', in *Ekonomicheskaya Gazeta*, No. 4, 1980, p. 9.
239 S. Vtorushin and V. Sevast'yanov, 'Tyumen': vtoroi etap', Part 2, in *Pravda*, 16/5/79, p. 2.
240 Shcherbina, 'Po toplivnym arteriyam'.
241 A. Shikin, 'Neftyanye magistrali Sibiri', in *Pravda*, 25/10/75, p. 2.
242 'Neftegazovyi kompleks Sibiri', in *Ekonomicheskaya Gazeta*, No. 7, 1978, p. 2.
243 V. Kuramin, 'Khotya sdelano po proektu . . .', in *Pravda*, 25/5/77, p. 2.
244 Lisin, 'Tugoi uzel'.
245 L. Levitskii, 'Bar'ery vdol' trassy', in *Pravda*, 23/2/77, p. 2.
246 S. Vtorushin, 'Poputnyi – ne brosovyi', in *Pravda*, 15/8/75, p. 2.
247 Levitskii, 'Bar'ery'.
248 V. Lisin, 'Gasnut fakeli na promyslyakh', in *Pravda*, 17/6/80, p. 1.
249 S. Vtorushin and A. Murzin, 'Industriya neftyanogo kraya', in *Pravda*, 10/6/78, p. 2.
250 S. Vtorushin, 'Gigant na Irtyshe', in *Pravda*, 8/10/76, p. 2.
251 Bogatko, 'Potentsial Sibiri'.
252 V. Dubrovin, 'Kontrasty dvukh stroek', in *Ekonomicheskaya Gazeta*, No. 29, 1980, p. 9.
253 Vtorushin, 'Poputnyi – ne brosovyi'.
254 V. Lisin and V. Parfenov, 'Tyumenskii sever segodnya', in *Pravda*, 5/5/80, p. 2.
255 Murzin, 'Gazovyi kontinent'.
256 *Ibidem*.
257 Aganbegyan, 'Territoriya i otrasli'.
258 Statement by V. Krasovskii, reported in V. Lavrovskii, 'Ob investitsion-nykh programmakh perspektivnogo razvitiya raionov Sibiri i Srednei Azii', in *Ekonomika i Organizatsiya Promyshlennogo Proizvodstva*, No. 6, 1971, p. 9.
259 See B. S. Semenov, 'Novye giganty neftekhimii', in *Ekonomicheskaya Gazeta*, No. 15, 1976, p. 11.
260 Vtorushin and Murzin, 'Tyumenskii gaz', Part II.
261 E. Kozlov, 'Byt severyanina', in *Pravda*, 2/7/79, p. 2.
262 S. Vtorushin and V. Sevast'yanov, 'Tyumen': vtoroi etap', Part 1, in *Pravda*, 15/5/79, p. 2.
263 Kozlov, 'Byt severyanina'.
264 Bogatko, 'Potentsial Sibiri'.
265 S. Vtorushin, 'S chego nachinaetsya gorod', in *Pravda*, 31/7/80, p. 2.
266 *Ibidem*.
267 V. Strizhov and R. Dadashev, 'Ekonomika severnogo gazopromysla', in *Ekonomicheskaya Gazeta*, No. 25, 1980, p. 16.
268 Bogatko, 'Potentsial Sibiri'.
269 V. Bakhilov, 'Lyudi i neft'', in *Trud*, 18/4/80, p. 2.
270 V. Lisin and V. Parfenov, 'Tyumenskii sever segodnya', Part 2, in

Pravda, 6/5/80, p. 2.

271 N. Federenko , 'Voprosy optimizatsii razvitiya i razmeshcheniya proiz-
     vodstva', in *Planovoe Khozyaistvo*, No. 8, 1968, p. 10.
272 V. M. Pushkarev, 'Rezervy povysheniya effektivnosti ispol'zovaniya
     trudovykh resursov tyumenskoi oblasti', in *Ekonomika i Organizatsiya
     Promyshlennogo Proizvodstva*, No. 2, 1972, p. 59.
273 A. Murzin and F. Chursin, 'Nastuplenie na Obi', Part II.
274 I. Dubovskii, 'V roli posrednika', in *Ekonomicheskaya Gazeta*, No. 30,
     1967, p. 20.
275 For a graphic description of the ingenuity with which permafrost
     problems are solved, see S. Vtorushin, 'Pod vechnoi merzlotoi', in
     Pravda, 23/5/75, p. 1.
276 'Ne chislom, a umeniem', in *Ekonomika i Organizatsiya Promyshlennogo
     Proizvodstva*, No. 2, 1979, p. 11.

7. Investment planning and investment strategy

1 For interesting material on this obscure issue see P. Hazlehurst, 'Russia
   ready to barter oil for Japan's aid on railway', in *The Times*, 29/3/74, p. 17;
   E. Stevens, 'Russia spurns foreign help to exploit oil', in *The Times*,
   29/5/74, p. 17; 'Doubts over US hold up Japan–Soviet talks on Siberia', in
   The Times, 23/7/74, p. 20; J. Earle, 'Montedison signs Soviet deal', in *The
   Times*, 3/12/75, p. 23.
2 M. Perlman, 'Party politics and bureaucracy in economic policy', in
   Tullock, *The Vote Motive*, pp. 72–3, quoting *The Sunday Times*, 15/2/76, pp.
   10–12.
3 For an interesting theoretical discussion of how problems of information
   and uncertainty could induce vertical integration under market conditions, see K. J. Arrow, 'Vertical integration and communication', in *The
   Bell Journal of Economics*, vol. 6, no. 1, Spring 1975.
4 Yu. Kazmin *et al.*, 'Sebe i potomkam', Part 3, in *Pravda*, 27/9/74, p. 2.
5 See E. R. Brubaker, 'A sectoral analysis of efficiency under market and
   plan', in *Soviet Studies*, vol. xxiii, no. 3, January 1972.
6 See any edition of the *Economic Survey of Europe*, New York, United Nations.
7 Leibenstein concludes a study of the ICOR based on western material
   with the statement that 'it would appear that the ICOR is really a function
   of growth, rather than the other way around'. See H. Leibenstein,
   'Incremental capital-output ratios and growth rates in the short run', in
   The Review of Economics and Statistics, vol. 78, 1966, p. 24.
8 For a discussion of this issue see S. H. Cohn, 'Deficiencies in Soviet
   investment policies and the technological imperative', in US Congress
   Joint Economic Committee, *Soviet Economy in a New Perspective*,
   Washington, US GPO, 1976, pp. 453–6.
9 See S. H. Cohn, 'A comment on Alec Nove, "A note on growth,
   investment and price indexes"', in *Soviet Studies*, vol. xxxiii, no. 2, April
   1981, p. 298.
10 See A. Nove, 'A note on growth, investment and price-indices', in *Soviet
   Studies*, vol. xxxiii, no. 1, January 1981; S. H. Cohn, 'A comment'.

11 Ustinov, *Statistika*, p. 25.
12 R. V. Greenslade, 'The real gross national product of the U.S.S.R., 1950–1975', in US Congress JEC, *Soviet Economy in a New Perspective*, p. 277.
13 S. H. Cohn, 'Soviet replacement investment: a rising policy imperative', in US Congress JEC, *Soviet Economy in a Time of Change*, vol. 1, p. 234.
14 For a detailed description of what is included under each title in the official Soviet industrial classification, see *Structure and Change in European Industry*, New York, United Nations, 1977, Appendix B, table B.1.
15 H. B. Chenery and T. Watanabe, 'International comparisons of the structure of production', in *Econometrica*, vol. xxvi, no. 4, October 1958, especially pp. 492–3.
16 Hirschman, *The Strategy*; Wilber, *The Soviet Model*, chapter v.
17 *Economic Survey of Europe in 1976*, Part II, p. 94; *Economic Survey of Europe in 1980*, p. 135.
18 *Economic Survey of Europe in 1976*, Part II, p. 104.

Appendix

1 *Metodicheskie Ukazaniya k Razrabotke Gosudarstvennykh Planov Razvitiya Narodnogo Khozyaistva SSSR*, Moscow, Gosplan SSSR, 1974, p. 595.
2 *Ibidem*.
3 *Ibidem*.
4 *Ibidem*.
5 V. Savost'yanov, 'Otsenka importnykh mashin i oborudovaniya', in *Planovoe Khozyaistvo*, No. 3, 1975.
6 *Ibidem*, pp. 79–80.
7 *Ibidem*, p. 82.
8 *Ibidem*, p. 80.
9 O. Rybakov, 'Ekonomicheskaya effektivnost' vneshnei torgovli', in *Planovoe Khozyaistvo*, No. 12, 1974, pp. 20–1.
10 Savost'yanov, 'Otsenka', p. 83.
11 *Ibidem*.
12 L. I. Mazurin, 'Organizatsiya upravleniya v stroitel'stve', in *Finansy SSSR*, No. 8, 1976, p. 43.
13 A. P. Krotov, 'Aktual'nye voprosy upravleniya stroitel'stvom', in *Ekonomika Stroitel'stva*, No. 11, 1980, p. 14.
14 V. Vitkovskii, 'Sovershenstvovanie upravleniya kapital'nym stroitel'-stvom', in *Voprosy Ekonomiki*, No. 6, 1977, p. 33.
15 D. I. Burkeev, 'Kakie organizatsii luchshe rabotayut?', in *Ekonomika Stroitel'stva*, No. 9, 1981, p. 71.
16 A. A. Patsuk, 'Kontsentratsiya sil', in *Ekonomika Stroitel'stva*, No. 2, 1981, p. 16.
17 A. S. Lukashevich, 'Voprosy sovershenstvovaniya khozyaistvennogo mekhanizma v stroitel'stve', in *Ekonomika Stroitel'stva*, No. 7, 1981, especially p. 24.
18 *Ibidem*, p. 24.
19 V. Sevast'yanov, 'Izderzhki popustitel'stva', in *Sotsialisticheskaya Industriya*, 4/10/81, p. 2.
20 Hanson and Hill, 'Soviet assimilation', p. 597.

Select bibliography

Baguzov, N., 'Effektivnost' kapital'nykh vlozhenii i proektirovanie', in *Ekonomika Stroitel'stva*, No. 2, 1966.

Beketov, V. and O. Latifi, 'Taktika i strategiya kompleksa', Parts I and II, in *Pravda*, 14/11/76, p. 2 and 15/11/76, p. 2.

Bergson, A., *The Economics of Soviet Planning*, New Haven, Yale University Press, 1964.

Bogatko, S., 'Potentsial Sibiri', in *Pravda*, 11/2/80, p. 2.

Borovoi, A. A., 'Novyi etap sovershenstvovaniya proektno-smetnogo dela', in *Ekonomika Stroitel'stva*, No. 6, 1981.

Charkov, M. I., 'Effektivnost' kapitalovlozhenii pri rekonstruktsii predpriyatii', in *Finansy SSSR*, No. 10, 1976.

Chentemirov, M. G., 'Povyshat' kachestvo stroitel'stva', in *Ekonomika Stroitel'stva*, No. 5, 1980.

Chirgadze, I. V., 'Mashinostroenie Tadzhikistana i Osnovnye Napravleniya ego Razvitiya', unpublished dissertation for the degree of Candidate of Economic Sciences, Dushanbe, 1965.

Dyker, D. A., 'Industrial location in the Tadzhik republic', in *Soviet Studies*, vol. xxi, no. 4, April 1970.

Economic Survey of Europe (annual), New York, United Nations.

Ferberg, A., 'O kapital'nykh vlozheniyakh na rekonstruktsiyu deistvuyushchikh predpriyatii', in *Voprosy Ekonomiki*, No. 1, 1966.

Galiaskarov, N., 'Ne otstavat' ot trebovanii zhizni', in *Ekonomika Stroitel'stva*, No. 4, 1966.

Galkin, I. (ed.), *Organizatsiya Planirovanie i Upravlenie Stroitel'nym Proizvodstvom*, Moscow, Vysshaya Shkola, 1978.

Geidarov, N., 'Dolgo – znachit dorogo', in *Ekonomicheskaya Gazeta*, No. 26, 1975, p. 9.

Hanson, P. and M. R. Hill, 'Soviet assimilation of western technology; a survey of UK exporters' experience', in US Congress Joint Economic Committee, *Soviet Economy in a Time of Change*, Washington, US GPO, 1979, vol. 2.

Hirschman, A. O., *The Strategy of Economic Development*, New Haven, Yale University Press, 1958.

Il'in, V., 'Uskorenie stroitel'stva – vazhnaya narodnokhozyaistvennaya zadacha', in *Voprosy Ekonomiki*, No. 1, 1976.

Il'in, V., 'Vmesto avansa – kredit', in *Ekonomicheskaya Gazeta*, No. 51, 1978, p. 9.

Isaev, V., 'Sovershenstvovanie planirovaniya kapital'nykh vlozhenii – vazhneishaya narodnokhozyaistvennaya zadacha', in *Planovoe Khozyaistvo*, No. 2, 1971.

Isaev, V., 'Puti povysheniya effektivnosti kapital'nykh vlozhenii', in *Voprosy Ekonomiki*, No. 8, 1973.

Kazhlaev, N. G., *Povyshenie Effektivnosti Kapital'nykh Vlozhenii*, Moscow, Ekonomizdat, 1963.

Khikmatov, A., *Rezervy Povysheniya Effektivnosti Kapital'nykh Vlozhenii*, Tashkent, Uzbekistan, 1969.

Kletsel'man, U. Kh., *Kompleksnoe Razvitie Promyshlennosti Tadzhikskoi SSR*, Dushanbe, Donish, 1969.

Krasovskii, V., *Problemy Ekonomiki Kapital'nykh Vlozhenii*, Moscow, Ekonomika, 1967.

Krasovskii, V., 'Ekonomicheskaya reforma i problemy kapital'nykh vlozhenii', in *Voprosy Ekonomiki*, No. 10, 1968.

Krasovskii, V., 'Oborot kapital'nykh vlozhenii i rezervy kapital'nogo stroitel'stva', in *Voprosy Ekonomiki*, No. 8, 1973.

Kulya, I. and I. Trushkin, 'Raschetam – stroinuyu sistemu', in *Ekonomicheskaya Gazeta*, No. 13, 1976, p. 9.

Latifi, O., 'Energiya Vakhsha', in *Pravda*, 4/8/79, p. 2.

Linskii, S. I. and V. U. Dubkov, 'Kreditovanie nezavershennogo proizvodstva stroitel'no-montazhnykh rabot', in *Ekonomika Stroitel'stva*, No. 4, 1980.

Mal'tsev, V. F (ed.), *Bratskaya GES. Sbornik Dokumentov i Materialov*, vols. I and II, Irkutsk, Vostochno-Sibirskoe Knizhnoe izdatel'stvo, 1964 and 1967.

Martsenitsen, N. and P. Temnov, 'Chto pokazala ekspertiza proektov', in *Ekonomika Stroitel'stva*, No. 7, 1965.

Metodicheskie Ukazaniya k Razrabotke Gosudarstvennykh Planov Razvitiya Narodnogo Khozyaistvo SSSR, Moscow, Gosplan SSSR, 1974.

Metodika Opredeleniya Ekonomicheskoi Effektivnosti Kapital'nykh Vlozhenii, in *Ekonomicheskaya Gazeta*, Nos. 2 and 3, 1981.

Murzin, A. and F. Chursin, 'Nastuplenie na Obi', Part II, in *Pravda*, 13/7/74, p. 2.

Narodnoe Khozyaistvo SSSR (annual), Moscow, Statistika.

Narzikulov, I. K. (ed.), *Problemy Razvitiya i Razmeshcheniya Proizvoditel'nykh Sil Tadzhikskoi SSR*, Dushanbe, Donish, 1967.

Nove, A., *The Soviet Economy*, London, Allen and Unwin, 3rd Edition, 1968.

'Ob uluchshenii planirovaniya i usilenii vozdeistviya khozyaistvennogo mekhanizma na povyshenie effektivnosti proizvodstva i kachestva raboty', in *Ekonomicheskaya Gazeta*, No. 32, 1979, special supplement.

Podshivalenko, P. (ed.), *Ekonomika Stroitel'stva*, Moscow, Izdatel'stvo Politicheskoi Literatury, 1965.

Podshivalenko, P., 'Usilenie roli finansovo-kreditnykh rychagov v povyshenii

effektivnosti kapital′nykh vlozhenii', in *Voprosy Ekonomiki*, No. 4, 1980.
Podskrebkin, V., 'Eksperiment v deistvie', in *Ekonomicheskaya Gazeta*, No. 48, 1975, p. 9.
Pogosov, I., 'V polnuyu situ!', in *Pravda*, 19/10/74, p. 2.
Probst, A. E. and I. K. Narzikulov (eds.), *Narodnokhozyaistvennoe Znachenie Nurekskoi GES*, Dushanbe, Irfon, 1964.
Savost′yanov, V., 'Otsenka importnykh mashin i oborudovaniya', in *Planovoe Khozyaistvo*, No. 3, 1975.
Sher, I. D., *Finansirovanie i Kreditovanie Kapital′nykh Vlozhenii*, Moscow, Finansy, 1972.
Shiryaev, G., 'O sovershenstvovanii proektno-smetnogo dela', in *Planovoe Khozyaistvo*, No. 8, 1969.
Shiryaev, G., 'Uluchshenie proektno-smetnogo dela – vazhnaya narodno-khozyaistvennaya zadacha', in *Planovoe Khozyaistvo*, No. 1, 1977.
Shtanskii, V., 'Tekhnicheskii progress i ekonomika proektirovaniya', in *Voprosy Ekonomiki*, No. 9, 1976.
Tipovaya Metodika Opredeleniya Ekonomicheskoi Effektivnosti Kapital′nykh Vlozhenii, in *Ekonomicheskaya Gazeta*, No. 39, 1969.
Tipovaya Metodika Opredeleniya Ekonomicheskoi Effektivnosti Kapital′nykh Vlozhenii i Novoi Tekhniki v Narodnom Khozyaistve SSSR, Moscow, Gosplan SSSR; Akademiya Nauk SSSR, Institut Ekonomiki, 1960.
Tregubov, A., 'Kachestvo – zabota obshchaya', in *Ekonomicheskaya Gazeta*, No. 42, 1975, p. 9.
Tullock, G., *The Vote Motive*, Hobart Paperback no. 9, Institute of Economic Affairs, London, 1976.
Ustinov, A. N., *Statistika Kapital′nogo Stroitel′stva*, Moscow, Statistika, 1980.
Vitkovskii, V., 'Sovershenstvovanie upravleniya kapital′nym stroitel′stvom', in *Voprosy Ekonomiki*, No. 6, 1977.
Vovchenko, N., 'Bystree osvaivat′ proizvodstvennye moshchnosti', in *Ekonomika Stroitel′stva*, No. 10, 1965.
Vtorushin, S. and A. Murzin, 'Tyumenskii gaz', Parts I and II, in *Pravda*, 26/2/77, p. 2 and 27/2/77, p. 2.
Wilber, C. K., *The Soviet Model and Underdeveloped Countries*, Chapel Hill, University of North Carolina Press, 1969.
Zen′kov, I. S. and M. A. Rusakov, *Ekonomika Stroitel′stva*, Moscow, Vysshaya Shkola, 1967.

Name index

Subject index

249